THE
FLYING
FRENCHMEN

THE FLYING FRENCHMEN

Hockey's Greatest Dynasty

by Maurice "Rocket" Richard
and Stan Fischler

A Stuart L. Daniels Book
HAWTHORN BOOKS, INC.
Publishers
New York

THE FLYING FRENCHMEN

1   2   3   4   5   6   7   8   9   10

Contents

PART III—RECORDS OF THE CANADIENS

Illustrations appear on pages 85–90 and 243–248

Introduction

As a Brooklyn-bred youngster, I had little exposure to Maurice Richard and the Montreal Canadiens except for bits and pieces of information that cropped up all too infrequently in the New York press. I vividly recall a 1943 newspaper article that dealt only with Richard's eyes. It had an accompanying photograph—a close-up showing only the area from Maurice's brow to the top of his nose.

If I was lucky, and weather conditions were right, I'd sometimes be able to pick up Doug Smith's broadcasts of the Canadiens' home games on radio station CBM-Montreal. It was then that I discovered the enormous magnetism of the man they called the Rocket. It wasn't Smith's beautifully frenetic description of Richard's goals that did it as much as the response of the Forum crowd. There has never been, and will never be, anything like it in terms of pure volume per fan—at least not in my experience. The noise was not thunderous, because the rumble of thunder gradually swells to a crescendo. It wasn't explosive either, for an explosion terminates in seconds. I guess it was a combination of both which made the response to a Richard goal so unique.

I finally managed to see Richard in action during the 1947–1948 season. It was in Madison Square Garden, and although his performance fulfilled my expectations, the response of the New York crowd was depressingly indifferent. I vowed then that it was my duty as a hockey fan to take a trip to Montreal to witness the Richard phenomenon.

Unfortunately, although I saw nearly a dozen games, both as journalist and as fan, I never saw the Rocket actually score at the Forum. It was unquestionably one of the bigger disappointments of my life and undoubtedly provided one of the motives for this book. For if I couldn't see Richard score a goal in person, I could at least see it vicariously through hearing the description given me by the Rocket.

Richard, the player, was never known for his amiability with the English-speaking press. The language barrier, coupled with his innate involvement with the game, made rapport impossible and created an image of Richard the Ogre.

Thus it was with immense satisfaction that I learned as a result of interviews for this book—and through other associations—that Maurice Richard is a perfectly delightful man: relaxed, informed, and predictably candid. I don't believe it is possible for a congenital fan like me to regard the Rocket without a little bit of awe, and I carried that feeling with me into this project, for better or for worse.

Writing an objective history of the Canadiens was another challenge. The plan was to avoid the pitfalls of earlier Montreal projects, which were both too superficial and based too much on the official team viewpoint. The Canadiens' management was deliberately not consulted in researching this book except where it was absolutely necessary.

Needless to say, much material will inevitably be overlooked in a dual book of this nature, but it is my feeling that Richard's version of the Canadiens' history is as essential to a book about Montreal hockey as General Eisenhower's version of World War II is essential to a discussion of that conflict.

What made working with Richard such a refreshing experience is that the Rocket has lost none of the unvarnished honesty that characterized his play on ice. In 1955 he believed that certain people—Lynn Patrick, for example—wronged him, and he feels the very same way about them today. More power to him for not being a slave to sentimentality. Interviewing him, I saw his piercing eyes bulge when we discussed a player named Bob Bailey who very nearly disfigured the

Rocket two decades ago. Richard remains passionate about the incident to this day.

There are those who will take exception to Richard's low opinion of contemporary big-league hockey. They will no doubt accuse him of a sour-grapes philosophy and observe that he is living in the past. It will do his critics well not to question the Rocket's motivation but rather to address themselves directly to Richard's points. Then, I believe, the validity of his arguments will be discerned.

I expect that the horde of new hockey fans who have emerged since the Rocket's retirement and the advent of expansion will also treat him with cynicism. That, of course, is their problem. Not having seen Richard in action automatically disqualifies a Johnny-come-lately from discussing the man.

If nothing else, this book is an attempt to treat a magnificent—although occasionally blemished—athletic institution as honestly as possible, both from within and from without. It was a pleasure to write, and I shall never forget my association with the Rocket.

S. F.
Boiceville, New York

PART I

*A HISTORY AND CRITIQUE OF
THE CANADIENS*
by *Stan Fischler*

1

The
Beginnings

*T*he story of the Montreal Canadiens is the story of hockey itself.

Historians have been unable to pinpoint the exact location of the very first hockey game played in North America, although partisans from Kingston, Ontario, and Halifax, Nova Scotia, have argued that hockey in some form or another was first played in their cities. Evidence suggests, however, that the first game took place in December, 1879, on ice adjoining the McGill University campus in Montreal, and there is no disputing the fact that the sport developed fastest in that city.

The earliest version of hockey bore little resemblance to the high-speed game seen today in the National Hockey League. Each team iced nine men. Sticks were crude one-piece hunks of wood, and the ice was barely skateable at times because of weather conditions, which caused irregular freezing and thawing.

Little by little, refinements were added later in the nineteenth century as organized hockey spread across Canada and teams were formed in various cities. In 1899 Arthur Farrell of the Shamrock Hockey Club drew up the first formal set of rules which, among other things, called for seven men to a team, a goal 6 feet wide by 4 feet high (the same as present-day dimensions), and a rink of at least 112 feet by 58 feet (today's minimum is 200 feet by 85 feet).

Perhaps more important than rule changes was the emergence of interest in the game among some of Canada's most distinguished citizens. One of them, Arthur Stanley, the son of Canada's Governor-General, Lord Stanley, participated in the formation of the Ontario Hockey Association in 1890. Three years later, the Stanley Cup, one of sports' most venerated trophies, was established with the assistance of Arthur's father.

Lord Stanley's full title was Right Honourable Sir Frederick Arthur Stanley, Baron Stanley of Preston, in the County of Lancaster, in the Peerage of Great Britain, Knight Grand Cross of the Most Honourable Order of the Bath. An English sportsman, Lord Stanley arrived in Canada in 1888 and almost immediately became infatuated with hockey, although his sons did most of the playing. On one occasion the Stanley boys, on a visit to Great Britain, played a pick-up game of hockey at Buckingham Palace. Their opponents included the Prince of Wales, later King Edward VII, and the Duke of York, who became King George V.

While his sons' interest in hockey gratified Lord Stanley, the father was even prouder of the Ottawa Hockey Club, which he followed as avidly as any National Hockey League spectator follows his favorite team today. In addition Lord Stanley had both influence and money. For ten guineas he had a silver cup struck and announced that henceforth it would be awarded annually for the hockey championship of Canada, starting in the winter of 1892–1893. Because of a dispute between the Ottawa and Toronto clubs over the site of the championship, the tournament was canceled for a year. The Montreal Athletic Association, predecessors to the Canadiens, won the first Stanley Cup a year later. At the time, there were three Montreal teams: the Montreal Athletic Association, known as Montreal, the Victorias, and the Shamrocks.

The game was so popular and had so many followers that new teams were constantly being organized. It was not unusual for a city to have more than one professional hockey team. In Montreal, a number of different teams made their appearance as the sport grew, and stayed on for a longer or shorter period of time in this pre-N.H.L. era.

Montreal's Victoria Rink hosted the first Stanley Cup game on March 22, 1894, but Lord Stanley wasn't around to see it.

He had been succeeded as Governor-General by the Earl of
Aberdeen, who preferred curling to hockey. Lord Stanley returned to England. Nevertheless, impetus to the game of hockey
had been generated by his donation of the trophy. The opening match between Montreal and the Ottawa Capitals lured
a crowd of five thousand to the venerable Montreal arena,
which, in time, would give way to other rinks and ultimately
the present Forum.

Following a pattern that would be observed several decades later, the Montrealers fell behind early in the game,
rallied to tie the score, and then won. The final score was
3–1 and the champions were carried off the rink on the shoulders of their bellowing rooters. Although nobody really knew
it at the time, Montreal's domination of the hockey world had
begun and it would continue—with a few brief lapses—right
up to the present.

As if to prove a point Montreal opened the 1894 season
by routing Quebec, 7–0, and concluded the campaign by defeating the Crystal Hockey Club, 2–1. Montreal then defeated
the Victorias, 3–2, and Ottawa, 3–1, to capture the Stanley
Cup once more. A season later the Cup was annexed by the
Montreal Victorias, who went on to lose it a season later to
the Winnipeg Victorias.

Montreal wasted little time regaining the trophy, which
was gaining more and more prestige as time passed. Montreal
won the Cup in December, 1896, and repeated the feat in
1897 and 1898. By now Montreal had clearly established itself as "the Hockey Capital of the World," and, as if to underline this fact, a magnificent new rink was opened on the corner of St. Catherine and Wood streets in downtown Montreal
on December 31, 1898.

"This was considered to be the last word in accommoda-
tion for hockey fans with a seating capacity of 4,300," notes
the N.H.L. historian Charles L. Coleman. "A refreshment buffet
and smoking rooms were provided and announcement made
that rugs would be available for rental which no doubt would
be appreciated by those who feared draughts."

The new rink was built just in time. Montreal now had two splendid hockey teams with the Victorias seriously challenged for hometown supremacy by the Shamrocks, an outfit that really began asserting itself in 1899. In a game at Montreal on February 4, the Shamrocks defeated Quebec, 13–4, and one of the first of the local heroes emerged as star of the contest. Harry Trihey captured the headlines of the day by scoring ten of his team's thirteen goals.

In later years Montreal's intracity rivalry would feature Les Canadiens and the Maroons, but at the turn of the century it was the Shamrocks and the Victorias. One of the most arresting victories ever accomplished was scored by the Victorias who demolished Ottawa, 16–0, on February 11, 1899, thereby setting a record that has never been equaled in the N.H.L., although the Detroit Red Wings came close when they routed the New York Rangers, 15–0, on January 23, 1944.

Like the Canadiens and Maroons, not to mention baseball's Brooklyn Dodgers and New York Giants, the Shamrocks and Victorias developed an intense competition that dramatically carried them down to the final week of the season tied for first place. Nearly eight thousand fans jammed the new rink for the showdown between the two clubs, and, as one might expect, betting was heavy, scalping was rife, and emotions were keen by face-off time.

For a change the Victorias wilted in the intense competition and star player Harry Trihey seized the opportunity to score the lone goal of the game. On the strength of that 1–0 victory the Shamrocks finished on top and went on to win the Stanley Cup.

The year 1900 saw no change in the balance of power. Paced by the ubiquitous Trihey, the Shamrocks conquered the league once more and this time went up against Winnipeg in a best-of-three series for the Cup. Winnipeg upset the home club in the opening match, but the Shamrocks were not easily rattled. Prior to the second game Trihey was presented with a bouquet of violets by the fans and he responded by scoring the winning goal as the Shamrocks rebounded, 3–2.

He repeated the feat in the third and final game which went to the Shamrocks, 5–4. The Cup-winners then played a series of challenge matches against Halifax and won them with consummate ease.

Winnipeg continued building on its superb club of 1900 and returned to Montreal a year later to challenge the Shamrocks once more for the Cup. This time, however, it was the western team that prevailed, sweeping the series with two straight victories.

All of this, natually, was regarded as sterling hockey and served as a prelude for the growth of the professional pastime that would inevitably intrude on amateur hockey as the game became more and more popular, as well as more and more intense among the rivals. The 1903 Stanley Cup final in Montreal set a new attendance record of eighteen thousand fans for the four-game series. The enthusiasm of Montreal fans continued mounting and it was not unusual for many rooters to accompany their teams on road trips to other cities. When the Montreal Wanderers, a team organized in December, 1903, visited Ottawa in 1909, more than five hundred followers journeyed to see the match.

Then, as now, brutality was as much a part of a big-time hockey game as the stick and puck. Hockey purists, particularly Canadians, have insisted that the jungle aspects of the game were introduced to appeal to the bloodlust of United States sports fans, but the fact is that games in Montreal then were as bloody as any played today, if not more so; and the Americans weren't even involved!

One time the Montreal Wanderers and a team from Ottawa engaged in a near massacre in a game at Montreal that had editorial writers running to their typewriters in indignation. A Montreal *Star* story that followed could well have appeared today. It complained, "They [the players] should get six months in jail is the opinion as to Saturday's hockey brutality. . . . Old players say it was the worst exhibition of butchery they ever saw. . . . Recorder Weir states that if he had been present he would have ordered arrests."

The editorial fears were valid. Not long after the newspapers bemoaned the ice brutality, Bud McCourt of the Cornwall sextet clashed with Art Throop of the Ottawa Vics. The donnybrook increased in intensity until McCourt fell to the ice, bleeding from a head wound. He was rushed to a hospital, where he died the following morning.

In an atmosphere not unlike the Ted Green-Wayne Maki court case of 1970, Charles Masson of the Vics was charged with manslaughter for striking the blow that allegedly killed McCourt. However, several witnesses at the trial testified that other Ottawa players had apparently clouted McCourt earlier in the fracas. This testimony clouded the case against Masson, and he was acquitted.

If anything, such savagery whetted the appetite of existing fans and stimulated the interest of new ones. All that the condemning headlines, editorials, and accounts did was provide hockey with more publicity which, in turn, created more fans. It was this burgeoning interest that resulted in the birth of Les Canadiens.

2

Les Canadiens
Are Born

"We don't own the Canadiens, really," said Senator Hartland Molson when he assumed the presidency of the club in 1957. "The public of Montreal, in fact the entire province of Quebec, owns the Canadiens. This club is more than a professional sports organization. It is an institution, a way of life."

Few would quarrel with the Senator's observation today, but back in 1909 Le Club de Hockey Canadien was nothing more than the germ of an idea nurtured by a few men involved in one of hockey's first interleague wars.

It was appropriate, to say the least, that hockey's most controversial team over the years should be born in the midst of a fierce battle between arena entrepreneurs in Montreal. It all started when officials of the Eastern Canada Hockey Association, the major league of its time, selected the Westmount Arena in Montreal as the site of its games. The decision was tantamount to the mayor of New York choosing Shea Stadium over Yankee Stadium for all New York home baseball games.

The decision infuriated the owners of the Montreal Wanderers Hockey Club and with good reason. The Wanderers were the property of the Jubilee Rink—which had the misfortune of utilizing only natural ice—and the Wanderers' backers immediately perceived they were being victimized by a hockey squeeze play.

Their suspicions were confirmed when the E.C.H.A. held its annual meeting on November 13, 1909. Representatives from Ottawa, Quebec, and Montreal complained about the sale of the Wanderers to P. J. Doran, who owned the Jubilee Rink, and who naturally wanted the Wanderers' games played there.

Opponents pointed out that the Jubilee was too small and generally too inconvenient, let alone unprofitable.

Hockey finances in the early years of the twentieth century varied from rink to rink. Club owners in the E.C.H.A. favored Montreal's Westmount Wood Avenue rink because the operators received 60 percent of the gate receipts while the clubs received 40 percent. In turn the teams handled such items as players' salaries and traveling expenses while the arena was responsible for practice ice, heating dressing rooms and showers, advertising, and other miscellanea.

The question perplexing the E.C.H.A. high command was how to outfeint the Wanderers. The ultimate strategy was an example of front-office chicanery that hasn't yet been matched by today's high-pressure moguls. On November 25, 1909, the E.C.H.A. simply dissolved itself and then reincarnated the league with the sobriquet "Canadian Hockey Association."

To create an aura of legality it went through the motions of "granting" franchises to Ottawa, the Montreal Shamrocks, Quebec, the Nationals, and All-Montreal. Each team paid an initiation fee of thirty dollars (today it costs a minimum of six million dollars to get into the National Hockey League) with an annual upkeep fee of twenty-five dollars.

Naturally, the Wanderers applied for membership. There was nothing particularly unusual about it other than the fact that P. J. Doran was advised that his application had been rejected! P. J. wasn't the only club owner who was upset about the reversal. George and Jim Barnett, owners of the Renfrew (Ontario) Millionaires, had also made a pitch for entrance into the C.H.A. Their representation was made by J. Ambrose O'Brien, a big man in Ontario mining circles and an "angel" behind a couple of teams in northern Ontario.

The events that day in the corridors of Montreal's Windsor Hotel would have made an excellent scenario for a Marx Brothers movie. O'Brien, who happened to be in town on other business, dropped over to the hotel, walked up to Room 135, and put in a bid for a Renfrew franchise. The C.H.A. governors treated his request with the same amusement they would reserve for a suggestion that hockey be played in mud.

Laughed out of Room 135, O'Brien was heading for St. Catherine Street when, by pure chance, he encountered Jimmy Gardner, an official of the Wanderers. The two losers-of-the-moment were exchanging condolences when they suddenly realized their respective team obituaries were a trifle premature. They quickly rented Room 129 in the Windsor Hotel, within shouting distance of the C.H.A. meeting, and began plotting the destruction of their oppressors.

The scheme was so rudimentary they both wondered why it had taken more than a minute to dream up. If the C.H.A. wouldn't have them, they would do the next best—if not the better—thing. They would form their own league. For starters they had the Wanderers, a respected and established outfit. O'Brien himself owned teams in Cobalt and Haileybury, Ontario, and his pals, the Barnett brothers, had title to the Renfrew club. That made four teams, which was a good start but not good enough for the ingenious O'Brien and Gardner. They agreed that a metropolis such as Montreal could support still another team, but not another team dominated by English players, as the Wanderers were.

"It was Gardner who suggested that a French team should go well in Montreal," O'Brien explained at the time of his induction into hockey's Hall of Fame. "Gardner also advised me to get Jack Laviolette as manager. Newsy Lalonde's name was mentioned as a likely player. There were several others who eventually joined the club."

If anybody could come up with French-Canadian hockey players, it was the French-Canadian Laviolette. Given such assurance from Laviolette, representatives from Renfrew, Cobalt, Haileybury, and the Wanderers convened in Montreal on December 2, 1909. In a "secret" conclave, they formally organized the National Hockey Association of Canada which ultimately became the National Hockey League, now embracing three Canadian cities and eleven in the United States.

Fred Strachan of the Wanderers, the association's first president, immediately sanctioned franchises in the original four cities. Right from the start the N.H.A. betrayed a vigorous survival instinct. Its life appeared very short-lived when the Barnett brothers developed second thoughts about the project and decided against participation, thus detonating the league's first crisis. This, however, was resolved with dispatch, not to mention a few thousand dollars, when J. Ambrose O'Brien and his father, M. J. O'Brien, took title to the Renfrew organization and reentered it into the league. And just to prove his good faith M. J. presented a brand-new trophy to the league which would be presented to the champions each year.

Unlike the relatively inexpensive Stanley Cup, the O'Brien Trophy was created by Hemsley's, the distinguished Montreal firm, and was composed of solid silver extracted from the rich veins of Cobalt, Ontario. The trophy was all well and good, but there was still the matter of a fifth hockey team, a project now in the hands of the flamboyant Laviolette.

Jack's assurance that he could produce the French-Canadian skaters was not a fragile promise. Thanks to his downtown Montreal restaurant, Laviolette was meeting athletes on a daily basis. What's more, a group of his cronies would convene regularly for exhibition games in and around Montreal.

The N.H.A. held another meeting on December 4 at the Windsor. Once again a bizarre tableau unfolded. The N.H.A. moguls gathered in Room 129. At that very moment officials of the established C.H.A. opened their meeting a few doors away in Room 135. Neither meeting was secret, and reporters from Montreal's English- and French-language newspapers patrolled the hotel for reports about the impending confrontation.

One possibility was that the C.H.A.'s antagonism toward the Wanderers would be reversed and the Wanderers would be welcomed back to the fold. Another was that the two leagues would merge into one big prosperous, if not happy, family. Still a third report had it that three clubs were prepared to bolt the C.H.A. and march down the hall to apply for membership in the baby league. However, none of these developments materialized.

The N.H.A. opened the meeting with the announcement that the fifth team, to be known as Les Canadiens, had applied for membership and that T. C. Hare of Cobalt, Ontario, would put up security for the franchise with a special proviso that the club be transferred to French-Canadian owners at the earliest possible date.

A dozen yards away owners of the C.H.A. teams rebuffed suggestions that the Wanderers be readmitted and became more and more intransigent in their discussions about the new league. While reporters suggested that the Wanderers had been pushed right out of the C.H.A., the league governors piously denied that any such thing had happened, although it obviously had. Little did they realize that their power play was inadvertently a death blow, although the coup de grace didn't immediately occur.

Whatever the case, the C.H.A. had its original wish. It had divested itself of the need to play in the Jubilee Rink and was prepared for another profitable season. Meanwhile, the N.H.A. agreed that both the infant Canadiens and the Wanderers would share the Jubilee ice and all that remained was the matter of signing up hockey players—which was when the fun really started.

The secret word was "money," and if the C.H.A. had it, then the spanking new N.H.A. had it with double digits. What made the intruders so strong was the bankroll of O'Brien who was coining money with his silver mines in northern Ontario not to mention assorted other enterprises in a growing Canada. Antitrust laws were unheard of in Canadian sport at the time, so nobody was particularly disturbed by the fact that the O'Brien family controlled four out of the five teams in the new league, the exception being Montreal's Wanderers. Besides, it was difficult to dislike Ambrose O'Brien. He had played hockey at the University of Toronto and betrayed a hyper-chauvinistic loyalty to Renfrew and its neighbors, particularly when the self-appointed sophisticates of Montreal would try to put him down.

"The ridicule of the cities," said Toronto *Daily Star* sports editor Milt Dunnell, "merely stiffened O'Brien's determination. It was his fierce pride in his hometown of Renfrew that led to the founding of the Canadiens and what now is the N.H.L."

O'Brien's intense motivation to make a success of his team was reflected in the bidding for hockey players. At the time, Lester Patrick, who later organized and ran the New York Rangers, was one of the most distinguished players in Canada. Patrick was playing in western Canada, and liking it, at the time O'Brien began developing his team. Naturally, Ambrose telegraphed an offer to Patrick who was highly amused by the temerity of a small-town team like Renfrew thinking it could afford his salary. But just to pursue the gag, Lester wired back a demand for $3,000, which by today's standards would be tantamount to $500,000. At the time, the highest-paid player in all hockey was Tom Phillips and he was receiving only $1,800 a year.

Lester went a step further and insisted that his brother, Frank, also be imported by the Renfrew club at a salary of no less than $2,000!

To the complete bafflement of the Patricks, O'Brien swiftly approved the terms and both Lester and Frank were soon on a train heading east. But Ambrose didn't stop there. He lured Hay Millar and Fred Whitcroft from Edmonton for $2,000 apiece. That was just for starters.

"By the time O'Brien was finished," said Baz O'Meara, former sports editor of the Montreal *Star*, "he had assembled the greatest galaxy of stars ever seen on one hockey team."

Odie and Sprague Cleghorn, Cyclone Taylor, Herb Jordan, and Steve Vair were a few of the members. Curiously enough, Renfrew never did win the Stanley Cup, a disappointment that O'Brien never overcame. "I guess," he once explained, "the trouble was that we had too many stars."

Nevertheless, O'Brien's freedom with the dollar inspired Laviolette who was zeroing in on the best French-Canadian talent available. His first coup was the signing of Edouard "Newsy" Lalonde, one of the toughest and most adept players available. Then he trained his sights on Didier Pitre, who was playing for the Nationals of the C.H.A. Pitre was a speedy right wing who seemed to be a natural for Les Canadiens.

Laviolette was well aware that Pitre had signed an eleven-hundred-dollar contract to play for the Nationals, so he responded by putting seventeen hundred dollars on the table. When Harry Trihey, the Nationals' attorney, learned of the counteroffer, he announced that Pitre was risking a two-thousand-dollar fine, not to mention a jail sentence, if he dared play for the Canadiens.

Now the Canadiens were on the spot, but they had no thoughts of backtracking. Laviolette huddled with Pitre and assured him that the seventeen hundred was his to keep no matter what happened.

On January 5, 1910, the Canadiens were scheduled to meet the Cobalt team on the natural ice of Montreal's Jubilee Rink. By this time Pitre's case had splashed across the papers, and the N.H.A. had captured just the publicity it required to launch its first season. Montrealers filled the venerable building, partly out of curiosity for the new Canadiens and partly for the excitement over whether or not Pitre would defy the Nationals and skate for Les Canadiens.

When Didier finally did step on the ice, a swelling roar developed among the crowd of five thousand and it was to continue virtually unabated as the Canadiens rebounded from 3–0 and 6–4 deficits to tie the game in regulation time and win the contest in a sudden-death overtime. But it wasn't only the pulsating triumph nor Pitre's appearance that captured the imagination of the crowd; there was also the essential element of quality hockey that the N.H.A. was offering, and needed to survive. Seasoned critics raved about the "speed, even balance, furious rushes, tension, skill, and combination play" that the match featured. If the opening game was any barometer, both the N.H.A. and Les Canadiens were there to stay.

Despite the legal threats generated by the Nationals, Didier Pitre remained with the Canadiens. Nothing came of the court action, and Didier developed into one of the first French-Canadian heroes of Les Canadiens. This right-winger had extraordinary get-away speed and quickly became the target of his slower rivals. Once, in a game against Ottawa's Senators, Eddie Gerard, the enemy captain, assigned his ace, Cy Denneny, to guard Pitre.

"No matter what I did," Denneny recalled, "Didier would get away for a shot on goal."

During the intermission Gerard suggested it might be more practical, if not prudent, to clout Pitre on the lower part of his legs, the theory being that this would enrage Didier and distract him from his pursuit of goals. When this strategem failed, Gerard suggested that Denneny try haranguing him with insults.

"There wasn't a name in the book that I didn't call him," said Denneny, "but that didn't seem to rile him either."

When the game finally ended, Gerard and Denneny consoled themselves with the knowelge that they had done everything in their power to needle Pitre. "A little later," Denneny revealed, "we discovered our mistake. Didier didn't fathom a word of English!"

Meanwhile, the interleague rivalry was turning into a war of attrition. Montreal was now loaded with five top-rated teams, and crowds soon began tailing off at some rinks. A C.H.A. match between the Shamrocks and the Nationals drew only eight hundred spectators and there were murmurings of merger once again.

The once-powerful C.H.A. betrayed signs of panic, and on January 15, 1910, both Ottawa and the Montreal Shamrocks "jumped" the venerable league for the new N.H.A. This signaled the beginning of the end for the C.H.A.

Despite such notables as Pitre, Joe Cattarinich, Ed Decarie, Art Bernier, and Richard Duckett, Les Canadiens finished in last place in their first season, with a poor record of two wins and ten losses. Their English-speaking rivals, the Wanderers, finished first with an 11–1 record and went on to win the Stanley Cup of 1910.

Controversy continued to follow Les Canadiens as the club prepared for its second season. A onetime wrestler and sports promoter by the name of George Kendall (who operated under the name Kennedy) took an ad in the Montreal *Herald,* asserting that the name "Canadiens" actually was the property of the Club Athlétique-Canadien, which was a registered and incorporated outfit. Since Kennedy owned the club he made it abundantly clear that he would demand the N.H.A. eliminate the name Les Canadiens.

But Kennedy was not a hard man to deal with if the deal was right. His plan was to obtain an N.H.A. team, which he did when O'Brien presented him with a franchise for $7,500. An entanglement of legal red tape over the rights to Newsy Lalonde developed into a head-on collision between Kennedy and O'Brien. The mining tycoon argued that Lalonde had become the property of Renfrew, but Kennedy countered that Newsy belonged to Les Canadiens. The league eventually resolved the dispute by ordering Lalonde to Montreal. It was a decision that would have a long-standing beneficial effect on the Canadiens' franchise.

A native of Cornwall, Ontario, Lalonde was nicknamed "Newsy" during a brief stint working in a newsprint plant. Canadian author Bill Roche once described him as "the greatest French-Canadian athlete of all time and one of the best who ever laced on a skate or fondled a lacrosse stick."

Lalonde broke into pro hockey with Sault Ste. Marie when he was only eighteen. In his first game against Pittsburgh he discovered that the defensemen had a habit of backhanding the puck into the air when they wanted to clear the puck from their zone. "Once I figured that out," Newsy revealed, "I made a point of getting in front of them and then, suddenly, swerving around so that I actually had my back to the defensemen."

Lalonde soon proved there was method to his madness. The next time a Pittsburgh player attempted to clear the puck, Lalonde executed his pirouette. The puck struck him in the back and slipped through his baggy hockey pants to the ice directly behind him. He then deftly spun around, captured the puck, and skimmed it into the net. Newsy executed the same maneuver twice in the same game, and Sault Ste. Marie came out on top, 3–1. "After that," he said, "I was in pro hockey for good."

With Newsy leading the team in scoring with sixteen goals in sixteen games, Les Canadiens finished second in their second season. But Lalonde wasn't the only ace on the team. By a strange coincidence the club had acquired a twenty-two-year-old goaltender from Chicoutimi, Quebec. His name was Georges Vézina, and he was to become so good the N.H.L. was ultimately to strike a trophy in his name to be awarded to the best netminder in hockey.

Like so many other Montreal stars who were to follow him, Vézina was a product of a small French-speaking city in the province of Quebec. Chicoutimi sits on the edge of the dark Saguenay River, which flows into the blue St. Lawrence at historic Tadoussac. It was in this setting that young Georges learned his hockey, although, admittedly, he learned it in a curious way.

Georges was an excellent goaltender—the best in Chicoutimi at the time—but he had developed a habit of playing without skates. For some peculiar reason he found the idea of wearing skates a bother, and it wasn't until two years before he graduated to Les Canadiens that he actually learned to wear skates while tending goal.

Conceivably, the Montrealers would never have discovered Vézina were it not for a chance exhibition game between Les Canadiens and the local Chicoutimi club on February 23, 1910. The match between the awesome professionals from

Montreal and the patchwork amateur outfit figured to be so one-sided that only a handful of fans turned out for it.

Chicoutimi hardly looked like a formidable foe, except for the six-foot goalie, wearing a red-and-white Habitant *toque* on his head. Leaning against the goalpost, the tall, lanky Vézina appeared almost too bored for words. But once the overpowering Canadiens sliced through the fragile Chicoutimi defense, Vézina suddenly responded with a peripatetic style that thoroughly dumbfounded the likes of Pitre, Lalonde, and Laviolette. Joe Cattarinich, who both goaled for and managed the Canadiens, began imploring his men for a goal as if his club were playing in a Stanley Cup battle, but Vézina would not be beaten. Vézina's overmatched teammates began rallying behind their goaltender and scored two goals against the Canadiens.

By the time the third period had begun, the Chicoutimi skaters had skated themselves to exhaustion. They had scored their goals and proved a point and now it would only be a matter of minutes before the stars from Montreal swept them off the ice. Wave after wave of Canadiens shooters swept in on Vézina, testing him with backhanders, forehanders, and short-pass plays around the net.

By the middle of the third period it was no longer a question of whether the Canadiens would win the game but rather would they ever put the puck behind Vézina? The young goalie seemed nonplussed by the whole affair—he was the only person in the building who showed no emotion—as he acrobatically fended off the enemy shots. When the game ended, the kid who was soon to be nicknamed "the Chicoutimi Cucumber" had prevented Les Canadiens from scoring a single goal.

Cattarinich was as impressed as he was flabbergasted and immediately urged George Kennedy to sign the youngster, although it almost surely meant the end of Cattarinich's own career in the Montreal nets. Kennedy obliged by inviting both Georges and his brother, Pierre, who had scored the winning goal, to Montreal. Georges made his debut in the *bleu, blanc, et rouge* Canadiens' uniform on December 31, 1910, and played for Montreal for fifteen years.

As personalities go, Vézina was as strange as any who have ever graced the N.H.L. He never signed a contract with the Canadiens, preferring a gentleman's handshake with his manager, first Cattarinich and later Leo Dandurand. Georges abstained from smoking and drinking, and was liberal to a fault when it came to "loaning" cash to friends. More often than not, it was never returned, but Vézina never seemed to mind. Certainly, as the father of twenty children, he could have used the money. One of his sons was named Stanley, having been born on the night the Canadiens won the 1916 Stanley Cup.

Vézina was beaten, 5–3, by Ottawa in his debut but went on to post a league-leading 3.9 goals against average in his rookie year as the Canadiens finished second to Ottawa. He didn't miss a game all season and played in every Canadiens game until November 29, 1925.

Thanks to Vézina, Lalonde, Laviolette, and Pitre, Les Canadiens rapidly obtained a distinctive image, which they have retained to the present day. "The Canadiens' charm is Gallic," observed Peter Gzowski, broadcaster-editor and one of the most perceptive writers on the North American continent. "And the headlong, passionate way they have always played hockey has helped to make them *the* national team of French Canada in a way no team representing *all* of Canada, with its diverse, unmelted ethnic strains, could hope to parallel, and I have sometimes wondered if their rallying cry, 'Les Canadiens sont là,' is not a better motto for the national spirit of French Canada than '*Je me souviens*.' "

This sensitivity to the French spirit of Les Canadiens was evident as far back as October 11, 1911, when the N.H.A. governors ruled that the Canadiens were to sign only French-speaking players. Conversely, all other teams, by rule, were forbidden to sign French-speaking skaters. Incidentally, at that same meeting the league responded to a request of W. E. Northey of the Montreal Arena and eliminated the position of rover, thereby reducing the number of players on each team from seven to six.

A cloud of anxiety hovered over the meeting when it was learned that Lester and Frank Patrick were organizing a Pacific Coast League that would directly compete with the N.H.A. for players. Having departed Renfrew, the Patricks began raiding the eastern teams for team members and it was the Canadiens who suffered some of the most severe losses, including Newsy Lalonde who signed with Vancouver. Without Lalonde, the Canadiens finished in last place, although Vézina once again produced the best goaltending average. A year later, however, the Canadiens entered negotiations with the Vancouver sextet and regained Newsy's contract.

By this time Newsy had earned a reputation as one of the roughest players in the game. His clashes with "Bad" Joe Hall, who later became a teammate on Les Canadiens, were studies in jungle brutality, but Newsy didn't reserve his venom for Hall. On December 22, 1912, the Canadiens played their hometown rivals, the Wanderers, in an exhibition game to unveil the new Toronto hockey rink. Midway in the game Lalonde dispatched Odie Cleghorn of the Wanderers into the boards with such force that Odie's brother, Sprague, charged across the rink and smashed Newsy across the forehead with his stick. The blow just barely missed Lalonde's eye and he required twelve stitches to close the gaping wound.

The episode didn't go unnoticed officially and a constable served a summons on Cleghorn. Sprague turned up in a Toronto court and was fined fifty dollars for his efforts, not to mention an additional fifty-dollar fine slapped on him by N.H.A. president Emmett Quinn. Cleghorn was also suspended for four weeks, but such was the laissez-faire atmosphere of pro hockey at the time that Sprague absented himself from only one game and then promptly returned to the Wanderers' lineup with impunity.

A year later Newsy was at it again. On December 30, 1913, the Canadiens were in Quebec City to help unveil the new hockey rink with a match against the hometown Bull-dogs. Lalonde bashed Joe Hall across the head with his stick, opening an eight-stitch wound. Hall, who had a craggy face and a neatly parted haircut, was not one to forget such a mis-demeanor. When the same two clubs clashed again on Jan-uary 14, 1914, in Montreal, there was no mistaking Hall's program for the evening. He had his eyes on Newsy from the start and finally connected with a lusty body check that crashed Lalonde into the boards so vigorously that Newsy required ten stitches to close *his* wound.

Lalonde's distillation of fury and finesse had a very ben-eficial effect on the Canadiens who became first-place threats by midseason. It was then that they became involved in big-league hockey's first classic overtime game.

It happened on February 18, 1914, in Montreal against Ottawa at a time when it was still commonplace for players to skate an entire game without substitution. On this night the two evenly matched clubs exchanged end-to-end rushes for the full three periods without a goal being scored, sending the match into sudden-death overtime. By the early minutes of the extra period skaters began collapsing on the ice even without being hit by an opponent; they were that tired. The agony was ended finally after six minutes and forty seconds of sudden death on a goal by Ernie Dubeau of Les Canadiens. Exactly a week later the Canadiens visited Ottawa and this time lost a sudden-death game to the home team after *thirty minutes* of overtime.

In later years Les Canadiens would be coached by men whose decibel count was as high as their boiling point was low. Both Dick Irvin and Toe Blake, Irvin's successor, often seemed to be on a treadmill to the N.H.L. office for one dis-ciplinary reason or another. What has generally been over-looked in the cases of Blake and Irvin is that precedent was set for vitriolic Montreal coaches as far back as 1914 when George Kennedy displayed a temper that would have made both Blake and Irvin appear decorous by comparison.

One of Kennedy's more flamboyant displays occurred at

the conclusion of an especially bitter contest with the Wanderers in which, oddly enough, Les Canadiens won, 6–5. In a scene that was later reenacted by Blake with referee Dalton McArthur, manager Kennedy assaulted referee Leo Dandurand as soon as the game ended. Interestingly, it was the same Dandurand who later helped purchase Les Canadiens from Kennedy's widow in 1921.

At the time, though, Dandurand was infuriated with Kennedy's behavior particularly because N.H.A. president Quinn's failure to suspend the Canadiens' manager appeared to suggest tacit approval of the assault. In those early days of pro hockey it was not unusual for either players or executives to fight their cases on the editorial pages of the local newspapers, and Dandurand did just that. He wrote a letter to Quinn in the Montreal *Herald & Daily Telegraph*, which printed it as follows:

The Wanderers vs. Canadiens match, decided Saturday night at the Arena, was full of incident. The worst part of it, no doubt, was the injurious manner in which I was treated by Mr. George Kennedy and the assault that he committed upon me as he left the ice when the game was finished. Obeying I know not what motive, Mr. Kennedy seized me and threatened me with blows, and at the same time speaking to me in terms unworthy of a dignified man. Mr. Kennedy failed in his duty as a sportsman, and accused me of not having fulfilled my functions as a paid umpire. He caught me by his fists before the spectators, players, and officers of the Canadien club.

I was afraid of receiving some severe blows and I believe that only my coolness under the circumstances saved me from an unpleasant assault.

Not content with having abused me in this manner upon my leaving the ice, the general manager of the Canadiens came back and insulted me in the worst manner in the umpires' room, calling me a ——— before Messrs. Waud of the *Daily Mail*, W. J. Morrison of the *Gazette*, E. C. St. Pierre of *Le Canada*, Mr. Robertson, proprietor of the Toronto Hockey Club, C. Hoerner,

John Dunlop, Tom Melville, Dave Power, Cecil Short and yourself. These are the facts and I hope you will take them into your serious consideration.

Mr. Kennedy may think himself authorized to consider me incapable, but I refuse him the right to insult me and my honor as a gentleman in the way he has done.

I have written enough to convince you that this time an end should be put to a deplorable situation among professional hockey players.

Quinn had more urgent matters to consider than Danrurant's letter. The season ended the day after the referee dispatched his missive to the newspaper, and both Les Canadiens and Toronto had finished in a tie for first place. Quinn ordered a two-game total goals play-off, opening in Montreal and closing in Toronto. The Canadiens sloshed their way to a 2–0 win in the first game on a soggy natural-ice surface made virtually unskateable by mild weather. In the second game, played on excellent artificial ice in Toronto, Les Canadiens were defeated, 6–0, and thus were prevented from playing in the first East-West competition for the Stanley Cup.

The truculent Kennedy was no more affectionate with his own players than he was with referees such as Dandurand, especially when it came to financial matters. By the beginning of the 1914–1915 season it was becoming fashionable for a few star players to think in terms of organizing hockey's first players' union.

Ironically, Art Ross, who later became manager of the Boston Bruins and was one of the most frugal moguls in hockey, started the stick-handlers' union movement in 1911 by launching a brief players' revolt. He feuded with owners again late in 1914 and this time was supported by Lalonde of the Canadiens. Newsy became one of Montreal's first hockey holdouts when he refused to accept a one-thousand-dollar contract from Kennedy. Kennedy replied by fining him one hundred dollars. The manager further announced that he would subtract one hundred dollars from Lalonde's salary for every week he refused to play. Les Canadiens launched the season without Newsy and promptly lost four consecutive games.

The impasse was broken when Lalonde signed a "secret" contract on January 9, 1915, but he played only six games before injuries compelled him to retire for the remainder of the season. Newsy's feud with management torpedoed the Canadiens as contenders and they finished the season in last place with an appalling 6–14 record.

In a sense the last-place trauma had a cathartic effect on the team. Newcomers such as Howard McNamara and Goldie Prodgers replaced Jimmy Gardner, Ernie Dubeau, and Harry Scott. Lalonde returned, apparently rejuvenated from the previous season's woes, and Les Canadiens appeared ready to spring themselves right back to the top of the N.H.A. With Prodgers leading the attack with two goals, the Canadiens launched the 1915–1916 season with a 2–1 victory on the road against the Toronto Blueshirts. They were on their way.

A week before the season had ended the Canadiens clinched first place and completed matters on March 18, 1916, defeating Toronto, 6–4. Newsy scored two goals in that game and won the scoring championship, finishing five points ahead of Joe Malone and Cy Denneny. The stage was now set for Les Canadiens to meet the Pacific Coast Hockey Association's champion Portland Rosebuds in a best-of-five series for the Stanley Cup in Montreal.

As play-offs go, the 1916 Stanley Cup final was one of the best of the early editions. The teams were tied two games apiece when they faced-off on March 30 in the rubber match. They matched goals early in the game and appeared destined for sudden-death overtime when Goldie Prodgers scored for the Canadiens. Georges Vézina was impregnable in the nets from that point on, and Les Canadiens won the game, 2–1, and captured the Stanley Cup. Each member of the winning team collected $238 while the losers rode home with $207 in their pockets.

To bolster his defense for the 1916–1917 campaign, George

Kennedy obtained Harry Mummery from Quebec. If nothing else, Mummery was distinguished for his size and girth, tipping the scales at 258 pounds. It was axiomatic that Harry had the appetite to go with it, a discovery made by Kennedy when Mummery checked in to his office after arriving in Montreal.

Harry shook hands with his new boss and in the next motion presented him a bill for $107, which covered his dining expenses from Brandon, Manitoba, to Montreal. (Remember that $107 in those days would be close to $600 in purchasing power today.) Kennedy was in no humor to tacitly accept such a toll and inquired just what Mummery had to eat on his jaunt across two provinces.

In a trice Harry itemized his six meals a day as well as a few side dishes, not to mention one quart of cream with every meal. Kennedy was prepared to concede the six meals a day but the cream was a bit much!

The two argued back and forth for several minutes until Mummery rose from his seat. Was he going to strike Kennedy? Nothing of the kind. "George," he said rather matter-of-factly, "I'm getting hungry. And I'm going to charge it to the club if you don't pay up pretty soon."

With visions of three-figure food bills in his head, Kennedy calmed his defenseman and promptly doled out $107 in crisp new bills. It was a wise decision because Mummery was soon to play an excellent defense for Les Canadiens, teamed with Bert Corbeau. However, Kennedy, perhaps because of the staggering food bills, traded Harry to Toronto the following season. He returned to Les Canadiens in the 1920–1921 season and scored a very impressive fifteen goals. The next year he was dealt to Hamilton, and Mummery finally retired after playing in Saskatoon for the 1922–1923 season. According to hockey people his food bills have never been matched, before or since.

But of the early Canadiens, Newsy Lalonde clearly established himself as the most distinguished of all. "He not only had class," says Elmer Ferguson, dean of Canadian sportswriters, "but Newsy oozed color. Once he scored nine goals in a game his team won with an eleven-goal performance. He was born about fifty years too soon."

With Newsy playing the best hockey of his life, Les Canadiens managed to beat Ottawa for the right to compete again for the Stanley Cup in 1917, only this time they traveled to Seattle for their defense of the world championship. After winning the opening game, 8–4, the host club took over and proceeded to smother Montreal by scores of 6–1, 4–1, and 9–1 to capture the Cup and end an era for Les Canadiens.

3

The

National Hockey League

World War I was reaching its climax when the player-stripped National Hockey Association convened for its annual meeting on November 10, 1917. Some of the foremost Canadiens players as well as stars from other N.H.A. teams had departed for the Canadian Armed Forces, and there was considerable talk about dropping pro hockey for the duration of the war. Petty feuding among the various team officials merely exacerbated the already deteriorating situation, and on November 17 officials of the Quebec franchise announced it was dropping out of the N.H.A.

The bombshell from Quebec shook the foundations of the N.H.A., and two more "crash" meetings were held within the week of the Quebec announcement. Apparently the remaining N.H.A. moguls believed a face-lifting was needed to restore hockey's stability, although the same teams—Ottawa, Canadiens, Toronto, and Wanderers—were still involved in the organization. The face-lifting took the form of a new name, the National Hockey League, which was officially created at a meeting on November 26, 1917, at the Windsor Hotel in downtown Montreal. As a result of the alteration, the only noticeable change in ownership involved the Toronto franchise. Otherwise it was the N.H.A. with a new sobriquet.

Once Quebec announced its abandonment of pro hockey, the entire roster of the dissolved team was put up for sale in a modified form of a draft system. This produced the second shock of the still unplayed 1917–1918 season when the Canadiens obtained from Quebec both Joe Malone *and* Joe Hall, two of the most formidable skaters on the continent.

Many respected observers regard Malone as the greatest all-round scorer who ever laced on a pair of skates. "He might have been the most prolific scorer of all time if they had played more games in those days," says Frank J. Selke, the former Canadiens managing director who remembers Malone as a young professional. "It was amazing the way Joe used to get himself in position to score. In that respect his style was similar to Gordie Howe's. Joe was no Howie Morenz as far as speed was concerned. But he was a clean player like Dave Keon and Frank Boucher. On the other hand, though, Joe never took a backward step from anybody."

The handsome native of Quebec City played his early hockey for teams in Ontario before being signed by the Quebec Bulldogs. His acquisition by the Canadiens for the 1917–1918 season was considered a coup of major proportions. A centerman, Malone could be equated as the Jean Béliveau of his day, although there was the inevitable difference in style.

"Quite often," Malone remembered, "I played fifty or fifty-five minutes a game. They didn't bother too much about changing lines, only individuals. There were only about nine or ten players on each team. I used to stick-handle in close and beat the goalie with a wrist shot. There was no forward passing allowed in the offensive zone and not as much scrambling as there is today. We wore shoulder and elbow pads, but the equipment wasn't too heavy and this was a good thing considering the number of minutes we had to play each game.

"The goalkeepers stood up a lot more. Vézina was a wonderful stand-up goalie who used to stop most shots with his stick. George Hainsworth and Paddy Moran were other good ones. There were no slapshots, but much more passing and stick-handling than today."

Malone's most notable achievement, which came later, was his record-breaking achievement of seven goals in a game scored on the night of January 31, 1920, in Quebec City. Three of the goals were scored within two minutes of the third period. Unfortunately, the game was played on a night when the temperature hovered around twenty-five below zero and only a handful of spectators turned up at the rink.

"There was no great fuss made about the seven goals at the time," said Malone. "It was only a night's work as far as I was concerned. The only thing I remember about it is that it was very cold outside."

As a member of Les Canadiens, Malone was no less spectacular than he was at Quebec. He missed two games of the twenty-two-game schedule in 1917–1918 yet managed to score a total of forty-four goals and scored in each of fourteen consecutive games and three times scored five goals in one game. "The funny thing is," said Malone, "there was more publicity about my record when Maurice Richard broke it than there was when I set it and all the years afterward."

Although Malone's record was shattered in 1944–1945, when the Rocket scored fifty goals in fifty games, nobody has been able to match his percentage of more than two goals per game. His compensation hardly matched his production. "My salary," Joe recalled "was about one thousand dollars a year with the Canadiens and then went up to two thousand dollars when I joined Hamilton in the early twenties. We could make another three hundred or four hundred by playing with a Stanley Cup-winner and maybe a few dollars more by endorsing hockey equipment. But there were no trophies or additional money for being leading scorer . . . and things like that."

If the acquisition of Malone was a surprise for the Canadiens, the signing of "Bad" Joe Hall was the height of irony, in view of the fact that his archfoe, Newsy Lalonde, had been named player-manager of Les Canadiens. Up until the day Hall joined the Monteral sextet it had appeared to many viewers of the pro hockey scene that Hall's sole ambition in life was to decapitate Lalonde. Now he was taking orders from the man!

Hall was born in England but learned his hockey in western Canada. He first achieved distinction—or notoriety—playing for Houghton, Michigan, in the bloodthirsty International Pro League in 1905 and 1906. Those who became close friends of Hall's insist that he was the victim of a newspaperman's overzealous typewriter and really wasn't a bad fellow after all.

"He wasn't mean," said Malone, "despite what a lot of people said about him. He certainly liked to deal out a heavy check and he was always ready to take it as well as dish it out. That in itself was remarkable when you consider that Joe weighed in at only a hundred fifty pounds. As far as I'm concerned he should have been known as 'Plain' Joe Hall and not 'Bad' Joe Hall. That always was a bum rap."

Whatever the case, Hall and Malone ignited the Canadiens to a successful first half of the 1917–1918 season and by midpoint the Flying Frenchmen—by now dotted with English-speaking players—were in first place. Then the roof literally fell in on them. On January 2, 1918, a huge conflagration gutted the Montreal Arena, reducing it to rubble. Both Les Canadiens and the Wanderers lost all their equipment—an estimated loss of $1,000 each—and the arena damage was put at $150,000.

Sam Lichtenhein, owner of the Wanderers, had been bemoaning his team's dearth of players since the beginning of the season. After surveying the fire damage he requested player help from the other teams. When they refused, he announced that the Wanderers would drop out of the N.H.L., leaving the Montreal hockey scene solely to Les Canadiens. Manager George Kennedy responded with the disclosure that his club would play out of the once-controversial Jubilee Rink.

By coincidence or otherwise, the fall of the Montreal Arena seemed to bring about the collapse of Les Canadiens. They soon lost their momentum, not to mention their poise, especially "Bad" Joe Hall. During a game at Toronto, Hall engaged Alf Skinner of the home club in so vicious a stick-swinging duel that they both received match penalties, were arrested by Toronto police, and subsequently charged with disorderly conduct. After appearing in court they received suspended sentences. Toronto won the game, 5–1, and went on to oust Les Canadiens for the right to meet Vancouver in the Stanley Cup play-offs.

Having adjusted themselves to playing in the Jubilee Rink for the 1918–1919 season, Les Canadiens regained their winning ways, defeated Ottawa for the right to go west, and challenge Seattle for the Cup. They soon rued the day they ever boarded the Pullman coach for the state of Washington.

The series opened on March 19. Seattle bombed Les Canadiens, 7–0, and appeared destined to sweep the series. But with Lalonde in command of his game, the visitors rebounded neatly to capture the second match, 4–2, and the teams settled down for what appeared to be a thrilling series. Seattle captured the third game, 7–2, setting the stage for what N.H.L. historian Charles L. Coleman has described as "the greatest match ever played on the Pacific coast."

Neither team scored in regulation time. One hour and forty minutes of sudden-death overtime was played before the game was called a draw. When the teams met again four nights later, the score was 3–3 going into overtime, but this time the Canadiens prevailed after 15:57 of extra play on a goal by Odie Cleghorn.

The game was significant in several respects. For one thing it made abundantly clear the fact that Les Canadiens had retained their flair for coming from behind, a trait that has remained with them into the present. "We were outplayed in the first two periods," said Malone. "At one point Seattle had a 3–0 lead but Newsy rallied the team with two goals and pretty soon we were right back in the game."

Equally meaningful was an incident that caught the eyes of some spectators as the teams battled for the winning goal. "Bad" Joe Hall, who in earlier games had battled vehemently with Seattle's Cully Wilson, appeared to lose his zest and finally left the ice and made his way to the dressing room.

Unknown to all the onlookers, it was to be the last time Joe was ever to step on a hockey rink.

Hall was rushed to the hospital, stricken with the flu bug that was causing an epidemic throughout North America. Immediately after the game several other Canadiens, including Lalonde and manager George Kennedy, were bedded with influenza but none as bad as Joe Hall. The belief was that the Montreal players had contracted the disease while sightseeing in Victoria, British Columbia, but this was never definitely ascertained.

With the series tied at two apiece an attempt was made to finish the play-off for the Stanley Cup. Kennedy requested permission to "borrow" players from Victoria to finish the series, but the hosts declined the bid and the play-off was canceled without a winner.

Six days after he had stumbled off the ice, Joe Hall died of influenza in a Seattle hospital. His friend and admirer, Joe Malone, was the most seriously affected by the news because he believed that Hall never had the opportunity to erase the bad name he had acquired. "There were plenty of huge, rough characters on the ice in Joe's time," said Malone, "and he was able to stay in there with them for more than eighteen years. His death was a tragic and shocking climax to one of the most surprising of all Stanley Cup series."

For the most part, though, life was fun and games for the Canadiens of that era. There were laughs galore and many of them came at the expense of the stars themselves. Once, the Montrealers "borrowed" a substitute player named Sam Goderre from the Ottawa sextet at the request of George Kennedy. Two weeks later Kennedy phoned Tommy Gorman, secretary of the Ottawas, and pleaded with him to reclaim Goderre before the youngster was lynched by the Canadiens players. "That kid," shouted Kennedy, "is a star poker player, *not* a star hockey player."

Sam eventually returned to Ottawa somewhat confused by the uproar he had ignited. Gorman was equally perplexed because he had known Goderre as a temperate young man not given to wild outbursts of gambling. "Now tell me, Sam," he asked the youngster, "what exactly happened with you and the Canadiens?"

What had happened was that the Montreal players were conducting a running poker game and were damned expert at it. When Goderre came along, they thought they had found a sucker and invited him to play. Not wanting to be unsociable with the veterans, Sam accepted the invitation and then developed an amazing run of winning hands. "After two weeks," said Gorman, "he had practically cleaned out all their wallets. That was the end of Sam's career with the Canadiens!"

Cattarinich, Letourneau, and Dandurand had been partners in a Cleveland, Ohio, racetrack when Les Canadiens were put on the auction block in October, 1921. Since the Musketeers, as they were known, were occupied with their thoroughbred venture, they were unable to be in Montreal at the time of the sale, but Dandurand was consumed with a desire to obtain the hockey team. He phoned a friend, Cecil Hart, in Montreal and asked if he would stand in for Dandurand and bid as high as possible for the Canadiens.

Hart agreed and went to the auction where he found himself in competition with Tom Duggan, who was representing both himself and the Mount Royal Arena Company. Duggan opened with a bid of $8,000 and Hart countered with $8,500. The auction was abruptly halted when N.H.L. president Frank Calder revealed that he was representing an Ottawa group intent on purchasing Les Canadiens. Calder said he wanted to contact his party for further instructions. At that point the bidding was temporarily postponed for a week.

When the second auction opened, Duggan startled the audience by placing ten $1,000 bills on the table. Calder said he would top that. Now it was Hart's turn and he was confused about his strategy on behalf of Dandurand. He asked for a time-out and dashed into the next room where he phoned Leo in Cleveland. There was no time to lose because obviously this was going to be the final auction. Unfortunately, neither Letourneau nor Cattarinich was around when Hart called

Dandurand. Leo decided to gamble and instructed Hart to go the limit.

The emissary returned to the room and raised the bid to $11,000, catching both Duggan and Calder unawares. The two adversaries looked at each other and conceded the decision to Hart who, in turn, ran out and phoned back Dandurand with the news. Leo didn't know whether to be jubilant or crestfallen but he had no choice but to tell his partners they had just acquired a professional hockey team. The investment paid off immediately because Les Canadiens collected a $20,000 profit the first year they owned it. However, a rejuvenation of the roster was needed.

"Leo was quick to see that the team was disintegrating," said Elmer Ferguson who was covering the Canadiens at the time, "and he quickly set about rebuilding. The accent in hockey in those days was largely on weight and power, though a few of the lighter-weight players had risen to stardom.

"Dandurand was thoroughly convinced that speed and skill were the real essentials. He had a keen eye for hockey-playing talent, having played the game himself. Out of the Mount Royal League he picked Pit Lepine, a fine scorer and one of the great defensive forwards of his era. He similarly secured the two Mantha boys, fast-skating Armand Mondou, Wildor Larochelle, Billy Boucher, Albert 'Battleship' Leduc, all from amateur ranks. Later he traded Newsy Lalonde for Aurel Joliat and beat the Toronto Maple Leafs to Howie Morenz by a few minutes."

It was hardly an accident that "the Three Musketeers" were able to thoroughly rejuvenate the Canadiens franchise. Each of the trio had had experience in sports ventures. Letourneau, a thickset, warmhearted little French-Canadian, always modestly described himself as "the least of the Three Musketeers" but he was as revered as his cronies.

"He would never tell his age while he lived," said a friend when Letourneau died in 1952 at the age of eighty-five. "He had such physical pride that he carefully concealed the fact that he was almost blind, and couldn't see the game clearly when he went to the Forum at the age of eighty-four to watch the Canadiens. In fact he was recognizing old friends who stopped to greet him by their voices only."

Cattarinich had come up the ranks as a player and Dandurand was both player and referee. Together, they had managed to scrounge up the capital ($11,500) for the franchise which they sold fourteen years later to the Forum interests for $165,000. Today, that same Canadiens franchise is worth more than $30,000,000.

The Musketeers didn't click immediately. In fact Les Canadiens "under new management" were walloped 5-2 in the opening game of the 1921–1922 season and followed that loss with a 10-0 debacle at the hands of Ottawa. When they lost their third straight—2-1 to Ottawa—Dandurand began worrying. He probed the roster carefully and decided, with many misgivings, that Newsy Lalonde was doing the Canadiens more harm than good.

Dandurand conferred with Montreal's perennial star, but rather than improving the situation, the conference appeared to set them further apart. Disgusted with his treatment, Lalonde abruptly announced his "retirement" on January 10, 1922, asserting that he was insulted by management, which charged him with not playing his best. Lalonde bolting the Canadiens was tantamount to Babe Ruth walking out on the Yankees. It was a national catastrophe and compelled N.H.L. president Frank Calder to intrevene and mediate the dispute. Calder didn't achieve a settlement overnight, but Newsy, after missing four games, was finally persuaded to return.

Newsy was never the same player for Les Canadiens after that. Later in the season the Montreal fans began razzing him and soon he was handed the supreme insult: he was demoted to a substitute's role and was eventually traded to Saskatoon for young Aurel Joliat.

Despite his brief clash with the Canadiens' front office, Newsy always regarded Dandurand as one of his closest friends. "He sure was good to me and my family," said

Newsy. "I'll never forget when he arranged that trade for Joliat. He got me a bonus for signing and a three-year contract at the most money I ever made in hockey—something like ten thousand dollars. Nobody in the East or West was getting money like that. Leo could strike a hard bargain, but there's never been a man in pro sport that did so much in so many ways for hockey."

The moment Newsy started slumping he was replaced on the front line by Sprague Cleghorn, who was a Montreal native and a big, capable leader. He had every much the fight in him that Lalonde possessed. "He was a product of a rough neighborhood," said the late Bobby Hewetson, curator of hockey's Hall of Fame, "where everything you got you had to fight for. And he played hockey the same way. You could be sure that Sprague was well fitted for it."

Anyone who had any doubts about Cleghorn's toughness should have been in the Ottawa rink on the night of February 1, 1922. Sprague had played three years for the Senators and saw no reason why the Ottawa sextet had dealt him to Montreal. He made no effort to conceal his hatred for the Senators' management, and on this night he took out his hostility on any member of the opposition who happened to get in his way. A sequence of events involving Cleghorn and the Senators is vividly described in *The Trail of the Stanley Cup.*

> A vicious swing at Eddie Gerard cut him over the eye for five stitches. Nighbor was charged and in falling damaged his elbow. A butt end for Cy Denneny required several stitches over the eye and some in his nose. This worked out to a match foul and fifteen-dollar fine for Sprague. The Ottawa police offered to arrest Cleghorn for assault. Referee Lou Marsh said in his report that he considered Sprague and his brother Odie a disgrace to the game.
>
> Gerard, Nighbor, and Denneny all missed two games as the result of Cleghorn's activities but President Calder did not seem to be unduly concerned. The Ottawa club

formally requested Cleghorn's explusion from the league but Hamilton and Toronto refused to support the demand. In fact Charlie Querrie (of Toronto) said there was too much hollering about rough play. He considered the players well paid and if they couldn't take the bumps they should quit. Calder's decision was that if Cleghorn drew another match penalty he would be out for the season.

If Sprague Cleghorn tended to blemish the Canadiens' reputation for "good sportsmanship," it was consistently restored and upheld by Georges Vézina. "The Chicoutimi Cucumber," apart from being a superb athlete, was the acme of gentility and a gentleman hockey player. Such displays as Cleghorn's tantrum against Ottawa grated Vézina's conscience. "He was," said hockey writer Bill Roche, "a deep thinker."

Although Vézina never attended college, he was nevertheless a gifted human who once took pen in hand and wrote a short essay called "Sport, Creator of Unity," which his boss, Dandurand, translated from French to English. It read, in part:

If fair play is the rule in the N.H.L., there will be no cause for worry. Speaking of fair play reminds me of the words of the noted English novelist John Galsworthy, who, despairing of what he termed "the present precious European mess," declared that he found only one flag that was flying high and true, and that was the flag of sport.

Athletes and sportsmen rejoice in this. . . . Around this outstanding British inheritance of two words—fair play—revolves Canada's powerful and precious asset, sport. It serves unfailingly, more than anything else, to impress Canadian youth with the importance of fair play. With those two words always in mind we are assured of what every thoughtful Canadian is striving for, and that is unity.

That sport, more than anything else, can bring this about was never brought home to me more forcibly than last year on our training trip to Grimsby, Ontario. I, a French-Canadian . . . being unable to speak English and living amongst men of a different creed and racial background, made many fast friends in Ontario, friends whom I would never have known if I had not been connected with the sport of hockey.

Quebec and its English-speaking sister provinces cannot have too many sports flags flying, because those flags always teach respect for rules and adversaries. Men who are able to live above the fog in public duty and private thinking are sportsmen inevitably. They are usually leaders also, not merely following the current but directing it.

Few were aware of Vézina's capacity for philosophy. The fans cared about only one thing, whether or not he was a good goaltender, and through the early twenties there was no question that Vézina was as good as he ever was. He proved his mettle in the 1922–1923 season in several episodes, some of which were defaced with blood.

During a game at Hamilton his former teammate Bert Corbeau smashed into Vézina with such force that the goaltender's head was cut open and his nose was broken. Vézina continued playing despite the wounds and continued to excel. A few games later he led the Canadiens to a win over Ottawa, allowing the Senators only one goal, although seventy-nine shots were hurled at him.

"After the game," wrote Canadian author Ron McAllister, "he left the rink a solemn, plodding figure, in sharp contrast to the wild hilarity of his teammates, who were already celebrating the victory that Vézina had won for them."

Another reporter observed, "Georges has a calmness not of this world."

The commentary was more prophetic than the writer had realized, for Georges Vézina's body was being tortured by the early symptoms of tuberculosis. "Beads of perspiration formed on his forehead for no apparent reason," said McAllister. "An expression of pain flitted momentarily across his face, but the

Great Vézina invariably settled down to the business at hand, turning in his usual matchless performance."

Whether or not Vézina himself was aware of the gravity of his condition is debatable. One thing is certain, and that was his determination to continue in the nets for Les Canadiens. There was no outward suggestion that Vézina was faltering.

He had a delicious sense of humor that somehow surmounted the language barrier, for Georges never learned to speak, read, or write English. "He wasn't completely ignorant of the language," explained Dandurand. "If he heard English spoken in his presence, he could figure out what was being said, more often than not, but he often gave others the idea that he didn't know what was going on."

Once when the Canadiens were heading for Ottawa on the Canadian National Express, Georges took a seat in the club car and began relaxing with a pipe and his favorite newspaper. He was just getting comfortable when a salesman for a beef-extract company walked in and sat down in the next seat.

Vézina ignored the man until he launched into an endless peroration on the benefits of his potion. The fact that the man was well into the grape *and* was speaking English distressed Georges who simply wanted to be left alone.

When it became obvious that the beef-extract salesman was not about to relent, Vézina beckoned to Dandurand and wondered whether Leo could somehow persuade the man to leave. Dandurand was perfectly willing to cooperate but, always the diplomat, Leo asked his goalie if there was anything special he might want him to say to the pest.

Speaking in French to his boss, Vézina replied: "Ask the fellow if he ever stopped to think what a good salesman he'd be if he confined his drinking to his beef extract!"

Although the Canadiens finished second to Ottawa in the 1923–1924 season, Vézina allowed only forty-eight goals in twenty-four games, including three shutouts, for a goals against average of 2.00. He then blanked Ottawa, 1–0, in the

N.H.L. play-off opener and sparkled as Les Canadiens swept the series, 4–2, in the second game, thus qualifying to meet a representative from one of the two western professional leagues.

A squabble between officials of the Western Canada Hockey League and the Pacific Coast Hockey Association resulted in a bizarre turn of events. Instead of one team coming east to challenge Montreal for the Stanley Cup, both Calgary and Vancouver showed up. Les Canadiens really weren't overly extended. They first dispatched Vancouver by scores of 3–2 and 2–1 and routed Calgary, 6–1 and 3–0. The final game was switched to Ottawa because of poor ice conditions in Montreal, but Vézina was never better. His Stanley Cup record was six goals against in six games for a perfect 1.00 average.

Proof that Vézina was outfighting his ailment was provided by his uncanny performance in the 1924–1925 season. Les Canadiens finished in third place behind Hamilton and Toronto, but Georges's 1.9 goals against average was easily the best in the league. His teammates rallied behind him in the first round of the play-offs to oust Toronto, 3–2 and 2–0, but Vézina enjoyed only one good game—a 4–2 win—at Victoria as the western champs dispatched Les Canadiens by scores of 5–2, 3–1, and 6–1 to win the Stanley Cup, the last time for a western professional team.

Whether Vézina was debilitated or not in the 1925 Cup series is uncertain, but when he showed up at the Canadiens' training camp in the autumn of 1925, he betrayed the signs of fatigue. "As this gigantic frame, in the grip of dread tuberculosis, gradually weakened, even his public sensed that their beloved goaltender was fading," wrote Ron McAllister. "If his color was a little higher than usual, no one remarked on it."

The 1925–1926 season was truly momentous for the National Hockey League. It had expanded into the United States, first accepting Boston the previous year, and now embracing New York and Pittsburgh as well. A second team, the Maroons, had been added to Montreal to provide an

English-speaking club as the natural rivals for the Canadiens. Needless to say, the outstanding attraction in the American cities among Montreal players was the redoubtable Vézina.

Pittsburgh, one of the new entries, provided the opposition for Les Canadiens in the season opener on November 28, 1925, at Mount Royal Arena. There were six thousand spectators in the stands on that rainy night who had come to see the great Vézina, ignorant of the fact that the lean goalie was suffering enormous discomfort as he took the ice for the opening face-off.

"No one knew," wrote McAllister, "that the great goaltender had struggled to the arena in spite of a temperature of 105 degrees. A deathlike chill settled over him; but with Pittsburgh forcing the play from the face-off, Vézina functioned throughout the entire first period with his usual dexterous ease, deflecting shot after shot. In the dressing room he suffered a severe arterial hemorrhage, but the opening of the second period found him at his accustomed place in goal."

Fighting desperately against the fatigue and fever that completely throttled his body, the great Vézina could no longer see the puck as it was skimmed from one side of the rink to the other. Suddenly, a collective gasp engulfed the arena. Vézina had collapsed in his goal crease! "In the stricken arena," said one observer, "all was silent as the limp form of the greatest of goalies was carried slowly from the ice."

It was the end of the trail for Georges and he knew it. At his request he was taken home to his native Chicoutimi where doctors diagnosed his case as advanced tuberculosis. On March 24, 1926, a week after the Canadiens had been eliminated from a play-off berth, Georges Vézina passed away.

An enormous funeral, held in the old cathedral at Chicoutimi, saw players and fans from all parts of the country deliver their final tribute to the gallant goaltender. A year later, Cattarinich, Dandurand, and Letourneau donated a trophy in his honor which is now given to the goaltender with the best goals against average in the N.H.L.

4

The
First Golden Era

*H*ad Vézina been healthy enough to play his normal game in the 1925–1926 season, Les Canadiens would surely have climbed to the top of the N.H.L. instead of finishing an embarrasing last, because the Three Musketeers had carefully collected some of the best young players in Canada. One of them was Aurel Joliat, a little French-Canadian who wore a black baseball cap and defied opponents to knock it off his head. The other was Howie Morenz, a youngster from Ontario with not an ounce of French blood in him.

The son of a railroad man, Howie was born in Mitchell, Ontario, a hamlet about thirteen miles from Stratford, in 1903. A little fellow, the young Morenz was often severely beaten by the older boys with whom he played hockey in the neighborhood games. From time to time he'd return home so badly cut and bruised he'd often consider quitting the game; but his love for hockey was so passionate he'd inevitably return to the rink. Soon he was the star of the Stratford team which journeyed to Montreal for a play-off game.

Dandurand happened to be in the stands on the night that Morenz dipsy-doodled around the hometown defensemen from the start to the finish of the game. Leo conferred with his aide, Cecil Hart, and both agreed it would be prudent to sign Morenz before the Maroons, Hamilton, Ottawa, or Toronto beat them to it.

Once again Leo was occupied with his horse-racing business, this time in Montreal, and again delegated Hart to handle the negotiating. Cecil was given two blank checks and two contracts, one to be signed by Howie and the other by his father. The offer was for three years starting at $3,500 for the first season with increases each season thereafter. Cecil took the first available train from Montreal to Stratford and expected little difficulty in signing the lad.

But when he arrived in Stratford, Hart was somewhat astonished to discover that Howie was working for the Canadian National Railroad with his father. What's more, his father had no intentions of permitting his son to forsake the good life of railroading for such nonsense as hockey. But the money was awfully big, and the elder Morenz finally modified his position. "If my boy thinks he'd like to spend his life that way," he said, "then it's up to him to say."

Howie paused for a moment, looked rather uncertainly at his father, and then said he would sign the contract. Both Hart and Dandurand believed their troubles were over when Cecil returned to Montreal with the Morenz signatures, but a month later Leo received a letter postmarked Stratford. It was from Howie and it read.

Dear Sir: I am enclosing cheque and contract to play hockey for your club. Owing to several reasons, of which family and work are the most to consider, I find it impossible to leave Stratford. I am sorry if I have caused you expense and inconvenience, and trust you will accept the returned contract in a sportsmanlike way.

Leo wasn't about to give up that easily. He phoned Howie and invited him to Montreal to discuss the matter at greater length. Morenz accepted and the next day told Dandurand face-to-face that he rather preferred his situation at home. He had a nice job in the railroad car shops and was able to play in the Ontario Hockey Association's Intermediate Division. He was, after all, a hero in Stratford and didn't mind telling Leo some of the stories about hockey back home. One night, he recalled, his opponents actually tried to use police force to stop him from scoring.

This happened when Howie's Stratford team was playing a game in the town of Preston. Between the first and second periods a constable appeared in the Stratford dressing room accompanied by what appeared to be a vigilante group of Preston rooters. The officer presented Morenz with a summons for malicious damage to property. The policeman charged that Howie, upon rounding the net at his usual breakneck speed, had *sliced the rubbers of the goal judge* who was stationed immediately behind the cage.

Strange as it may seem, the constable was dead serious about his mission and planned to haul Howie off to court. Stratford supporters offered five dollars for the rubbers provided they were delivered to the Stratford dressing room.

Milt Dunnell of the Toronto *Daily Star*, himself a native of the Stratford area, reported that the charge was dropped after the offer to repay the goal judge was made.

"The goal judge kept his damaged rubbers," said Dunnell. "After all, he had his pride."

Dandurand was suitably impressed with these tales and told Morenz so. But Leo was operating a hockey team for profit as well as for fun, and he told Howie that there was a contract that had to be honored. He expected Howie to honor it. Morenz couldn't control himself. He burst into tears and, in the process, revealed to Leo what was *really* bothering him. He didn't think he was good enough to play in the N.H.L. What's more, Dandurand was told that he would have to accept the consequences if he *forced* Howie to play and thereby lose his job in the car shops.

"The kid touched a soft spot," Leo admitted later, "and I had all to do to keep from letting him off the hook. But something inside of me said, 'No, don't you do it.' And when we were through talking I told him I was certain he could make our team and that I expected him to show up at training camp that November."

Morenz *did* show up at camp and, for a while, seemed certain that he had made the wrong move. The veterans, as was the custom then, tried their best to intimidate the rookie, and each day his bruises multiplied. But it was also obvious that his skills were enormous, and soon the veterans were finding it more and more difficult to keep up with "Lightning Legs." Anyone who saw Morenz play in that rookie year was quick to admit he was a star.

"He was the picture player," said Nels Stewart, himself a member of the Hall of Fame. "Howie had the grace and speed to finish off plays like no one else could."

Raw speed was Howie's forte as he gained a varsity center ice berth on Les Canadiens. Within weeks he was dubbed "the Stratford Streak," "the Mitchell Meteor," and assorted other appellations that almost but never quite described his presence on the ice. "The kid's *too fast*," said one observer. "He'll burn himself out."

Morenz scored his first goal in the *bleu, blanc, et rouge* uniform of Les Canadiens against Ottawa on December 26, 1923, before 8,300 spectators at the spanking new Ottawa Auditorium, a curious-looking egg-shaped rink. Ottawa's Senators dominated the N.H.L. that season, thanks in part to a miniscule defenseman by the name of Francis "King" Clancy who would go on to become one of hockey's most delightful personalities as a referee, coach, and vice-president of the Toronto Maple Leafs. Clancy vividly recalls his first clash with Morenz.

"Weeks before I ever played against him," said Clancy, "I had read story after story about this kid and I couldn't believe any boy that age could be *that* good. The stories also said he was making a lot of the veteran defensemen look like fools. I made up my mind that Clancy wasn't going to be one of them."

Clancy gave Morenz a once-over in practice and concluded there was nothing very special about him. "He was only an inch taller than I was," said Clancy. "That gave me the confidence I needed for starters."

Inevitably, Morenz captured the puck and launched a rush in Clancy's direction. King's linemate covered the other Canadiens' forward, enabling Clancy to get a dead bead on Howie who, by this time, was under a full head of steam. King had sized up the situation as well as he could. Morenz was a left-handed shot; he figured to cut to his left when he reached poke-checking distance; everything perfectly calculated for King's riposte.

"I remember telling myself," Clancy recalled, " 'get nicely set on your feet, watch a quick reverse and you got him.' "

Morenz barreled right in on King and neither zigged nor zagged. He released a snapshot, skated right into Clancy, and bowled him on his derriere. Howie didn't score on the play, but as he returned to center ice Clancy pulled himself together and warned the rookie: "One more run like that and I'll knock your block off."

The kid was singularly unimpressed. After digesting Clancy's warning, he replied that he planned to pull off the very same play as soon as he received the puck again. "Believe it or not," said the King, "he did *exactly* what he said he'd do."

Dandurand took a paternal interest in Morenz even to the point of boarding him with an elderly Scottish lady who ran a rooming house in Montreal. Leo asked her to keep an eye out for Howie should he get homesick and decide to depart for Stratford. Sure enough, early one morning Dandurand was awakened with a phone call from the lady.

"Young Morenz is gone," she said, half-weeping. "He left last night and hasn't returned since."

Thinking Morenz might have been sight-seeing on the town, Leo suggested the landlady go back to sleep and phone him again later in the morning. But by 9 A.M. Howie had not returned and now Leo was genuinely worried.

There were several possibilities. One, naturally, was that Howie had decided to leave the big city and return to Stratford. Another, that he had gone on the town and was still collecting himself. Or possibly the kid was simply overwrought from the previous night's game and had to unwind somehow.

It was Dandurand's custom to hold a meeting the morning after the game, followed by a luncheon with his players. Leo decided to go straight to the Mount Royal Arena in the hopes that Morenz would be there. Sure enough, he was in the dressing room, looking none the worse for wear.

He had gone on a tour of Montreal from Bonaventure Station to the Canadian National Railways yard in Point St. Charles and finally back to the city. It was to be a standard operating procedure for Morenz in years to come and one that would amaze both his teammates and sportswriters alike.

Morenz scored thirteen goals in his rookie season to finish in a tie with Jack Adams for seventh place in scoring. He was well on his way to becoming the glamour boy of hockey; a man admired as much by his opponents as by his teammates and fans. Howie played the game as cleanly as was possible in those rambunctious days of chronic stick fights and butt ends.

In a game at Madison Square Garden he knocked out four of Bun Cook's front teeth with the end of his stick as the pair was battling for the puck. Howie immediately dropped his stick and helped Bun off the ice. Later Cook explained, "It was just an accident. Howie wouldn't pull anything like that intentionally."

Morenz was a superstar in his second year of big-league play. He finished second in scoring to Cecil "Babe" Dye of Toronto and was doing things with the puck that astonished even such skeptics as Conn Smythe, founder of the Maple Leaf empire and the venerable dean of hockey in Toronto.

"The trouble is," said Smythe, "that writers are always talking about what a great scorer Morenz is. Which is true enough. But they overlook the fact that he's a great two-way player."

According to Smythe, Morenz executed "the most amazingly impossible play" he had ever seen in hockey up until that time. It was accomplished against the Boston Bruins who had a big, rugged team and had managed to ram Morenz forcefully into the boards on more than one occasion. Somehow, Morenz responded to the battering by skating even faster than he had before he was hit. Finally, Eddie Shore and

Lionel Hitchman of the Boston defense prepared to sandwich
Morenz between their powerful bodies as he tried to split the
defense. Suddenly Howie leaped forward and crashed through
like an auto speeding past two closing railroad gates at a
crossing.

Just then a Bruin forward swerved in behind his defense
to intercept Morenz. Seeing that he couldn't elude the checking
wing, Howie released his shot from twenty-five feet in front
of the net. The shot missed the goalpost by a few inches and
caromed off the end boards right back to the blue line and
onto Shore's waiting stick.

The Bruin defenseman, one of the speediest rushers
hockey has ever known, orbited into a breakaway with all
the Montreal players caught in Bruin territory along with
Morenz. "I was watching Howie all the time," said Smythe,
"and I saw him follow up his shot with a long leap in prepara-
tion to circling the net. To this day I can't figure out how he
managed to stay on his skates as he rounded the cage."

Meanwhile, Shore was away at top speed for the Canadiens' goal. Nobody in the rink, let alone Smythe, doubted
that the Bruin would have plenty of time for an easy play on
goal and a likely score. That is, all but Morenz. He had put
his head down and dashed in pursuit of Shore. "He flashed
from the net to the blue line," said Smythe, "faster than I can
say 'blue line.' "

Shore was about to enter the final stages of his maneuvering when Morenz suddenly cut directly *in front* of him, released the puck from the Boston player's blade, and immediately changed direction for another play on the Bruin goal.
"Shore," said Smythe, "was absolutely dumbfounded. As for
me, I actually was unable to move my mouth, I was so awed
by the play. Morenz had done what he was to do for years to
come—he took my breath away!"

Many respected hockey observers claim that Morenz was
singly responsible for the successful expansion of the N.H.L.
into the United States in the 1920's. It was no secret that New

York promoter Tex Rickard became a hockey fan the moment he spied Morenz in action. Not long afterward Rickard introduced the Rangers to New York.

"There isn't a team in the league that has not in some way been affected by some aspect of Montreal hockey," wrote Peter Gzowski, "even if the link is as tenuous as the Detroit Red Wings' crest, which is based on the old Montreal Athletic Association's winged wheel."

But Gzowski was quick to point out that Morenz was the leader of "the most exciting team in hockey from the mid-1920's to the mid-1930's." He adds. "While most fans remember Morenz mainly for his blistering speed and his headlong rushes on goal, he also provided one of the most remarkable examples of the passionate dedication to the game—to winning—that has been another characteristic of Canadien teams. Many people say, of course, that Morenz's fierce involvement in hockey, and in the Canadiens, led to his untimely death, although Morenz's dedication is not unique in the annals of the Montreal team."

Few opponents ever got the better of Morenz when Howie was in his prime, although Joe Primeau, the crack Toronto center, did just that one night when Les Canadiens and the Maple Leafs were locked in a Christmas Eve match. The teams were tied, 1–1, after regulation time and nobody scored in the overtime. When the siren sounded to end the game, both clubs headed for the dressing room until they were halted by the referee. Apparently the timekeeper had erred by ten seconds and the referee ordered the players back to the ice to play out the remaining unused time.

This act of recall nettled Morenz who was anxious to get home to his family. Before the referee dropped the puck, Howie urged Primeau not to touch it after it hit the ice; that way the ten seconds would be squandered and everybody could quit for the night. Primeau understood Howie's point but had no intentions of complying. Once the puck hit the ice the Leaf center slapped it to the left side where his winger, Busher Jackson gathered it in and roared toward the Montreal goal. His shot fooled goalie George Hainsworth and Toronto won the game, 2–1.

This necessitated another face-off and now Morenz was furious. He glared at Primeau as they went through the ritual of the last face-off and then told him in no uncertain terms that he would get even, which he did less than a week later when the teams clashed again. Nobody could touch Howie for the three periods of regulation time, but he, in turn, couldn't get the puck past the Leaf goalie.

At last the teams went into overtime and Morenz took possession of the puck immediately after the opening face-off. Bobbing and weaving through the Leaf defense, Howie worked his way right up to the goal mouth before depositing the puck where it belonged. Primeau, who was known as "Gentleman Joe," recalled that Morenz never said a word to him after scoring. "He had promised to get his revenge," said Primeau, "and he did. There was nothing more to say."

The episode reflects the competitive spirit of Morenz that was matched by perhaps only one other member of Les Canadiens—Maurice Richard. But in the twenties, the fires of competition burned fiercest in the heart of Morenz, and only those who were with him at the time can honestly portray the quality of his emotion. One of them was Elmer Ferguson, the veteran Montreal writer who had traveled to Boston one weekend with the Canadiens.

"It was a dark, muggy sort of morning," Ferguson recalled, "the way Boston gets when fog rolls in from the sea on March days and nights. But it didn't seem possible it could be time to get up, and still be this dark, when the knock sounded on my hotel room."

Ferguson rubbed his eyes and wearily strode to the door. When he opened it, there was Morenz fully dressed as if ready to take an early-morning stroll along the Charles River. "Howie," asked Ferguson, "don't you think it's a little early to be getting up? It's still dark. Where are you going?"

"I'm not getting up," said Morenz. "I haven't been to bed yet. I've been out walking around the streets, thinking about that play I missed. I lost the game for the team, and there's no use going to bed, because I won't sleep."

The play that so disturbed Howie was a face-off he had lost to Cooney Weiland of the Bruins. A split second after the referee had dropped the puck it flew into the air. Weiland batted it down with his hand and promptly shot it into the net in the same motion. The goal won the game for the Bruins. Eight hours later a sobbing Howie was still blaming himself for the goal as he slumped into the chair in Ferguson's hotel room. "He buried his face in his hands," said Ferguson. "His shoulders shook because he was crying like a little boy. He was heartbroken. He felt that he alone was responsible for the defeat. . . . In all the history of hockey there never was a more sincere competitor."

A Morenz ritual was to arrive at the dressing room at least an hour before game time. "He'd restlessly pace around the long promenade," said Ferguson, "as high-strung as a thoroughbred that is being readied for a race."

It was easy enough for Montreal players and writers to wax ecstatic about Morenz and it was not uncommon for opponents to do likewise. But when the opponent happened to be Eddie Shore, the fiercest defenseman in the game, *then* Morenz knew he had arrived!

"He's the hardest player in the league to stop," Shore admitted. "Howie comes at you with such speed that it's almost impossible to block him with a body check. When he hits you he usually comes off a lot better than the defenseman. Another thing that bothers us is his shift. He has a knack of swerving at the last minute that can completely fool you. Everybody likes Howie. He's one player who doesn't deserve any rough treatment."

Howie's ascendancy came at a fortuitous time for the Canadiens because they were about to be challenged for patronage by the newly formed Maroons. In 1924 Dandurand sold half of the Canadiens' territorial rights in Montreal to the owners of the Canadian Arena Company who owned the new Montreal Forum. Dandurand's asking price was fifteen thousand dollars. When Chicago and Detroit applied for franchises, the N.H.L. formally announced that the league was to receive fifty thousand dollars in return for entrance into the league. Dandurand later admitted that his generosity in permitting the Maroons to become N.H.L. members wasn't as altruistic as it looked on paper. "I figured that having an English team to compete with the French Canadiens would make for a great rivalry," he said later, "and I was proven right."

Dandurand's shrewd wheeling and dealing brought the Stanley Cup to Montreal in 1924 following victories over Ottawa, Vancouver, and Calgary. The feat was hailed in Montreal with appropriate enthusiasm but with a dignity and hilarity that has never been matched in the team's long history.

Instead of the traditional ticker-tape parade that greets the contemporary Stanley Cup champions, the 1924 Canadiens were honored by no less august an institution than the University of Montreal. A public reception was held at the city's national monument, during which each player received what amounted to an honorary degree from the university. The highlight of the civic affair, of course, was the presentation of the Stanley Cup.

That formality dispensed with, Dandurand herded his players to his home for a private party. Members of the team made the trip in private cars, including Vézina, Sprague Cleghorn, and Sylvio Mantha, along with Dandurand, in Leo's Model T. Ford. En route to Chez Dandurand, Leo's automobile broke down and required a rather hefty push. One by one the Canadiens emerged from the car, including Cleghorn who had been nursing the Cup on his lap. When Sprague got out of the car, he placed the Stanley Cup on the sidewalk and joined in the pushing brigade. It took several minutes to get the car up and over the hill, and when this was accomplished the quartet jumped into the car and jubilantly drove off to Leo's house.

Madame Dandurand was delighted to see her husband

and the players when they arrived, but she was anxious to pour some of her newly concocted punch into the Stanley Cup. She asked Leo where it was and he, in turn, asked Cleghorn where he had put it. Sprague nearly collapsed with anguish when he remembered that he had left it at curbside. An hour had passed but Leo and Sprague returned to the site and found the Cup sitting there undisturbed.

Theoretically, Morenz, whose ancestry was Swiss, should have been playing for the Maroons. However, the Canadiens had their share of French-Canadian stars to complement Howie, and the one who did it best was the smallest of all, Aurel Joliat. Morenz and Joliat worked together through the years, and when they retired, they had identical scoring totals of 270 goals.

Like Morenz, Joliat was a native of Ontario, having grown up in the New Edinburgh district of Ottawa. He learned his hockey on the frozen Rideau River along with Bill and Frank Boucher who also were to achieve enormous fame in the N.H.L. In time Joliat graduated to a fast league in western Canada and arrived in a Canadiens uniform when Dandurand decided to unload the aging Lalonde.

Aurel weighed 135 pounds, at his heaviest, but his size never bothered him. It apparently motivated him to compensate with a vast repertoire of stick-handling maneuvers and pirouettes. "He transported the world of ballet to the hockey arena," said one admirer. To which Aurel replied, "A fellow *needs* finesse when he weighs only 135 pounds!"

Joliat teamed up with Morenz in the 1923–1924 season. The pair jelled perfectly right from the start, although Aurel was to prove that season that he could excel with or without Morenz at his side. The Canadiens had gone up against Calgary in the play-offs and Morenz's shoulder was broken after he was hit successively by Red Dutton and Herb Gardiner. That's when Aurel took over. In the third period he intercepted an enemy pass and circled his own net to gain momentum.

"I traveled through the entire Calgary team," said Joliat,

"and faked a shot to the far corner of the net. But even as I let it go I sensed I was covered on the play. So I kept going, rounded the net, and backhanded a shot into the open corner. I tumbled head over heels after that one. We went on to win the Cup and I consider it the best goal I ever scored."

Joliat was a constant source of annoyance to his larger opponents. Once, after Aurel had thoroughly confounded Toronto's Babe Dye with a series of fakes, the distressed Dye skated over to Dandurand at the Canadiens' bench and said: "I'm tired of chasing that shadow of yours—that Frenchman, Joliat. Move him over to center, Leo, hold a mirror to each side of him—you'll have the fastest line in hockey."

Morenz and Joliat didn't travel together only on the ice. In the summer of 1926 the two went to work together in the mutuels department of Washington Race Track in Chicago, which just happened to be run by Dandurand and Cattarinich. Joliat was the more prudent type while Morenz was a wild better with very little self-control.

One day that summer, Howie bought a pair of fifty-dollar straight tickets at odds of 7½–1. When he got home in the evening, he suddenly decided to check his racing program with the mutuel tickets he had in hand. He discovered those that had been bad bets but realized that his winning tickets were gone. Then it all came back. He had inadvertently tossed them away with some losing tickets that afternoon and had not claimed the winners.

He quickly dressed, hailed a cab, and told the driver to take him out to the track, although it was now the middle of the night. The somewhat perplexed driver drove right up to the racetrack gate, which, naturally, was closed. Nonplussed, Morenz pleaded with the watchman to open the gate and promised that if he found the ticket he'd give everyone a reward.

The obliging watchman hauled out a kerosene lamp and watched the great Morenz crawl around on his hands and knees until he actually found both winning ducats. With a typical Morenz turn of generosity he gave fifty dollars to the watchman and another fifty to the cab driver. The next day he cashed in his ticket and instructed the racetrack treasurer to turn one hundred dollars of it over to his favorite charity.

Dandurand was like a father to Morenz and had pleaded with Howie not to gamble, but like any good father he had excellent insight into the young man and had said, "He'd take all sorts of gambling chances in hockey games and he was inclined to do the same in money matters."

Leo should have known. He had been wheeling and dealing all his life at both the racetrack and the hockey rink. Dandurand was one of the most lovable characters in Montreal sport, always willing to lend a hand to anyone who'd come along and ask. When the Pacific Coast and Western Canada leagues collapsed in 1926 and the players were sold by Frank and Lester Patrick to the N.H.L. clubs, it was Dandurand who helped arrange some of the deals for the Patricks. Frank and Lester respected Leo and were particularly appreciative of his help in arranging the player transfer. It was just this altruism that inadvertently resulted in the Canadiens acquiring *another* star who contributed to their first Golden Era.

The player was defenseman Herb Gardiner, of the Calgary sextet, who was somehow overlooked by the other N.H.L. teams when they were stocking up on Western players. One night the Patricks and Dandurand were dining at Leo's home when Dandurand casually mentioned that Gardiner was certainly good enough for the N.H.L. "I agree," said Lester Patrick, "and you can have him for one dollar!"

This was the Patricks' way of repaying Dandurand for all the help he had given them. The trio completed the deal on the spot and Gardiner, in turn, developed into one of the most formidable defensemen in the history of Les Canadiens. "This had to be my best bargain," said Dandurand.

Well stocked on offense and defense, Dandurand realized that his major project would be finding a replacement for the legendary Vézina. Immediately after Vézina collapsed at the start of the 1925–1926 season, the Canadiens replaced him with Alphonse "Frenchy" Lacroix who obviously couldn't handle the job. After five games Lacroix was removed, and Herb Rheaume played twenty-nine games for Les Canadiens but also left much to be desired.

Once again luck played a hand in the Canadiens' favor. When Newsy Lalonde was traded to Saskatoon for Aurel Joliat, Lalonde went searching for a goaltender and found an exceptionally courageous young man playing in Kitchener. The son of a plumber, George Hainsworth soon persuaded Lalonde that he was major-league caliber and Newsy signed George to play for the Saskatoon Sheiks of the Western Canada League.

But Newsy, like so many of the Canadiens before and since, had strong ties to his alma mater in Montreal. One day he wrote a letter to Dandurand, advising him that it would be worthwhile keeping Hainsworth in mind. "This kid," wrote Lalonde, "could be the one to take Vézina's place if Georges ever retires."

This was not exactly startling news to Dandurand because he and Vézina had watched Hainsworth play for Kitchener a few years earlier when Georges had actually entertained thoughts of retiring. Vézina was greatly impressed with Hainsworth and Dandurand knew it. "That night, " Leo once told Bill Roche, "Vézina really chose his own successor in the Canadiens' net."

Dandurand launched his pursuit of Hainsworth in earnest as soon as Vézina entered the hospital. But since Hainsworth was under contract to Saskatoon through the 1925–1926 seasons, Leo's hands were tied. As soon as the Western League dissolved, Dandurand was free to negotiate with the little goalie and Leo was right there with a bid.

Dandurand didn't sign Hainsworth without some grave reservations. After all, there was the delicate matter of finding a *suitable* replacement for the venerated Vézina. Unlike his predecessor, Hainsworth was an English-Canadian who measured only five foot six inches, compared to the tall, distinguished Vézina. And furthermore, at thirty-three years old, Hainsworth seemed to be approaching the end, rather than the beginning, of his major-league career.

Hainsworth's debut was something less than impressive. He was beaten, 4–1, in the season's opener at Boston and returned to Montreal where Ottawa outscored Les Canadiens, 2–1. This was followed by a 2–1 loss to the Maroons, thus confirming the suspicions of Canadiens fans that Hainsworth was an unworthy successor to Vézina.

"From their point of view," observed Ron McAllister, "everything George did was wrong. Their loyalty to Vézina was a living thing."

The criticism notwithstanding (one sportswriter referred to him as "a lowly substitute"), Hainsworth played every one of the forty-four games on the Canadiens' schedule and finished the season with a goals against average of 1.52, topped only by Clint Benedict of the Maroons who registered a 1.51 mark. But George led the league in shutouts with fourteen and outgoaled Benedict in the first round of the Stanley Cup play-offs.

Little by little the Canadiens fans began warming to Hainsworth. He won the Vézina Trophy in the 1927–1928 season with a remarkable 1.09 goals against average and managed to improve on that in 1928–1929, this time allowing only forty-three goals in forty-four games for a 0.98 mark. It would be presumptuous to suggest that Hainsworth ever commanded the same total adulation of Montreal fans that Vézina enjoyed, but by January, 1929, Hainsworth had certainly become a hero to many French-Canadians. It was a single performance, however, that captured their imagination.

On the night of January 24, 1929, the Toronto Maple Leafs were visiting the Forum. As the Canadiens were peppering Hainsworth in the pregame warm-up, a practice shot caught the goaltender unawares and smashed into his nose, knocking him unconscious. A bloody mess, Hainsworth was carried to the dressing room and a call went over the Forum loudspeaker for the Canadiens' spare goalie. He couldn't be located.

Meanwhile, the team physician worked over Hainsworth's broken nose, attempting to reduce the swelling around his eye and cheeks. But the blow was so severe there was little the doctor could do, and within a matter of minutes the swelling had completely shut one eye. "Bandage me up," Hainsworth insisted, "I want to get out there."

Neither the doctor nor the Canadiens had much choice. Ten minutes later George skated out to his position for the opening face-off. The Forum crowd reacted with a distillation of jubilation and fear. The goal-hungry Maple Leafs immediately swarmed to the attack and bombarded Hainsworth with every variety of shot at their command.

"George appeared to be enjoying himself," said one viewer. "He seemed to laugh with mad glee after stopping each shot."

Veteran reporters could hardly remember the fans sitting down throughout the game as Hainsworth portrayed a hockey version of Horatio at the bridge, and soon George himself was yelling and screaming along with his fans. "His face," wrote McAllister, "one-sided and bulging, feverish and red from excitement and injury, loomed livid and macabre above the forest of sticks and whirling forms crowding close about him. This was his night of nights!"

The Maple Leafs managed to jam one shot behind him, but the inspired Canadiens scored a goal, too, and the game ended in a 1–1 tie. From that point on Hainsworth was a Forum hero and played seven full seasons until he was forty years old.

Hainsworth seemed to improve with age. In 1928–1929 he recorded twenty-two shutouts in forty-four games and continued to excel for the Canadiens until the 1932–1933 campaign. The entire Montreal team from Morenz to Hainsworth was in the trough of a slump that year. It reached a climax on February 21, 1933, when Les Canadiens visited Boston and were demolished, 10–0, by the Bruins. Dandurand was furious with Hainsworth, who had given up several "easy" goals and made up his mind to trade him at the earliest opportunity. The result was one of the quickest deals in hockey history.

It happened after the season in which the Canadiens were quickly dispatched from the play-offs by New York. Dandurand had been brooding over Hainsworth's play for a long time when one afternoon, in a Toronto hotel room, he picked up the telephone and called Conn Smythe, manager of the Maple Leafs, whose goalie was tall Lorne Chabot.

"Would you be interested in trading Chabot for Hainsworth?" Dandurand asked.

"Certainly," replied Smythe, who promptly hung up.

Dandurand could be forgiven if he thought the whole brief sequence had been a bizarre dream. He phoned Smythe again to be sure the whole idea wasn't a gag in the mind of the Toronto boss. Thus assured, the two agreed to announce the trade the next day and the deal was completed.

Chabot played only one season for Les Canadiens and registered a 2.15 goals against average, whereas Hainsworth's mark was a less impressive 2.48. But Hainsworth lasted three full seasons in Toronto, during which the Leafs twice led the league, before returning briefly to Montreal in 1937, where he played a few games before retiring.

"George was one of the greatest goaltenders," said a Montreal observer, "but he had the misfortune of battling the ghost of Vézina as long as he played for the Canadiens."

The seeds of the world championship team that Dandurand had planted in the mid-1920's finally bore fruit in the play-offs of 1930. Les Canadiens went up against the Chicago Black Hawks in the first round of a two-game total goals series and emerged with a 1–0 win at Chicago before 17,476, the largest crowd to see a game in the Windy City until then, and returned to Montreal where the teams played a 2–2 tie. Thus, the Canadiens came off with a 3–2 edge in goals and moved on to the semifinals against the Rangers.

Paced by Gus Rivers, who scored at 68:52 of sudden-death

overtime, a new record, Les Canadiens won the opening game, 2–1, and Hainsworth shut out New York, 2–0, in the second and final match, giving Montreal the right to meet the Boston Bruins in the Stanley Cup final. Boston was heavily favored to rout Les Canadiens, but Hainsworth was too much for the Bruins in the opener and stopped Boston, 3–0. The Bruins hadn't lost two consecutive games that season and were expected to rebound in the second game of the best-of-three series, but the Canadiens prevailed, 4–3, and captured the Cup.

Dandurand wasn't one to stand pat. He embellished his lineup with a small slick French-Canadian forward named Johnny Gagnon. Swarthy and black-haired with quick darting moves, Gagnon was placed on the line with Morenz and Joliat and immediately dubbed "the Black Cat." He was to become one of the foremost Canadiens forwards in the years ahead.

With the Gagnon-Morenz-Joliat line leading the way, Les Canadiens finished first in the Canadian Division of the N.H.L. and faced Boston, champions of the American Division, in the first round of the best-of-five series. As expected it was a superb series that went down to the fifth game with the clubs tied at two apiece.

Montreal grabbed a 2–0 lead in the finale at the Forum, but the Bruins counterattacked and tied the score, forcing the game into sudden death. It was finally resolved after nineteen minutes of furious skating when Marty Burke passed the puck to Wildor Larochelle who beat Tiny Thompson in the Bruin goal.

In the meantime, the Chicago Black Hawks coached by Dick Irvin, a man who was to play a major part in the Canadiens saga, reached the finals against Montreal. Cleverly directed by Irvin, the Black Hawks stunned the Canadiens by taking a 2–1 lead in games and a 2–0 lead in what could have been the fourth and Cup-winning game for them. But "Black Cat" Gagnon rallied Montreal with two goals and Pit Lépine followed with two more as Les Canadiens triumphed, 4–2.

The finale was the type of match that has since been referred to as "typical play-off hockey." Both teams accented a close-checking defense game, also known as "kitty-bar-the-door," waiting for the one break that would lead to a score. The Canadiens finally got it and the Black Cat once again was the scoring hero, with Morenz supplying the second goal, giving Les Canadiens their second straight Stanley Cup.

A year later the Canadiens led the Canadian Division again, but this time they were wiped out in the opening Stanley Cup round by the American Division champion Rangers, three games to one. Like the more contemporary Montreal teams, the Canadiens of that era accented style rather than strength. They were an artistic bunch with one collective flaw: size was always against them. The Morenz Line, for example, was nothing more than a collection of half-pints compared with the behemoths on the other teams. Consequently, whenever an opposing coach planned strategy against Les Canadiens, he would give serious consideration to mauling the smallest of the Flying Frenchmen. Boston's Bruins, then as now, typified the manslaughter theory of hockey and on January 24, 1933, gave a vivid demonstration of how it works.

Big, bruising Eddie Shore started the brawl by cross-checking miniscule Johnny Gagnon across the bridge of his nose with his stick. Minutes later Sylvio Mantha of the Canadiens clashed with Shore and a bloody fight developed with referee Cooper Smeaton in the middle trying to separate the pair. The peacemaker Smeaton took three of Shore's hardest blows and fell to the ice with two broken ribs!

Faced with the possible extinction of his team unless the league intervened, Dandurand protested the Bruins' behavior to both N.H.L. president Frank Calder and Charles Adams, president of the Boston sextet. Dandurand had the naiveté to expect Adams to punish Shore, a suggestion that received a huge laugh in Boston. Calder responded by fining Shore one hundred dollars, and Adams protested that Shore was not permitted the right to defend himself.

Adams continued feuding with Calder and finally resigned as an N.H.L. governor on February 11, 1933. The decision was regarded as both a triumph for Calder and Dandurand and a

curious thing for hockey in general. The essence of Adam's resignation was his displeasure with the N.H.L. "gag rule," which
provided a one-thousand-dollar fine for criticizing another
N.H.L. official. By resigning, Adams cleverly placed himself
beyond the ken of the rule yet in a position to denounce Calder and Dandurand as much as he pleased.

The Bruins weren't the only players taking runs at the
smaller Canadiens. Conn Smythe's big Maple Leafs also had
their strategy settled when the teams clashed. Since Gagnon
had developed into one of the most formidable scorers on
Montreal, Smythe decided that the Black Cat should be
softened up, and he chose his husky forward Harvey "Busher"
Jackson to handle the job. From the opening face-off Jackson,
for no apparent reason, would crash headlong into the surprised Gagnon. The Black Cat knew Jackson as a pleasant
chap off the ice and asked him why he was battering him so
violently.

"Sorry, Johnny," Busher replied, "that's orders."

Each time Jackson floored Gagnon, the Leaf would look
down at the crumpled Canadien and repeat, "That's orders."
Finally, in utter desperation, Gagnon shot back: "Hey, Busher,
how long these goddamned orders for?"

Gagnon, like so many of his teammates, had a sparkling
sense of humor that was briefly abetted by a huge French
Canadian named Jean Baptiste Pusie. Considered the funniest
man to lace on a pair of skates, Pusie played briefly for the
Canadiens in 1931, 1932, and 1936, and was never at a loss for
words, although his English was often fractured beyond re-
pair. Once, after a losing game a teammate berated Jean
Baptiste in the dressing room for his lack of teamwork.
Specifically, he wanted to know why Pusie hadn't passed the
puck to him.

"I skate h'up de h'ice," said Jean Baptiste, "I no see you.
I skate around' de net; I no see you. Den I look h'up; an' I see
you. But I cannot pass de puck, because you are park' in de
penalty box!"

Dandurand wasn't doing much laughing in those days.

His dynasty began crumbling in the 1932–1933 season, and for no apparent reason. The Morenz Line was intact, the goaltending and defense appeared to be sound, and the rest of the roster could hardly be considered inferior. Some of the players, including Gagnon, later charged that they couldn't get along with Newsy Lalonde, who was coaching the team at the time. The behavior of some stars confirms this thinking. Overlooking Lalonde's part in the slump, Dandurand threatened to shake up the team and even went so far as to put Morenz on the trading block. At one point late in the season it was rumored that Leo had fined Gagnon two hundred dollars for indifferent play. Leo clearly established himself in support of the coach and immediately began probing the minor leagues for potential replacements. Oddly enough, he took Morenz with him on a trip to Hamilton, Ontario, and it was Howie's advice that led to a vital acquisition for Les Canadiens several years later.

Dandurand had heard some good things about a forward line with the Hamilton Tigers, of the Ontario Hockey Association's Senior League, and after watching the Tigers in action, he asked Morenz whom he liked best. "Toe Blake and Herbie Cain," Morenz replied.

"I agree," said Dandurand.

A day later Leo phoned the N.H.L. office and requested that the pair be placed on the Canadiens' reserve list, thereby reserving them for his club. As a philanthropic gesture, Dandurand agreed to permit Cain to play for the enfeebled Maroons and later agreed to have his intracity rivals sign Blake. But in each case, Leo reserved the right of recall, a stipulation that was to be very significant in the late thirties because both Blake and Cain were to become two-hundred-goal scorers in the N.H.L.

Such Maroons-Canadiens amity was never reflected on the Forum ice. The English-French rivalry had been well established in the thirties with the bigger Maroons having the edge in the fighting if not in the scoring. On February 22, 1934, the Maroons edged Les Canadiens, 1–0, at the Forum in a game enlivened first by a bout between Morenz and Cy Wentworth and then accentuated by a melee around the Canadiens' bench when Lalonde attempted to behead Hooley Smith, the Maroons' captain, with his stick. Dandurand couldn't restrain himself either and connected with a few well-placed jabs at Smith while referee Mike Rodden was trying to haul the Maroon out of danger.

In a startling turn of events Frank Patrick, a managing director of the Canadiens, disclosed the following day that both Lalonde and Dandurand would be fined a hundred dollars apiece for their belligerence. More significant was the fact that fights such as the Morenz-Wentworth affair were beginning to take a toll on the Canadiens' star. His physical condition continued to deteriorate in the play-offs, won by Chicago, when he crashed into the end boards and broke a thumb. Proof of Howie's eroding scoring abilities was evident in the final statistics of the 1933–1934 season: he finished forty-eighth on the list with only eight goals in thirty-nine games.

Dandurand was a sentimentalist, but he was also a businessman. He knew Morenz was slipping, and he also realized that the Morenz name could command some interesting players in a trade. Dealing the Stratford Streak was probably the most difficult decision of Leo's long career in sports. But Howie himself was despondent about the booing he was receiving from the Montreal fans and suggested to Dandurand that he be traded.

Morenz was thirty-three years old at the time and had obviously slowed down to a point where he could be more easily stopped by the opposition. Just prior to the 1934–1935 season Dandurand dropped his bombshell—Howie Morenz was traded to the Chicago Black Hawks!

After eleven years with Les Canadiens, the most popular Montreal hockey player since Vézina was being cast adrift. In addition, Dandurand dispatched Lorne Chabot and Marty Burke to the Black Hawks in exchange for Lionel "Big Train" Conacher, Roger Jenkins, and Leroy Goldsworthy.

In honor of his friend, Dandurand tossed a farewell dinner

for Morenz and solemnly told the audience, "As long as I'm associated with the Canadiens, no other player will wear Howie's number seven." Dandurand's promise was kept by his successors, and to this day the Montreal management has honored that vow.

The shake-up was beneficial to both Les Canadiens and Morenz. Although he was admittedly unhappy in Chicago, Howie played a scintillating game for the Black Hawks and finally scored against his old teammates in the final game of the season at the Forum in which Chicago triumphed, 4–2. Howie received a standing ovation from the Montreal crowd. A season later Morenz was dealt to the Rangers, but he was a shadow of his former self and New York's Lester Patrick was happy to return him to Les Canadiens for the 1936–1937 season.

Wearing the *bleu, blanc, et rouge* once more proved to be a tonic for Morenz. True, he had lost his old get-away power, but he was reunited with his old buddies, Gagnon and Joliat, and every so often he'd bring the Forum crowd to its feet with one of the exquisite Morenz rushes.

He was doing just that on the night of January 28, 1937, at the Forum when a Chicago defenseman caught him with a body check, sending Morenz hurtling feet-first into the end boards on the Atwater Street side of the north-end net. It wasn't a normal spill and Howie had lost all control as he skidded toward the boards. When his skate rammed into the wood, a snap could be heard around the rink and Morenz crumpled in excruciating pain.

Howie was rushed to the hospital with a badly broken leg, and there was some doubt that he would recover in time to return for another season of play. Once in the hospital, the thirty-six-year-old Morenz began brooding about his fate. Instead of recuperating, he suffered a nervous breakdown. Then he developed heart trouble.

Nobody is quite sure what transpired in the hospital to bring about the utter deterioration of Howie's condition. One theory has it that he was overwhelmed by well-intentioned friends who filled his room with flowers, books, and candy. "The hospital," said one visitor, "looked like Times Square on a Saturday night. The continual stream of visitors tired him."

Perhaps too late, hospital officials forbade all but Howie's immediate family from visiting him. Then, early on March 8, 1937, Morenz was given a complete checkup. It appeared he was rallying. It was a deceptive analysis. A few hours later Howie Morenz was dead.

In his book *Hockey Heroes*, Ron McAllister theorized:

> Probably Morenz realized that even if he did recover, he would never be able to make a second comeback. And when he could no longer see visitors—his one link with the game that had become a whole life to him—the future must have looked terribly black. The terrific strain under which he played that last season, against younger and fresher men, had brought him to a complete breakdown; only genius and drive and know-how had kept him abreast of the game at all.

The funeral service for Morenz was held at center ice of the Forum where thousands filed silently past his bier. Andy O'Brien, of *Weekend Magazine*, was there at the time and recalls the scene as thousands of hockey fans lined up outside the rink that Morenz had made famous:

"Outside," said O'Brien, "the crowd was so great, we of the press had to enter through the boiler room on Closse Street. As I walked below the north end, profound silence left an impression of emptiness, but at the promenade I stopped in breathless awe. The rink was jammed to the rafters with fans standing motionless with heads bared."

The N.H.L. paid an official league tribute to Morenz on November 7, 1937, by sanctioning an All-Star Game at the Forum. In it the Canadiens and Maroons combined forces to challenge a select squad of N.H.L. stars including Frank Boucher, Charlie Conacher, Eddie Shore, et al. The All-Stars won, 6–5, before some 8,683 fans who contributed $11,447 to a fund for the Morenz family. Howie's uniform was presented to his son, Howie Morenz, Jr.

The death of Morenz signaled the end of a significant era in Montreal hockey history and was also the prelude to the downfall of Les Canadiens in the N.H.L. They reached their nadir in the 1939–1940 season, finishing dead last in the seven-team league. Leo Dandurand had sold his interest in the club and the new management realized it was time for a major housecleaning. The first and most important move of the 1940–1941 season was the signing of Dick Irvin as coach.

5

Rebuilding
the Empire

Curiously, it was to be James Dickenson "Dick" Irvin, an English-Canadian from Limestone Ridge, Ontario, who would remold the Flying Frenchmen into the most awesome team in hockey. It didn't come easy to the white-haired Irvin but nothing ever came easy to him. As a youngster Irvin couldn't afford a pair of ice skates so he simply joined the neighborhood games wearing an old pair of overshoes.

In time, he earned some money working in a butcher shop, bought a pair of skates, and matured into a player who would be accomplished enough to star in the N.H.L. Dick's career was shortened when he suffered a fractured skull after being checked by Red Dutton of the Maroons. He turned to coaching, first with the Black Hawks and then the Maple Leafs. He coached Toronto for eight years—always a winner —and would probably have been there for another decade were it not for a dispute with his managing director, Conn Smythe. The Irvin-Smythe rupture turned out to be the best break Les Canadiens could have hoped for.

Frank Selke, Sr., who was later to emigrate from Toronto to Les Canadiens as managing director of the Montreal sextet, summed up the prevailing opinion about Irvin: "No one man but Irvin could have restored order out of chaos in so short a time."

Dick's first order of business was to separate the wheat from the chaff on the Canadiens' roster. He obtained goalie Bert Gardiner from the Rangers and dropped goalies Wilf Cude and Claude Bourque. One of his most important additions was a young rambunctious defenseman named Ken Reardon who would be the "policeman" of the Montreal blue line for years to come. Later that season defenseman Jack Portland was acquired from Chicago, soon to be aligned with Emile "Butch" Bouchard, a gangly youngster who came to training camp on a bicycle.

"When most critics laughed at the clumsy rookie, Bouchard," said Selke, "Irvin kept boosting him. After a while Bouchard became the number-one defenseman in hockey."

On the offense, Irvin inherited one solid line comprised of Hector "Toe" Blake, whom Morenz and Dandurand had originally scouted, Charlie Sands, and Ray Getliffe. He obviously needed new blood and managed to secure Erwin Groves "Murph" Chamberlain from Toronto and three youngsters—Joe Benoît, Johnny Quilty, and Elmer Lach, each of whom would prove valuable additions. For goaltending insurance he obtained Paul Bibeault to complement Gardiner and wasted no time with a netminding innovation that would be adopted for occasional use thirty years later. During a game against the New York Americans, Irvin alternated Gardiner and Bibeault at seven-minute intervals and came off the experiment with a stunning 6–0 victory.

By the end of his first season it appeared that Irvin had jelled the Canadiens into a cohesive if not overwhelming team, although they finished in the sixth and last play-off berth out of seven teams (in those days the first six out of the seven teams were eligible to compete for the Stanley Cup). Still, they weren't strong enough to challenge for the Stanley Cup and were eliminated, two games to one, by the Black Hawks in the opening round.

If there was one quality Irvin sought in a player it was speed. "As long as they play this game on skates," he'd say, "you have to be able to skate to win. Personally, I'll take a young pair of legs over an old head anytime." He then underlined his point by signing Gerry Heffernan, Pete Morin, and Buddy O'Connor, three speedy youngsters who worked under the label "the Razzle Dazzle Line." Most observers who studied their kaleidoscopic maneuvers agreed that it was an apt label.

Irvin's tongue was as sharp as his mind and through the years he managed to antagonize just about every opponent in the league. One of his earliest sparring partners was Detroit's coach, Jack Adams, who wasn't particularly enamored of Irvin, nor his frugality.

"That Irvin," said Adams, "even washes his own socks on the road."

Advised of the remark, Dick countered, "Adams doesn't even wash *his*. He wears 'em till they fall off."

In his spare time Irvin was a pigeon fancier and once declared that there was a similarity between his hockey players and his birds. "Pigeons are just like the skaters," he explained. "You send one out and he's back in a minute, huffing and puffing. You send another one out and he has no idea where he's going or what he's doing. You send a third one out and he knows exactly where he's going and what he's doing."

One of those who fit the latter category was Toe Blake, a hard-nosed left wing who scored enough goals to be nicknamed "the Old Lamplighter." Blake was cut from the Irvin mold. He played hard and talked loud, something that didn't endear him to many referees around the circuit. Blake managed to be penalized by referee Mickey Ion more than by any other arbiter and soon developed a feud with the veteran whistle-blower.

During the 1940–1941 campaign the Blake-Ion relationship had reached razor's edge. In a game at Toronto the referee sent Toe off for a couple of minor penalties which really disturbed the Montrealer. Blake was so incensed after the second infraction was called that he referred rather indelicately to Mickey's ancestry and was given both a misconduct penalty and a match-misconduct.

Blake fumed over the incident all the next day and remained in a snit that night prior to the game against Chicago. His anger wasn't the least tempered when he discovered that Ion was the referee again.

"As a matter of fact," Blake said later, "I probably went into the game with a big chip on my shoulder."

Early in the game a Black Hawk defenseman high-sticked Blake and Toe responded in kind. As so often happens in these incidents the referee only noticed the retaliatory blow and Ion promptly whistled Blake off the ice with a two-minute penalty. When Blake realized what was happening, he erupted like Krakatoa and headed straight for Ion with every indication that manslaughter would be an appropriate response.

Ion realized this, and when Blake reached shouting distance, the referee snapped, "One word—just one word—out of you, Toe, and you're out of this game!"

In that split second Blake was torn over whether he should follow through on his anger or whether to control his fury and stay in the game. Finally, he couldn't stop himself any longer and blurted: "I'm not going to say a word, Mickey, but you sure as hell know what I'm thinking!"

That was enough for Ion. He perceived the humor in Blake's retort but not enough to win him over. "You're damned right I do," the referee shot back, "and you can go straight to the dressing room 'cause you're through for the night!"

Nobody else in the rink knew at the time what had happened, but when the Canadiens filed into the dressing room later they asked Blake what transpired and he recounted the dialogue. Instead of getting sympathy he received a torrent of laughs.

Toe later admitted that he enjoyed the episode in retrospect and had the utmost admiration for Ion. "I hope he lives to be a hundred," he once told author Bill Roche. "He was not only a great referee; he was the best mind reader in the business."

Blake was an apt student of Irvin's technique let alone his emotional responses. When Toe eventually became coach of the Canadiens, he earned a reputation as one of the most difficult losers in sports; but he was no match for Irvin. The word "sportsmanship" was not in Irvin's vocabulary and

Dick made no apologies for it. One spring, after losing to the Red Wings in a play-off, he retired to the dressing room and barred the foreign press from visiting him. "I'm not a good loser," he explained later. "What's the use of trying to kid people?"

He never kidded his players, unless he was trying to make a point. One of his classic chalk sessions occurred after his team had been having a seige of errant shooting. Dick ordered a rink attendant to haul a goal net into the Montreal dressing room. Then he assembled his players and delivered a one-sentence lecture. "This is what the game is all about." With that, he took the puck, tossed it into the net, and walked out.

Irvin's lecture was irrelevant to Toe Blake. Toe was one of the few outstanding young players willed to the new coach and had already established a reputation as a scorer and worker. While the Canadiens were finishing last in 1939–1940, Blake led the league in scoring. His awards included the Hart Trophy as the N.H.L.'s most valuable player, not to mention two nominations to the All-Star Team. "When Irvin became coach of the Canadiens in 1941," wrote Charles L. Coleman in the official N.H.L. history, "his rebuilding job was done around Blake."

His accomplishments earned Blake the expected accolades in Montreal, but he discovered that the range of his popularity was of a surprisingly small radius. Once, after having an especially fruitful year, Blake returned to his hometown in northern Ontario. He was feeling pretty good about the whole thing and admitted to himself that he would not be at all surprised if there was a brass band at the railroad station to greet him. To Toe's surprise, however, he discovered that the railroad station was empty but for an old friend who happened to amble by. Blake expected the chap to ask a few dozen questions about life in the N.H.L. and possibly ask him to recount the details of some of his more elaborate goal-scoring efforts.

As the chap pumped Blake's hand, Toe's face dropped a few inches when his old chum remarked, "Geez, Hector, what've you been doing these days?"

At the start of the forties, Blake was used on a line with Johnny Quilty and Joe Benoît, but Irvin was soon to change that with an accidental "gift" he received a few years earlier when he was coaching the Toronto Maple Leafs. The "gift" turned out to be center Elmer Lach.

Another of the superlative English-speaking Flying Frenchmen, Lach learned his hockey in the province of Saskatchewan, starring for the Weyburn Beavers in the 1937–1938 season. It was then that Maple Leaf scout Beattie Ramsay discovered him and cabled Conn Smythe back in Toronto that he was sending young Lach on the next train east for a tryout. For good measure Ramsay added two other players, Harvey Barnes and Doug Bentley, just in case Smythe wasn't enthused about Lach.

Dick Irvin was coaching the Leafs at the time, and he could have warned Ramsay to save himself the trouble. Smythe's philosophy was "If you can beat 'em in the alley, you can beat 'em on the ice," and it was apparent that the kid trio hardly had the dimensions of tough guys.

Standing next to such behemoths as Charlie Conacher and Bucko McDonald, the Saskatchewan rookies looked like a collection of pygmies. That's exactly the impression Smythe received when he walked into the Leaf dressing room and saw Bentley, Barnes, and Lach. "I thought that guy Ramsay was sending me some *men*," blurted Smythe. "He's sent me three little peanuts!"

Lach and friends were understandably humiliated. They picked up their gear and returned to the hotel. Irvin realized Smythe was being typically impetuous and attempted to phone them the next day, but the boys had taken a night train to Regina and were finished as prospective Maple Leafs. But Irvin never forgot them and when, two years later, Canadiens' scout Paul Haynes touted Dick on Lach, as well as

Kenny Reardon and Glen Harmon, Irvin realized that Smythe had erred in the first place.

For Lach was an extremely talented young hockey player and a lot tougher than Smythe suspected. Elmer proved this early in his Candiens career by staging a couple of kamikaze raids against Earl Seibert, the battleship who played defense for the Chicago Black Hawks. On his first foray, Lach clipped Seibert across the eye with his stick. Uncertain about the rookie's intentions, Seibert skated over to Elmer before the next face-off and snapped, "Okay, Lach, we'll consider this an accident. But don't let it happen again."

Normally, that would be enough of a deterrent for any opponent of Seibert's, but one period later Lach charged the Chicago defenseman and further bruised his eyebrow. "You asked for it, kid," snarled Seibert. "Just be sure your head's up next time you're in this end of the ice."

Lach appeared to give Seibert a wide berth until the last period when he made the mistake of riveting his eyes on the puck as he carried the disk over the blue line and into Chicago territory. Seibert was awaiting him, like an infantry battalion about to ambush an unsuspecting enemy. Elmer was so vulnerable it wasn't even necessary for Seibert to resort to foul play. He merely hurled his 210-pound body into Lach's gut, sidelining the young Canadien for three months.

Irvin rapidly developed an appreciation of Lach's resilience, although the young center was to be victimized by injuries from the beginning to the end of his career. The coach, who had an Argus eye for physical conditioning, would occasionally zero in on Lach to the amazement of outsiders who couldn't quite understand how Dick knew so much about his players.

"Irvin knows his stars so well," said Toronto *Daily Star* sports editor Milt Dunnell, "he can almost tell them by watching them skate whether they had a second helping of pumpkin pie with whipped cream for dinner a week last Wednesday."

Lach, who didn't mind a bit of whipped cream now and

then, knew exactly what Dunnell was talking about. In a dressing room tête-à-tête one afternoon Irvin berated Lach for not very obvious reasons, at least not to the naked eye. "Elmer," growled Irvin, "you must be about two pounds and six ounces over playing weight. Step on the scale and let's find out right now."

The tall center obliged. "See, it's not two pounds and six ounces," Lach shot back. "It's two pounds *eight* ounces. I noticed it yesterday, and I was hoping I could skate it off before you caught up to me."

Irvin wasn't partial. After another of his stars had scored two goals in a winning effort for Les Canadiens, the player expected a pat on the back from Irvin when the coach entered the dressing room. Dick's reply was typical: "Son, you're four pounds overweight. You'll have to take it off to make this team."

Irvin's psychology was not original with him. It is not generally known that Dick had patterned himself after the legendary Knute Rockne whom he accidentally met when Rockne was coaching football at Notre Dame. It happened when Dick took over the Black Hawks in 1929–1930 and Tom Shaughnessy was manager of the Chicago sextet. Irvin very vividly recalled the episode that molded his style.

"Shaughnessy was a graduate of Notre Dame," said Dick, "and a friend of Rockne's. He asked Knute for permission to have the Black Hawks hold their training camp on the South Bend campus and Rockne agreed. We did our calisthenics and running on a corner of the campus before football practice. Then I'd wait around to see the practice, which gave me a chance to watch and study Rockne's methods.

"Knute was suffering from a leg infection that fall. He was so crippled by phlebitis that he couldn't walk, and he sat in a car near one of the sidelines directing the practice through a loudspeaker. He had a brusque and commanding voice and was a great believer in discipline. He was also a stickler for perfection and was a man of infinite patience, but he could laugh, too.

"I remember one occasion when he was watching the first team in a practice game against the freshman team. At one point he stopped the game and called over Hunk Anderson, his line coach, and told him to give the ball to the first team and run off certain plays. The freshman team stopped the first team cold. At first Rockne was mystified, then worried, and finally he called over both teams and began to bawl out the first team with fine sarcasm. One of the freshman laughed, and Rockne broke off and demanded to know what he was laughing about.

" 'You forget that you were sitting right there before the amplifier when you told Anderson what plays to use, sir,' the freshman explained. 'We knew what was coming every time.'

"Rockne himself led the laugh that followed. It was a relief to him to know that the fault wasn't with the plays or with the first team, as he must have suspected."

Veteran critics of the Canadiens later detected the similarity in the styles of Rockne and Irvin. "Rockne had the ability to catch up a general truth in a brief phrase," said Montreal *Gazette* columnist Dink Carroll, "and Irvin could do the same thing."

As soon as he was hired by Les Canadiens from Toronto, Irvin had one big strike against him: he was an English-Canadian and he would be viewed with skepticism by the French-Canadian press, not to mention one Montreal player. The skater in question discussed his dismay over Irvin with a French-Canadian sportswriter not long after Dick had taken over the coaching reins, and soon several members of the French-language press had united in a demand for Irvin's dismissal. A day or two after Les Canadiens departed Montreal for a road trip the clamor over Irvin's ouster reached a high point and one arch foe even suggested he would burn down the Forum if it would speed Dick's departure.

Irvin had his players in Toronto for a game against the Maple Leafs when the burn-the-Forum threat made the headlines and Dick responded in a manner that betrayed his genuine sense of humor. He visited a local service station and filled his shopping bag with giveaway prizes the gasoline company was dispensing to its customers. That night Dick unloaded the premiums in the dressing room and shortly thereafter Les Canadiens skated out on the ice wearing imitation fireman's helmets. The practical joke apparently extinguished any incendiary attempts on the Forum and Irvin scored another few points against his critics.

Irvin might have been more constrained were he not complemented in his direction of Les Canadiens by a rollicking Irishman named Thomas P. Gorman, who managed the Chicago Black Hawks, Ottawa Senators, New York Americans, and Montreal Maroons before moving in as manager of the Canadiens. "He was," said Bill Roche, "one of hockey's all-time executives."

Tommy was also one of the funniest men in the sport and exceptionally creative. There was a time when Gorman was obsessed with the idea that too many of his veterans were lugging the puck *behind* the net before heading for enemy territory. His lectures on the subject proved fruitless and finally Tommy decided that more drastic or vivid measures had to be taken. So, just prior to a practice session he walked out onto the ice armed with a couple of hundred yards of thick rope. With the help of some rink attendants, Gorman attached the rope to the goal net and then extended it to each of the sideboards, thereby creating what amounted to a roadblock from the goal line to the end boards. The theory was simple enough: the players were not to skate behind the net before orbiting on a rush.

Unfortunately, Gorman neglected to inform all his players of the scheme, and Herb Cain, who was the first on the ice, had no idea a barricade had been erected. Typical of an enthusiastic skater, Cain leaped on the ice and pursued the puck, which happened to be sitting a few feet *behind* the rope. Herb's interest was so consumed with the puck he completely ignored the rope. By this time Cain had picked up speed and was hurtling at about twenty miles an hour when he started what was to be a circling of the net with the puck.

Before the startled rinksiders could shout a warning, Cain struck the rope at neck level, became enmeshed in the twine, and, with the momentum behind him, began whirling upside down like a miniature Ferris wheel. He ultimately landed on his back, knocked unconscious when his head struck the hard ice. Luckily, his injury was only temporary and Cain soon returned to action. The rope was never seen again at the Forum.

Cain played only one season for Les Canadiens before being dealt to the Bruins where he went on to become the league scoring champion in 1943–1944. But Montreal was a team in transition at the time, an organization desperately trying to find its place in the N.H.L. sun. In the 1941–1942 season they managed to reach a play-off berth only by the grace of the New York Americans who were the perennial doormats of the league.

In 1941–1942 Les Canadiens opened the season with a 3–2 loss to Detroit and ended the regular schedule by thrashing Toronto, 7–3. Their overall record was eighteen wins, twenty-seven losses, and three ties, which gave them thirty-nine points to thirty-five for the last-place Americans. By now World War II had involved both Canada, which had entered the conflict in 1939, and the United States. The Canadiens, curiously, managed to benefit by the wartime regulations imposed in both countries.

Although many players were quick to enlist in the armed forces, others took jobs in war plants and managed to continue playing in the N.H.L. In some cases, players who had certain jobs in Canada were forbidden to cross the border to play games in the United States. Boston defenseman Terry Reardon was one of them. The Canadiens obtained his services for games in Canada by trading goalie Paul Gauthier to the Bruins.

It was obvious at the time that Les Canadiens could be a threat in the N.H.L. if they could fortify themselves in goal. Neither Paul Bibeault nor Gardiner proved adequate enough, and at one point Gorman made a pitch for Davey Kerr, the retired Rangers' goalie, but Kerr rejected the offer. Struggling along with Bibeault and Gardiner, the Canadiens suffered some of the worst defeats of the season. Chicago trounced them, 9–2, with Gardiner in the nets, and later in the season Bibeault was humiliated, 10–0, by Detroit.

If the Canadiens were weak in goal, they were strong in the pugilistic department, mostly because of the Reardon brothers, Kenny and Terry. In a game against Toronto on January 29, 1942, Bingo Kampman, of the Leafs, who was so strong he would often lift a bridge table with his teeth, challenged Terry to a battle. Kenny soon intervened on his brother's behalf, and soon Buddy O'Connor and Pete Morin, of the Canadiens, had joined the battle along with Sweeney Schriner and Lorne Carr, of the Leafs, for one of the better tag-team matches of the year.

The more important contest, for the sixth and last play-off berth, dragged on between the Americans and Canadiens until late in the campaign when Montreal defeated New York, 8–3, at the Forum and then tied the Americans, 1–1, at Madison Square Garden. Les Canadiens then embarked on a three-game winning streak that put them into the postseason playdown against the Red Wings.

Detroit took the opener at Olympia Stadium, 2–1, but Bibeault blanked the Red Wings, 5–0, in the second game, this time in Montreal. However, the Habitants' goalie faltered in the third and final match, which the Wings easily captured, 6–2, at Detroit, and once again Les Canadiens were on the outside looking in.

There was no evidence at the time to suggest any renaissance in Les Canadiens' fortunes; but the blue horizon was actually just around the calendar. The first suggestion of the dawning of the second Golden Era came at the start of the 1942–1943 season with the arrival of two seemingly awkward hockey players—goalie Bill Durnan and right wing Maurice Richard—and the development of defenseman Emile "Butch" Bouchard.

6

The Second Golden Era

*I*nsightful scouting and judicious trading enabled Les Canadiens to approach the early 1940's with a formidable defense and an attack that was more than adequate. But the club's weak underbelly remained goaltending. Paul Bibeault had won the job from Bert Gardiner, and coach Irvin gave the tall French-Canadian the entire 1942–1943 season to prove himself. Bibeault played all fifty games for Les Canadiens and emerged with a 3.82 goals against average. This was quite an embarrassment to the Montrealers because Gardiner, who had been shunted to the Chicago Black Hawks, topped Bibeault with a 3.60 average, although the Black Hawks were clearly an inferior team.

Finding a competent goaltender, as other clubs had discovered, was a needle-in-the-haystack problem in those mid-war years. The Rangers, for example, went through a half-dozen possibilities and found one goalie worse than the next. Once, the New Yorkers went so far as to import a young man who had worked for the Dominion Agricultural Service in Saskatchewan. After being beaten 14–1 along with other ridiculous scores the Rangers replaced him with another western Canadian product, and this one went down to defeat by the modern record-breaking count of 15–0.

Once again, the break for Les Canadiens came as a result of poor judgment by the Toronto Maple Leaf organization. The Leafs normally had a good line on prospects developing in the Queen City of Canada. They should have rushed to sign a youngster named Bill Durnan whose approach to goaltending suggested the late Georges Vézina.

Like Vézina, Durnan played without a pair of skates until his teens, when a friend "borrowed" his father's unused blades and urged Bill to wear them. Durnan protested that it made little sense wearing the blades even if he was playing goal because he really couldn't skate.

"Don't worry," his friend insisted, "you're a big guy and you can fill the nets. The skating will come."

Durnan accepted the challenge and, in time, he became the outstanding player on the North Toronto Juniors, a Maple Leaf farm club. When the N.H.L. club displayed a conspicuous lack of interest in his services, Durnan decided to go north and took a job in the mining town of Sudbury, Ontario, where he also played for the Sudbury Wolves, a splendid junior team that eventually won the Memorial Cup, emblematic of Canada's junior championship.

Once again the Leafs trained their eyes on Durnan, but this time he injured a knee wrestling with a friend. Not long after that he fractured a leg in a softball game, and Bill himself acknowledged that he'd never play hockey again. There was only one thing to do—get a job—so he returned to northern Ontario and went to work as a millwright with the Lakeshore mine in Kirkland Lake.

Late in the autumn, as the ice began forming on the local ponds, Durnan's leg began feeling no pain, the urge to play hockey returned, and he applied for a tryout with the Kirkland Lake Blue Devils, a senior team that just happened to have some of the best nonprofessionals in Canada. To Bill's surprise, his legs didn't bother him at all and he won the first-string goalie's job. In 1940 the Blue Devils startled Canada by defeating the best senior teams in the country and winning the Allan Cup. En route to the senior championship, the Blue Devils routed the Montreal Royals, the early Allan Cup favorites, and Durnan thereby caught the attention of Canadiens scouts. They promised him a job in Montreal as well as the varsity goaltender's position with the Royals. The Leafs also expressed a renewed interest in Durnan but they were too late.

"We weren't impressed with Durnan at first," said Tommy Gorman, "but he seemed to get better with every game. As goaltenders go he was big and hefty but nimble as a cat and a great holler guy."

Les Canadiens assumed that Durnan would fit right into the lineup for the 1943–1944 season, especially when it was learned that Bibeault had received his call from the Canadian Army. Gorman invited Bill to the Canadiens' training camp at Ste. Hyacinthe, Quebec, and the elderly "rookie" quickly impressed Irvin with his ability to glove shots. It was a throwback to his softball-playing days when Durnan was first a catcher and later an excellent pitcher.

"Sign him up," Irvin urged, "and we'll open the season with Durnan in the nets."

An hour later Gorman approached the goalie, anticipating an enthusiastic response to his offer. Instead, Durnan rejected it out of hand. The money was immaterial to him. "I've got a good job in a war plant," he told Gorman, "and I kind of like playing for the Royals. Besides, I'm a little too old to be starting in the National Hockey League."

Durnan meant business. Day after day he displayed big-league quality goaltending, and with each offer he became more adamant in his refusal to turn pro. Finally, training camp had ended and Les Canadiens were ready to open their home season against the Boston Bruins at the Forum. But still no Durnan. An hour before game time Gorman invited Bill into his office.

"He was hesitant, very hesitant," Gorman has said. Durnan trotted out all the old arguments—his job, his age, and his affection for the Royals—and the manager listened patiently.

"I don't know just what turned the tide," said Gorman. "But Durnan finally put his name on the dotted line just ten minutes before game time! Bill hadn't even put down the pen when I informed him that he was going into the nets that very night, and I pointed at the clock."

Durnan shook Gorman's hand, bolted from the office,

and dashed past the startled spectators who were entering the rink. Irvin greeted him at the dressing room and reiterated that, yes, he was going to start the game for Montreal, if he was willing. Certainly, he was. After all, he hadn't charged halfway across the Forum for nothing!

A half hour later Durnan skated out onto the Forum ice and was greeted with mixed emotions by the crowd. His debut was reminiscent of George Hainsworth's many years earlier. Like Hainsworth, Durnan was an English-Canadian from Ontario who had supplanted a French-Canadian. The crowd wasn't terribly enthused about that, particularly because Bibeault had managed to return to the N.H.L. and was now playing for, of all teams, the Toronto Maple Leafs.

It took Durnan approximately an hour to persuade the capacity crowd that Les Canadiens had not made a mistake. Although he permitted two goals and the game ended in a 2–2 tie, his goaltending was so spectacular that the critical Montreal audience could offer no legitimate complaint. "He won the respect of his teammates and fans alike," observed one writer, "because Durnan was playing the finest hockey of his life." Three nights later, he limited the Rangers to a single goal, the Canadiens triumphed, 2–1, and both Durnan and Les Habitants were off and running to one of the most extraordinary seasons that any team ever enjoyed in the N.H.L.

Durnan's life was made a lot easier by a tall French-Canadian defenseman, Emile "Butch" Bouchard, who had learned his hockey on the sidewalks of Montreal not far from the Forum. At first, Bouchard was considered too awkward to be an effective hockey player. His long arms and legs suggested an octopus trying to maneuver on the ice, and when young Butch had tried out for the team at Académie Roussin, he literally fell on his face.

To start the audition Roussin's captain asked young Bouchard to skate around the rink a few times and then come to a stop next to the end boards. Butch started out by cruising to the other end of the rink with flawless strides. This was easy

The ancestors of the contemporary Montreal Canadiens were the members of the Montreal Hockey Club. They won the Canadian hockey championship in 1894. Note the antique skates and curved sticks, which were prototypes of the modern "banana-blade." The 1894 team members sported more mustaches than are seen in all of professional hockey today (and that's a lot of mustache).

Left: Handsome and poetic Georges Vézina was a legendary goaltender in his time. "The Chicoutimi Cucumber" starred for the Canadiens in the early twenties. It was no fluke that the Vézina Trophy, symbolic of goaltending supremacy, was named after him. *Right:* The goal of every French Canadian youngster was to wear the "*bleu-blanc-et-rouge*" of Les Canadiens. Dashing Billy Boucher achieved that pinnacle and poses here in a typical off-season portrait outside the Montreal Forum.

Canada Wide Photo

Thoroughly disarmed and partially disrobed, these members of the Canadiens line up for mug shots in a Montreal gymnasium. A frequently asked question was who was the more bowlegged, Albert "Battleship" Leduc (sixth from left) or Sylvio Mantha (second from right).

"Les Canadiens *sont là!*" The Canadiens are the greatest and proved it in 1946 by winning the Stanley Cup. Seated in the front are Glen Harmon, Ken Reardon, and Maurice "Rocket" Richard. On the far left is coach Dick Irvin. As far as can be determined, there is not an unhappy fellow in the lot.

Cat on a cold thin ice. Ranger goalie Emile Francis ("the Cat") loses a battle to both gravity and the puck as Claude Robert (number 4) fires the disk past him in March, 1951. This rare photo is a Robert heirloom, since it represented his first and last goal in the National Hockey League. The score ignited a Montreal rally, however, which enabled the team to overcome a 5–2 deficit to tie the Rangers and ultimately eliminate the New Yorkers from a play-off berth. Robert, ironically, soon returned to the minors and wound up as a policeman in Quebec, where he justifiably boasted to friends about his monumental score. The victim went on to become general manager of the Rangers.

Here's Elmer. Chicago Black Hawk goalie Al Rollins would have preferred it if the Canadiens' great center were less ubiquitous. Lach sprints past defenseman Bill Gadsby to flip the puck over Rollins and into the net during a 1947 game.

He shoots, he scores! Burt Olmstead, one of the Canadiens' most efficient left wings, flings a backhand shot through New York Ranger goalie Gump Worsley's legs during a Stanley Cup play-off game in the late fifties. Rangers Dean Prentice (left) and Ivan Irwin move in too late to thwart Olmstead's drive.

Photogr

Expansion it is. Lowell MacDonald bounces the puck off goalie Gump Worsley while defenseman J. C. Trembley moves in to thwart the attack.

Seeing Red! Ranger center Red Sullivan (top left) is on a collision course with Montreal goalie Jacques Plante. The Montreal player on his derriere is the perennial all-star, Doug Harvey. The Ranger on the left is Andy Hebenton.

Canada W

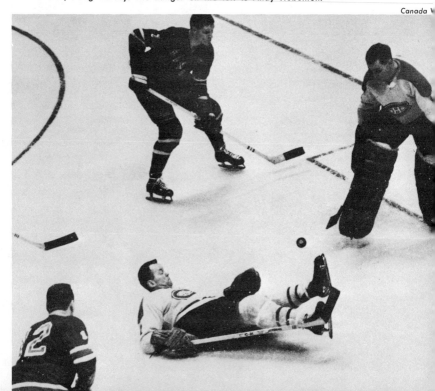

enough; but to impress the captain he decided to pick up speed on his return and dazzle the older boy with a snowy display of two-skated stopping. Gradually, Butch accelerated until he was skating at top speed. Suddenly, the captain loomed directly in front of him. Butch applied the brakes but they wouldn't hold and he plowed headfirst into the boards, a dazed and thoroughly humiliated youngster.

The older players stood around laughing as Butch pulled himself together. "Don't worry, kid," the captain said. "You may not make the team this year but stick with it and you'll be all right."

There was no next year at Roussin. The Bouchard family moved and Butch enrolled at St. Francis Xavier School where he easily won a berth on the team. His style continued to improve, and before long, Paul Stuart, a Montreal sports commentator, invited Bouchard to join his amateur team. In time Bouchard was signed to play for the Verdun Maple Leafs, along with another promising young man named Joseph Henri Maurice Richard.

From the Maple Leafs, Butch graduated to senior hockey where Dick Irvin spotted him and assigned Bouchard to Providence of the American Hockey League. "He wants to play in the N.H.L. so badly," said Irvin, "he'd probably do it for nothing if we asked him."

After a season at Providence, Bouchard was signed to a Canadiens contract, although some members of the Montreal front office weren't as enthused about the gangly defenseman as their coach. At least one official of the Canadian Arena Company urged Irvin to demote Bouchard once more, but Dick replied succinctly: "That kid will be with the Canadiens as long as I am." Which is precisely what happened.

In his first game against the Toronto Maple Leafs, Butch was confronted by the slick-skating Sweeney Schriner. The Leaf forward tried an assortment of head and stick feints but Bouchard held his ground like a seasoned pro. The one-on-one challenge became an obsession with Schriner, but each time Butch stopped him cold. With each rebuff, Toronto coach

Hap Day became more and more frustrated. "Listen, Sweeney," he demanded, "next time you get into Canadiens territory, go around the *other* side."

Schriner accepted the advice and on his next expedition toward the Montreal goal he skated face-to-face with the veteran Red Goupille. The Leaf ace, faked to the left, went to the right, left Goupille standing in his tracks, and scored easily. "At that time," noted a Toronto observer, "Bouchard became a marked man."

When Butch and the Canadiens visited Boston Garden, Bouchard so emphatically mauled the Bruin forwards that an irate female fan jabbed him in the derriere with a hat pin that felt like a harpoon. "Please don't do that!" pleaded Butch with all the discretion at his command. To Bouchard's amazement a collection of Boston policemen moved in and attempted to arrest *him* for bothering the lady. But before they could reach Butch, his teammates pushed him onto the ice and the incident appeared to have ended.

After the game Irvin charged Bruin manager Art Ross with fomenting "the plot" to get Bouchard, although it was later established that Ross was ill in bed at the time and was nowhere near the scene of the "crime."

It soon became apparent that the only way to stop the marauding Canadiens was by wholesale arrest. On successive nights in November, 1943, they routed Toronto, 7–2, and Boston, 13–4. When it was learned that center Phil Watson of the Rangers would have difficulty crossing the Canadian-American border because of passport problems, the New York club traded him to Montreal for Charlie Sands and Dutch Hiller. Soon after the deal it was learned that Watson could travel with impunity and now the Canadiens were stronger than ever.

When Montreal visited New York on January 9, 1944, Les Canadiens boasted an arresting 19–2–3 record and the New York *World-Telegram* ran a headline: "LES CANADIENS —WONDER TEAM OF ICE SEASON." In the accompanying story, the *World-Telegram* hockey critic observed:

What makes them go? In a phrase, their wonderful balance. They have the league's most effective goalie, a rugged defense, and three forward lines which mount a sizzling attack, and also back-check faster and in more robust fashion than any other threesomes.

The first line of Phil Watson, Murph Chamberlain, and Ray Getliffe is two-way dynamite when they have the puck, or when the other side has it. Watson very likely stands next to Bill Cowley of Boston among the league's centers. Chamberlain and Getliffe are crack shots, particularly the latter, and both have that rare forward line ability to dish out the body checks. The trio forms the roughhouse line. There's not a weak spot in the lot, and that's the main reason Les Canadiens lose a game only about once a month.

Ironically, the only game Les Canadiens lost in the month of January occurred on the night of January 11 at Maple Leaf Gardens in Toronto. The man who did the damage was none other than Paul Bibeault. Needless to say, "the Roughhouse Line" was in trouble that night. Watson fought with linesman Jim Primeau and then engaged in a wrestling match with Tom O'Neill of the Leafs. His reward was a major penalty and a match misconduct. League president Mervyn "Red" Dutton suspended Watson, pending a report from referee Bert Hedges. The referee was lenient with Watson, and the fiery center returned to action missing only one game.

Since Montreal could not be thwarted on the ice, opponents did their best to throttle them in the public press. Art Ross of the Bruins was one of the foremost Canadien-baiters. At one point during the season a dispatch carried by the Canadian Press quoted Ross at length in an anti-Montreal diatribe. The gist of it was that the Canadiens refused to play in a fund-raising game at Quebec City, whereas his Bruins had a habit of giving away thousands of dollars for charitable purposes.

Ross later insisted that he was misquoted, and an attempt by the Canadian Arena Company to sue the Bruin orator was eventually dropped. The fact is that no team in the league was more charitable than the Canadiens. At one point during the season Lester Patrick, manager of the player-starved Rangers, appealed to the league governors for assistance. The Montrealers responded by sending Johnny Mahaffey and Fern Gauthier to the Rangers from their regular roster. Some observers cynically remarked that Les Canadiens really gave away two bodies, not two hockey players. Gauthier, not known for his blazing shot, was later involved in a publicity stunt after going several weeks without a goal. The prevailing wise-crack had it that Fern couldn't shoot the puck in the ocean.

A creative New York Rangers publicist got the idea of bringing Gauthier down to the sands of Coney Island accompanied by some newspaper photographers and have him prove that he *could*, in fact, deposit the puck in the Atlantic. According to the legend, Gauthier took a swipe at the puck, just barely got a piece of it, and the rubber trickled a few yards in the sands but failed to reach the surf.

Obviously the contribution of Mahaffey and Gauthier to the Rangers did nothing to stop the Canadiens' onslaught. By late January it was apparent that they had no challengers, and on February 26, nearly a month before the season's end, Les Canadiens clinched the championship with a 10–2 victory at Boston. All that remained for them was a "cooling out" period before the Stanley Cup play-offs, but Irvin wasn't about to ease up on his warriors.

Despite the clinching, Irvin regarded every match as if it were a Stanley Cup final and his men responded in kind. During a game at Chicago on March 9, with absolutely nothing at stake, Chamberlain charged referee Norm Lamport and was ejected from the arena with a match-misconduct penalty. Earlier in the game Glen Harmon of the Canadiens smashed Chicago's Doug Bentley to the ice, leaving the Black Hawk star with a broken nose and three facial cuts requiring six stitches. In addition, Harmon's burly teammate, Mike Mc-Mahon, drew a major penalty for hitting Bentley with his stick. Dutton penalized Chamberlain with a two-game suspension, and left it at that.

When the season ended on March 19 the Canadiens had amassed a record-breaking thirty-eight wins, seven ties, *and only five losses*. Their margin over second-place Detroit was twenty-five points. They had scored a league-leading 234 goals and permitted only 109, thus giving Durnan the Vézina Trophy with a goals against average of 2.18 in his rookie season.

The Canadiens did not, however, produce the league scoring champion. That honor went to Herb Cain of the Bruins. Montreal's best point-producer was center Elmer Lach who finished in a tie for fifth place with Chicago's Clint Smith. Next in line, buried in twelfth place, was Toe Blake.

With such a formidable record the Canadiens appeared destined to romp through the play-offs as unchallenged as a lion in the African plains. Their first-round opponents were the Toronto Maple Leafs with onetime Canadien Paul Bibeault in goal. The Leafs stunned Montreal with a 3–1 defeat in the opening game at the Forum, but the Canadiens regained their composure and easily swept the series, winning the next four games in a row. Meanwhile, the Black Hawks wiped out the Red Wings in five games and skated on Montreal ice April 4 hoping for an upset. The Chicago club had finished in fourth place, thirty-four big points behind Les Canadiens, but the Hawks realized that the brief best-of-seven series was conducive to an upset.

Their hopes were immediately dashed in the first game as Les Canadiens thoroughly bedazzled the visitors with a 5–1 win. Montreal captured the second game, 3–2, and then moved on to the Windy City where they wrapped up the series with 3–2 and 5–4 decisions and Montreal's first Stanley Cup success in fourteen years.

Nobody was particularly surprised at the outcome of the series, nor was there anything unusual about the Canadiens' romp through the season, once it became obvious that they were the class of the hockey world. But there were several raised eyebrows over the play of Joseph Henri Maurice Richard, the thick-browed Montreal right wing. "Richard has the speed of Howie Morenz," said one sportswriter, "but hardly his daring." That line was to be a classic of poor judgment.

7

The Rocket Takes Off

"*M*aurice Richard," summed up a writer for the *Star Weekly* magazine, "was the most exciting athlete I have ever seen. So much has been written about Richard that for me to offer a flood of new praise would be roughly equivalent to a Ph.D. candidate announcing he is going to prove *Hamlet* is an interesting play."

In the beginning, though, there was no suggestion that fourteen thousand Forum fans would someday be chanting "*vas-y Maurice*" whenever Richard would boom along the boards in a wide-eyed rush. The son of Onésime Lucien Richard preferred baseball to hockey, although when winter arrived in Montreal, he would lace on his skates and play shinny on the treacherous Rivière des Prairies (the Back River) near his home in Bordeaux in the northern section of town.

Some of his neighborhood chums suspected that Maurice would make a better boxer than either a baseball or hockey player. At one point in his teens Richard entered the Golden Gloves tournament in Montreal, and according to one report, handled himself quite well. It was a portent of things to come on the ice.

Richard's interest in hockey intensified while he attended St. François de Laval School in Bordeaux and continued after he graduated to Montreal Technical High School. In summer he would play ball in the fast Provincial League and in winter he'd play hockey for the Paquette Club of Montreal's Intermediate Hockey League. Four men who were to play a significant role in Richard's future entered his life at this time.

His manager was sports commentator Paul Stuart, who

immediately detected the spark of a supercompetitor in Richard and began touting him to coaches around the city. Georges Norchet, the trainer, would soon become Richard's father-in-law. It was while Richard skated for the Paquette Club that Aurel Joliat, the former Canadiens ace, and Arthur Therrien recommended Maurice as a candidate for the Verdun Maple Leafs, one of Montreal's most distinguished junior teams.

By the late thirties hockey had just about pushed baseball and boxing into the background as far as Maurice was concerned. In one season he managed to play for Verdun as well as a team in the Parc Lafontaine League, not to mention a couple of other teams which could use him when his other clubs weren't scheduled to play. Given seven days of ice a week, young Maurice was able to perfect the art of playing right wing while shooting left-handed, a feat that would play a significant role in his N.H.L. development. He led the Verdun team in scoring during the 1939–1940 season and was soon commanding double the attention of his teammates.

While admiring Richard most hockey scouts agreed that it was much too soon to determine whether or not he had the capabilities to cut the ice with the professionals. His physique had not completely filled out when as a nineteen-year-old he was promoted to the Montreal Canadiens of the crack Quebec Senior Hockey League. And there was some doubt whether or not he could handle the more severe body checking and assorted illegalities of minor-league hockey. The suspicions were almost immediately confirmed in his first game with the Senior sextet when he crashed heavily into the boards and broke his left ankle. Maurice was finished for the season and, possibly forever.

Fortunately, his injury healed perfectly and he returned to the Senior Canadiens for the next season. This time, after about twenty games, he was careening down the ice in one of his headlong dashes that were later to characterize his N.H.L. style, when he tripped and slid headfirst into the steel upright of the goal cage. He was able to thrust his arm in front of his face before striking the net, but his human bumper, while protecting his head, absorbed too much of the blow and he was carried off the ice with a broken left arm.

That was all the bird dogs had to see. Word soon filtered up and down the hockey grapevine that Richard was too brittle to get anywhere in the pros. Several scouts who had expressed a keen interest in the kid turned attentions to more substantial types.

"By this time," said Ron McAllister, "Maurice was wondering if his frame was too fragile for this rugged. close-checking game. Moody and self-conscious, he seriously considered hanging up his skates for good, more from a sense of fairness to the men for whom he played than for his own well-being."

Significantly, Richard's recovery came about a lot sooner than it had the first time he was injured and he was welcomed back to the lineup at play-off time. His response was six goals in a four-game series and an invitation from Dick Irvin to attend the Canadiens' autumn training camp.

The slick-haired kid had little trouble making the N.H.L. team in his first try, but he was overshadowed by such new Montreal additions as Gordie Drillon, who had been obtained from Toronto, and Dutch Hiller from Boston. Richard's significance to the Canadiens at the time was summed up in the official N.H.L. history with only one line: "Another new face was a fast-skating right wing named Richard."

Irvin inserted Richard on a line with the veteran Tony Demers and young center Elmer Lach. The line clicked immediately and Demers scored two goals as the Canadiens won their opening game from Boston, 3–2. The result was especially appealing to one of the game's linesman—Aurel Joliat.

On November 8, 1942, Richard played his third N.H.L. game. Montreal's opponents in the Forum that night were the Rangers who had beaten them on the previous night in New York. This time Les Canadiens were the winners by a score of 10–4. The highlight of the game was a pulsating end-to-end rush by Richard who made his way through the Ranger defense like a pinball bouncing its way past the obstacles to the goal. Richard's shot beat Ranger goalie Steve Buzinski, and even so critical an analyst as Newsy Lalonde raved about the rookie.

After fifteen games Richard had played commendably, if not always spectacularly. His record was five goals and six assists for eleven points, and the Canadiens, as a team, appeared refreshed by his vitality. Then, in the sixteenth game, it happened again. The Canadiens were skating against the Bruins when Jack Crawford, a big but clean defenseman, collided with Richard and sent Maurice sprawling to the ice in pain. He had suffered a clean break just above his right ankle and was finished once again for the season.

"It looked as though the Flying Frenchmen had picked an easily-bruised-and-busted lemon," said Bill Roche. "Richard seemed destined only to be number one on the Canadiens' injury list."

Only a young man with exceptional perseverance and grim determination could surmount such a collection of injuries. Richard was troubled by his misfortune and again seriously considered quitting hockey, but neither Irvin nor Gorman was persuaded that he was through. They bided their time through the summer of 1943 and eagerly awaited the start of training camp when Irvin announced that he was forming a new forward line with Richard as the balance wheel.

More than anyone it was the short-tempered, vitriolic Irvin who convinced Richard he would become a star. "Not only will he be a star," Irvin predicted at the start of the 1943–1944 season, "but he'll be the biggest star in hockey!"

Irvin had theorized that Lach was the ideal center for Richard but he wasn't so sure about left wing. He finally decided that Toe Blake would be worthy of an experiment on the unit, and in no time the line was made—for keeps. The trio, soon to be named "the Punch Line," finished one-two-three (Lach, Blake, Richard) in scoring on the team with Richard collecting thirty-two goals and twenty-two assists for fifty-four points in forty-six games.

He was, however, buried in fifteenth place on the scoring list and certainly wasn't regarded with the same awe as his two linemates. That is, not until the first round of the Stanley Cup play-offs against Toronto. In the opening game Richard was held scoreless by the Maple Leafs' expert checking forward, Bob Davidson. But in the second game, on March 23, 1944, Davidson's most determined efforts proved feeble against Richard's towering performance.

Maurice scored three goals in the second period, breaking a scoreless tie, and added two more in the third period. The final score was *Richard* 5, Toronto 1! The last time a player had scored five or more goals in a Stanley Cup match was in 1917 when Bernie Morris scored six against Les Canadiens for Seattle.

After disposing of Toronto, the Canadiens challenged Chicago and, once again, Richard dominated an entire game. The Montrealers defeated Chicago, 3–1, on April 6 in the second game of the final round and Richard scored *all three goals!* Just to prove it was no fluke, Maurice practically single-handedly saved Montreal in the fourth and last game of the series after Chicago had mounted a 4–1 lead after two periods.

Richard's second goal of the game tied the match 4–4, sending it into sudden-death overtime. Then his pass to Blake set up the winning goal, and minutes later Richard, Blake, and Lach were sipping champagne from the Stanley Cup.

As for the kid from Rivière des Prairies, in his first full season in the N.H.L. he had set two big records. One for scoring five goals in a single game (a modern record), and another for amassing twelve goals in the complete play-off series.

Oddly enough the reaction to Richard's accomplishments was not totally enthusiastic. Some viewers suggested that the "injury jinx" would soon catch up with him again. Others predicted that he would burn himself out. "He won't last" was a familiar cry whenever Richard was discussed. "Let's see what he'll do *next* year" was another.

When "next year" arrived, Les Canadiens iced virtually the same team they had when they won the Stanley Cup in April with only a few exceptions. Phil Watson was reluctantly returned to the Rangers and the Canadiens received Gauthier and Hiller. Another key addition was Ken Mosdell, a tall rangy forward who had just been released from the armed forces. The Punch Line remained intact and launched the season with the same syncopated attack that had stirred the fans in 1943–1944. Richard seemed particularly bolstered by a full season under his belt without serious injury and he broke from the post like an overzealous thoroughbred. His scoring was becoming so prolific that opposing coaches began mapping specific strategies to stop Maurice alone, on the theory that if you could blockade Richard you could beat Les Canadiens. These stratagems took on many variations as they would over the years. One of the favorites was simply to goad Maurice into a fight. This was not exactly difficult since the brooding French-Canadian still couldn't speak English and was rather sensitive and self-conscious about his language barrier.

One of the most effective methods for inciting Richard to riot was for an opposing coach to select one of his less-effective hatchet men to pester Maurice with an assortment of words, elbows, high sticks, and butt ends until Richard retaliated. Both players would then likely be penalized, but at least Richard would be off the ice. The Rangers tried this ploy in Madison Square Garden on December 17, 1944.

Midway in the second period Bob "Killer" Dill, a young Ranger defenseman, challenged Richard a few seconds after Chuck Scherza of the Rangers and Leo Lamoureux of the Canadiens had started their own private war. Up until then Dill's chief claim to fame was the fact that he was a nephew of Mike and Tom Gibbons of fistic fame. From that night on, however, Dill became renowned as the man who lost two knockouts to Maurice in one period!

In the first bout, Richard disposed of Dill with a hefty right to the jaw. When the Ranger recovered, referee King

Clancy sent him to the penalty box with a major penalty for fighting and doled out the same sentence to Richard. In those days the penalty benches were constructed without a barrier separating players of opposing teams, so it was not unusual for the combatants to exchange insults while they awaited their release.

Still smarting from his knockout, Dill challenged Richard to a return bout. Maurice didn't quite understand Bob's English but there was no mistaking his sign language. Dill tossed the first punch and the two were off and swinging on the dry wood of the penalty box.

"Here Maurice the Mauler again measured his man," wrote Dan Daniel. "Roberto suffered a cut left eye and other bruises and contusions."

Richard's performance against Dill intrigued the imagination of New York sportswriters. One suggested that boxing promoter Mike Jacobs arrange a return fight between the pair in the ring rather than on the ice. Another described it as "the most interesting wartime set-to on local ice." Opinion was unanimous that Maurice was one of the best one-two punchers to come along since Joe Louis. "Richard scored two widely separated but emphatic knockdowns," said a boxing writer, "and he won on points!"

There was no longer any question that Richard had orbited into a very special position among the galaxy of hockey stars. Hy Turkin, of the New York *Daily News*, dubbed him "the Brunette Bullet," and added that his sidekick, Lach, was a "sandy-haired stick-handling Svengali." On Richard's first return to New York following his decision over Dill more than fifteen thousand fans jammed Madison Square Garden to see him. One newspaper carried a two-column photo of Richard's eyes alone and added, "He is the main event wherever he goes." For the first time in Richard's career he was being favorably compared with such Hall of Famers as Howie Morenz and Aurel Joliat.

"He may prove to be one of the great players of history," suggested sportswriter Joe King. "Those who saw Morenz will remember him for his flashing straightaway speed and his boundless daring. He was an arrow whizzing through the defense. He did not know caution. No momentary gap in the defense was too small for him to attempt.

"Richard is extremely speedy, but he is not the breathtaking adventurer that Morenz was. He is on a different pattern, with more guile in his makeup. . . . Maurice makes much more use of the change-of-pace, the trickery of speed and stick-handling than did Morenz. Richard swoops around the defense, while Morenz dared the guards to stop him dead on."

Ranger manager Lester Patrick, who was in a position to know, said Richard was more a copy of Jack Laviolette than of Morenz. Phil Watson echoed Patrick's sentiments. "There's no doubt," Watson asserted, "that Richard is the best wingman in hockey today." *Daily News* columnist Jim McCulley referred to Les Canadiens as "Richard & Co." And, needless to say, Maurice reinforced his reputation on each visit to New York.

With four games remaining in the season, Les Canadiens, snug in first place, invaded Madison Square Garden and routed the Rangers, 11–5. Banging two shots past goalie Ken McAuley, Richard lifted his goal-scoring mark to an astonishing forty-eight in only forty-seven games. "McAuley," observed Hy Turkin, "acted shell-shocked."

Overlooked by most readers consumed with the uproar over Richard was a small item out of Montreal carried by the Canadian Press. It said: "Howie Morenz, Jr., who a few weeks ago was warned that he would have to cut down on his hockey because of 'athlete's heart,' has sliced his playing time in half with encouraging results, his doctor said today. Young Morenz had been playing with Catholic High School and with the Junior Canadiens. He has dropped the Canadiens."

Acclaim for Les Canadiens was not as warm in Detroit and Toronto as it was in New York. The Red Wings peppery manager Jack Adams sniped at both Irvin and Richard, calling Montreal's coach Dick Irvin "a poor sport" and suggesting that Richard was becoming too self-important and far too touchy when checked by opposing players. Toronto's manager Conn Smythe criticized Richard for his weak back-checking.

Such commentary was regarded as so many sour grapes by Tommy Gorman who launched a verbal counterattack. Gorman accused Richard's foes of deliberately fouling Maurice and singled out Smythe's Maple Leafs as the worst offenders.

Maurice seemed to rise above the smog of blather and cruised speedily along at a goal-a-game pace. He had surpassed Joe Malone's goal-scoring record, for which he received a standing ovation at the Forum, and the pressing question remaining was whether or not Richard would reach the hitherto unattainable plateau of fifty goals.

He scored number forty-nine on March 15 with only two games remaining on the schedule. In the next-to-last game, against the Black Hawks on Forum ice, Les Canadiens triumphed, but somehow Maurice was thoroughly blanked. That left only one more match, the final game of the season at Boston Garden. This time Richard came through in a 4–2 win over the Bruins and he finished the season with fifty goals in fifty games, a modern hockey average that has never been and will likely never be equaled.

Having defended their first-place championship with ease, the Canadiens now turned to the business of defending their hold on the Stanley Cup. Toronto's Maple Leafs, the robust third-place finishers, would be the opening-round opposition and it didn't take very long for Conn Smythe's outfit to prove they had come to play.

Leaf coach Hap Day once more assigned Bob Davidson the thankless job of manacling Richard and this time he succeeded. Toronto upset Montreal, 1–0 and 3–2, in the first pair of games on Forum ice and Richard was completely neutralized. Although Montreal won the third game, in Toronto, by a score of 4–1, Richard was held scoreless. The Leafs captured the fourth game of the series with a 4–3 win and Richard

finally scored. Maurice then exploded for four goals in the
fifth game in which Toronto was routed, 10–3. Richard's inflationary output created the mirage that Montreal was about
to dispose of the upstart Leafs, but when the teams met on
March 31 in the sixth game, Richard was nullified and Toronto
came away with a 3–2 win, stunning Les Canadiens with
elimination.

The fact that Toronto went on to win the Stanley Cup
hardly consoled the Canadiens' front office. But Irvin was
quick to guard against a panic shake-up and decided to launch
the 1945–1946 season with virtually the same lineup that he
had employed the previous season. There was one very significant addition, Ken Reardon. A boisterous prospect who had
quit hockey to join the armed forces, he had returned to
Montreal, and Irvin immediately invited him to training camp.

Reardon was a rare bird. Taken at face value, his hockey
skills were minimal. In fact he never so much as betrayed
the likes of a star as far back as anyone could remember. As
a youngster in Winnipeg, Manitoba, he played second fiddle
to his older brother, Terry, and appeared content to watch
his sibling develop into a big-league defenseman. "Ken had
courage," said a friend of the family, "but little else as far
as hockey was concerned."

Yet, somehow, his brother's success inspired Ken to pursue a hockey career. He would slog his way through sub-
zero temperatures to find a practice rink where he could hone
his game to sharpness. Despite a seemingly innate clumsi-
ness, he pursued his goal and obtained a tryout with the
Edmonton Athletic Club after writing a letter to the team
executive requesting a chance to play. He made the team and
at one point was closely scouted by the New York Rangers,
but the Garden bird dogs finally rejected him because of his
abject skating failures. Not long after the Ranger experts had
departed, a Montreal scout took up the trail. He found Reardon's truculence to his liking. Working on the assumption that
Kenny would never lose his guts and *would* improve his
skating, the scout recommended that Reardon be signed. Rear-

don's first two seasons in Montreal were inconsequential and before he could make a hockey name for himself, he joined the 86th Bridge Company of the Canadian Army and was next heard from in dispatches from the front.

One of them told how Reardon stood in a drizzling rain to receive a Certificate of Gallantry from Field Marshall Bernard Montgomery. Another indicated that he was rarin' to rejoin the Canadiens at war's end to display his hockey skills. Reardon was discharged from the army in 1945 and immediately returned to the N.H.L. to open up his own war on ice. "He has built a fearsome reputation," said one observer. "His feuds are becoming of national interest."

Forum fans immediately took him to their hearts while spectators in out-of-town rinks were quick to despise him. In one of his earlier games in New York, Reardon was severely heckled by a fan sitting in a seat along the boards. During a stoppage in play, Ken gathered together a hunk of ice shavings, pressed them into a ball, and tossed it in the fan's face.

That, more or less, was what the Canadiens did to their opponents in the 1945–1946 campaign, despite dire predictions that they would be routed by the rejuvinated opposition. World War II had ended and many of the stars of Boston, Detroit, New York, Chicago, and Toronto had returned. It was assumed that the opponents *had* to get better while the Canadiens would inevitably slip.

It would prove to be more wishful thinking than reality.

8

Postwar
Prosperity

*A*ubrey "Dit" Clapper, the professorial player-coach of the Boston Bruins, was one of the more outspoken detractors of Les Canadiens. It was Clapper's boast that his Kraut Line, composed of Milt Schmidt, Bobby Bauer, and Woody Dumart, would obliterate the Punch Line in the eyes of postwar hockey fans. Clapper could be forgiven for his optimistic outburst. After all, the Krauts were one of the best offensive units before the war, and Boston fans nurtured the hope that they would regain their touch after being mustered out of the armed forces.

When Irvin declared, "Only an atomic bomb can stop the Punch Line," Clapper countered, "And we have that atomic bomb in our Kraut Line."

Dick realized he was being suckered into the brand of argument that would do his club no good. He was convinced that he had the best club in the N.H.L., but Irvin kept telling himself he would be better off keeping his mouth shut when it came to discussing the league's balance—or imbalance—of power. "If the other clubs make up their minds that we have the best team," he reasoned, "they'll all gang up on us."

But it was the Canadiens who did the ganging up. They routed Chicago, 8–4, in the opening game of the 1945–1946 season; then swept past Toronto, 4–2, and Detroit, 3–1. However, they had yet to be tested by Clapper's Krauts, and on November 4, 1945, Les Canadiens invaded Boston Garden ice for what was to be the first chapter in a new Boston-Montreal grudge series that seems to have been replayed almost every year since then. Clapper proved prophetic this time as the

Bruins prevailed, 6–5, handing Les Canadiens their first defeat of the season.

Less than a week later the Canadiens returned the compliment with a 5–3 triumph at the Forum. One of the grating aspects of the feud, from the Montreal viewpoint, was the presence of Paul Bibeault, who had been *loaned* to Boston because of the wartime goalie problems. When Clapper revealed that Frankie Brimsek, Boston's prewar goalie, was being mustered out of the U. S. Coast Guard, Irvin swiftly demanded that Bibeault be returned to Montreal. As expected, the Bruins balked at the demand, and the level of enmity between the two clubs reached a new high.

This hostility was translated to the ice when the teams collided at the Forum on January 5, 1946. Goalie Bill Durnan, already acclaimed the greatest since Vézina and possibly even better than Vézina, had to leave the game with a double fracture of the hand. Boston captain Milt Schmidt, who collided with Durnan, injured his hip and soon the chaps had more or less decided to forget the puck and run at each other. Elmer Lach, who was regarded as the number-two center in the league after Bill Cowley, took care of the ratings by crashing the Bruin, Cowley, to the ice with a heavy body check. Cowley left the rink with a compound fracture of the wrist. Les Canadiens then took their toll of another third of the Kraut Line when Ken Reardon checked Bauer, injuring the Bruin's shoulder. By the time the final buzzer had sounded, Pat Egan, of Boston, had twisted his knee, and Murray Henderson had hurt his shoulder. Practically overlooked in the mayhem was the result of the game—4–2, Montreal! The Canadiens also scored a victory over Ross and Clapper. Now that Durnan was injured and Brimsek was back in the Bruins' lineup, the Boston club was compelled to return Bibeault to Les Canadiens.

Durnan's temporary absence braked the Canadiens Express. With the less proficient Bibeault in goal the Montrealers slipped to third place in mid-January. What's more, Irvin's gravest fears about opponents ganging up on Richard were borne out. Maurice, who by this time had been nicknamed "the Rocket," staged a stirring bout with Murray "Muzz" Patrick, of the Rangers, who was once heavyweight champion of Canada. A few weeks later huge Reg Hamilton of the Black Hawks slugged toe-to-toe with Richard for three minutes before the linesmen could separate the pair.

When Durnan finally returned to the nets on February 9, Les Canadiens launched their successful offensive that would carry them to first place. The Punch Line led the attack, with Toe Blake motivated by his approach to the two-hundred-goal plateau. He achieved it on February 17 at Madison Square Garden, scoring a spectacular goal with less than a minute to play. The score was tied, 4–4, as Irvin dispatched the Punch Line to the ice with the overhead clock ticking away the final sixty seconds.

"In a violent rush," commented Kerr N. Petrie writing in the New York *Herald Tribune*, "Elmer Lach smashed through the Rangers' defense and forced the opening. Blake salvaged the puck and will remember the game it won for many years to come."

Kenny Reardon, who in subsequent years was to battle with numerous Rangers, reopened his war with the Garden spectators by scuffling first with a Ranger and then a railbird in the front row. "The crowd appeared to think Reardon should have been hung, drawn, and quartered," said Petrie, "but beyond the usual shower of paper and minor refuse there was no scene worthy of the name."

Having defeated the Rangers, Les Canadiens took a firm hold on first place and didn't relinquish it for the rest of the season. They clinched the league championship on March 14 and gamboled along the rest of the route as individual players fattened their averages and collected the usual awards. Durnan won the Vézina Trophy for the third successive time and was now regarded as superior to Vézina. Blake, who received only one minor penalty all season, was awarded the Lady Byng Trophy, for combined ability and gentlemanly conduct, and Les Canadiens prepared for another march to the Stanley

Cup, fully aware of the previous year's disappointment.

Paced by the Punch Line, they demolished Chicago, 6–2, in the opener of the best-of-seven semifinal. The Black Hawks sent several players on marauding missions against Richard, and Don Grosso of the Hawks emerged with a major penalty for fouling the Rocket. In the second game Chicago's truculent defenseman Johnny Mariucci clashed with Richard, but the Rocket would not be daunted; nor would the Canadiens, who easily triumphed, 5–1.

"No player in hockey history has been so illegally shackled and interfered with by a host of personal checkers and shadows as has Rocket Richard," said Bill Roche. "Small wonder that he occasionally blows his top. Maurice should know a lot about the sour science of pro wrestling, for he has had nearly all the headlocks, arm scissors, and other grips and grabs applied on him in ice action. Further, if all the high sticks that have been thrust at his head were laid end to end he'd have quite a flourishing lumberyard."

The avalanche of wood notwithstanding, Richard & Co. eliminated the Black Hawks with 8–2 and 7–2 wins and prepared for their meeting in the Stanley Cup finals with the hated Bruins.

The Bruins tossed a scare at the Canadiens in the curtain-raiser at the Forum on March 30 when they held a 3–2 lead late in the third period. But Murph Chamberlain tied the score before the final buzzer, and the Rocket escaped from his check to blast home the winner in sudden-death overtime.

Boston obviously wasn't about to wilt. Goals by Pat "Box-car" Egan and Bobby Bauer sprung them up to a 2–1 lead with less than ten minutes remaining in the second game, when Butch Bouchard released a long shot that escaped Frankie Brimsek. Once again the teams were thrust into the caldron of overtime and now it appeared the Bruins would prevail.

Speedy Don Gallinger found an opening in the Montreal defense early in the overtime period and dashed unmolested toward Durnan. "The Canadiens goaltender waited coolly for the Boston winger," said the Associated Press dispatch, "and just as Gallinger was preparing for his shot Durnan snatched the puck from him."

Minutes later, Jimmy Peters of Les Canadiens virtually duplicated Gallinger's effort except that when Brimsek lunged for the puck, Peters slipped a low shot under him and the Montrealers won the game. The Canadiens then won the third match, 4–2, but Terry Reardon, now wearing a Boston uniform, snapped Montreal's winning streak with a sudden-death goal in the fourth game.

The Bruins fought gamely to avert elimination and managed to hold Montreal to a 3–3 tie after two and a half periods of the fifth game. It was then that Blake, despite an ailing back, drove in the winning goal. Chamberlain and Hiller added scores later in the period, and Les Canadiens had won the Stanley Cup for the sixth time in the team's history.

Irony continued to pile on irony in the Toronto-Montreal relationship and, as always, the Canadiens benefited from the curious exchange. Perhaps one of the most significant developments, which would have reverberations right up to contemporary hockey, occurred at the start of the 1946–1947 campaign when a quiet, pleasant man named Frank J. Selke was named manager of Les Canadiens.

Few men have been more steeped in hockey lore than the little man from Berlin (now Kitchener), Ontario. Selke broke into the hockey business like most Canadians, as a player. His profession, until hockey permanently intruded, was electrician, but Frank became more and more enamored of the game, and when old-time Montreal Wanderers' star, Hod Stuart, presented him with a gift stick at the end of a game in Berlin, young Selke was hooked for keeps. By 1912 he was managing City League teams and he continued climbing the hockey ladder while working at non-ice jobs on the side.

He eventually made his way to Toronto where it was inevitable that he would come into contact with Conn Smythe. In time Smythe appointed Selke his aide-de-camp, a decision that proved rather fortuitous for Smythe, Selke, and the Toronto

Maple Leafs. When Smythe went overseas to serve with the Canadian Armed Forces in World War II, it was Selke who ably filled the breach and guided the roster-riddled Toronto sextet. However, one of Selke's smartest moves in Toronto led to his downfall as a member of the Leaf hierarchy and his "deportation" to Montreal.

The coup de grace was rooted in a decision Selke made in 1944 while Smythe was overseas. At the time the Leafs had signed Frankie Eddolls, a young defenseman who had learned his hockey in Verdun, not far from where Rocket Richard had played his junior games. Dick Irvin had seen Eddolls play and liked what he had seen. Since Dick was on speaking terms with Selke, he mentioned that he wouldn't mind having the Montreal lad in the Canadiens' system.

Selke's mind was turning. He knew that Les Canadiens had the rights to a tenacious center playing in nearby Port Colborne, Ontario. "We'll let you have Eddolls," said Selke, "if you give up Ted Kennedy."

The proposal was both intriguing and perplexing to both sides and very nearly foundered on the rocks of uncertainty. At last, the parties agreed to the swap and Ted Kennedy put on the royal blue and white uniform of the Maple Leafs. In time, young "Teeder" would become the darling of Toronto hockey fans, one of the most proficient centers in N.H.L. history, and the captain of the Leafs.

There was only one thing wrong. In his haste to complete the deal Selke neglected to obtain the green light from Smythe who happened to be in war-torn France at the time. When the vitriolic Smythe finally learned about the trade, he made nearly as much noise as the cannons that were booming around him. He promptly cabled Maple Leaf Gardens demanding that the deal be erased and Eddolls return to the Toronto fold. This, of course, could not be arranged, and when Smythe was so advised he blasted off again to no avail.

"The deal spelled finis to my usefulness as assistant to Conn Smythe," Selke later reflected in his autobiography, *Behind the Cheering*.

The wisdom of Selke's decision would be underlined in years to come. Eddolls eventually became a member of the Canadiens but only as a mediocre defenseman soon traded to the Rangers. Kennedy was eventually voted into the Hockey Hall of Fame.

Smythe's return to Toronto at war's end generated open warfare at Maple Leaf Gardens. He publicly roasted Selke for the Leafs' demise in the 1945–1946 season, overlooking the fact that Toronto had annexed the Stanley Cup in the previous season. Smythe still rankled over the Kennedy deal, and the Major, a stern advocate of discipline, inspired Selke to resign from the Maple Leaf organization in May, 1946. By autumn, Selke had obtained a job with the Montreal sextet.

In his first months as managing director of Les Canadiens, Selke had little to worry about. Montreal opened the 1946–1947 season at home with a 3–0 triumph over the Rangers, and the Punch Line appeared to have more verve than ever. The Rocket scored two goals and his linemates, Lach and Blake, dazzled the New Yorkers with their footwork.

Under Dick Irvin's guidance, Les Canadiens had distilled a combination of accurate shooting, hard skating, and the kind of roughhouse deportment one would expect in a Pier Six brawl. The leading advocate of belligerency, naturally, was crazy-legs Kenny Reardon, who had found a favorite foe in Toronto's Wild Bill Ezinicki. Reardon took the opening decision in an early season game at Maple Leaf Gardens.

"Reardon was given the thumb for attempting to 'strangle' Ezinicki," wrote Jim Vipond, sports editor of the Toronto *Globe and Mail*. "The Montreal rear guard applied a full nelson on Ezinicki twice within a matter of seconds. . . . Butch Bouchard boarded Joe Klukay and then climbed on the Toronto player's back, jockey style. The aggressive Murph Chamberlain joined the fray, and when a spectator grabbed at his stick, the terrible-tempered Mr. Chamberlain slashed wildly across the boards, narrowly missing a woman's head."

While all this was going on, Richard had climbed into the scoring lead, ahead of Detroit's Billy Taylor and, of all people,

Ted Kennedy of Toronto! The Rocket also was learning something about guerrilla warfare on ice. "The Rocket," complained
Toronto defenseman Gus Mortson, "has a habit of hanging on
to you until the referee looks around and then he drops his
grip."

The Leafs didn't accept the punishment without retaliation.
Early in February, 1947, the Canadiens and Leafs erupted in
one of the most acrimonious feuds in their long history. It
started when Toronto forward Don Metz collided with Elmer
Lach and sent the Montreal center sprawling to the ice. Ex-
amination later revealed that Lach had suffered a fractured
skull and would be lost to the team for the rest of the season.

When the serious nature of the injury was revealed, it
raised several pertinent questions, not the least of which was
the legality of Metz's check. The Toronto player had received
a minor penalty from the referee but maintained that the
check was legal and that he should not have been penalized. "I
struck Lach from the side," said Metz, "but did not see him
fall." Smythe also insisted that Lach had been struck fairly.

Rather than diminish the flames of anger, the Leafian com-
ments merely served to fire one of modern hockey's bitterest
feuds. Few of the Montreal newspapermen were prepared to
believe the Metz-Smythe version of the collision and their reports increased the intercity passions.

Baz O'Meara of the Montreal *Star* declared that Metz was
given a "ridiculous minor penalty for what probably was intended to be a charge, if not, indeed, a planned effort to put
Lach out of action."

"The way we saw it," wrote Montreal *Gazette* sports
editor Dink Carroll, "and the way 90 percent of the people we
have discussed it with saw it, he (Lach) was 'speared.' Don
Metz tore into him from the side and knocked him heavily to
the ice. Elmer never saw Metz and it was entirely unexpected."

Apparently, N.H.L. president Clarence Campbell was satisfied that the minor penalty imposed on Metz was sufficient for
the crime. Campbell investigated the accident and reported
that "the incident is closed with the unfortunate result that

occurred. . . . My own presence at the game, plus the referee's report, was enough."

But it wasn't enough for Smythe. Never one to shirk a battle, he counterattacked with both guns, citing an episode in the same game when Ken Reardon was given a two-minute penalty for high-sticking Metz. "No Toronto player has ever done a trick like Reardon did," snapped Smythe, "when he charged at Don Metz when the Leaf player was up against the boards with his back turned."

Now the fight was in full force. Brawls predominated the next time the teams met. Toronto's archruffian was Ezinicki, and the ubiquitous Chamberlain was at the forefront of Les Canadiens' brigade. Jim Coleman, witty columnist of the *Globe and Mail*, said Chamberlain "set a new world's record for the broad jump as he piled Bill Barilko into the boards."

Coleman was one of the few viewers to extract some drops of humor out of the tankful of rancor. The respected Toronto writer was particularly bemused by the efforts of Montreal's Ken Mosdell to goad the referee into giving Toronto a penalty.

"Mosdell's actions apparently were inspired by the impression that referee Gorgeous George Hayes is a devotee of the drama. Mosdell died oftener than Camille, and at any second we expected to see him dab his dry lips daintily with a cambric kerchief. Once, when someone creamed him against the boards he died with almost as many gestures as were displayed by the late Sir John Martin-Harvey in *The Only Way*. . . . All in all it was the best acting that Toronto has seen since John Gielgud trod the boards at the Royal Alex."

The Canadiens proved to be better hockey players than fighters and relentlessly pulled away from the second-place Maple Leafs. Richard, who had led the league in goal-scoring but never in total points, was in a neck-and-neck battle with Max Bentley of the Black Hawks as the season approached the finish line.

By now every team in the league, even the lowly New York Rangers, was taking dead aim at the Flying Frenchmen.

A week before the end of the season Les Canadiens and the Rangers played in Madison Square Garden. Before the night was up the teams had engaged in what many seasoned observers believe was the longest, most vicious and all-encompassing brawl in N.H.L. annals.

It exploded late in the game in rather innocent fashion when Bryan Hextall of the Rangers checked Ken Reardon. As Reardon rebounded from the check he was apparently struck in the mouth by Ranger Cal Gardner's stick. His mouth bleeding and aching, Reardon made his way to the infirmary for repairs, but en route to the first-aid room he walked past the Ranger bench. A few unpleasant remarks were passed by the Rangers, then embellished by a fan, none of which Reardon appreciated.

Reardon swung at the fan and a Ranger swung at Reardon. From their vantage point across the ice the Canadiens believed that their rugged defenseman was being outnumbered. With coach Irvin's blessing they clambered over the boards and made their way en *masse* to the tiny corridor leading to the the first-aid room.

They were preceded by their teammates on the ice, led by goalie Durnan who was brandishing his big goalie stick as if it were a machete. Soon the battlers moved out from the corridor and onto the ice with three main-eventers going on at one time. At first the rest of the players simply stood around and watched the brouhaha develop, but *this time* there would be no spectators. One by one, the players were drawn into the whirlpool of flying fists. Sticks were being swung like baseball bats as referee Hayes stood helplessly on the side, hoping that a battalion of New York City police would invade the ice.

According to Dink Carroll there were four main events: (1) Maurice Richard vs. Bill Juzda, (2) Bill Moe vs. Bill Durnan, (3) Hal Laycoe vs. Leo Lamoureux, (4) Butch Bouchard vs. Bryan Hextall.

In his punch-by-swing account, Jim Coleman noted, "The Moe-Durnan and Laycoe-Lamoureux bouts were orthodox boxing exhibitions. Richard broke his stick over Juzda's head and

Juzda swarmed in and wrestled him to the ice. Bouchard ripped Hextall's stick away from him and flattened him with a punch. Moe broke a stick over Bouchard's head and Bouchard didn't seem to notice that he had been hit. When it was over, Reardon had ten stitches in his face, the bald-headed spectator had three stitches, and Buddy O'Connor had a fractured cheekbone, allegedly a result of being hit by Juzda's stick."

There were, of course, a number of fascinating side bouts, including one which featured Chamberlain and Joe Cooper. The Ranger defenseman scored a TKO when his right cross deposited Chamberlain clear over the sideboards and onto the New York bench.

Even coach Frank Boucher, of the Rangers, was involved, which was rather unique because Boucher won the Lady Byng Trophy so many times as a player that the N.H.L. finally gave him the award and struck another trophy. At one stage Boucher was clinging desperately to two Canadiens sticks while attempting to dodge wild blows tossed by Ken Mosdell. Curiously, Reardon, who instigated the furor, never actually participated in the major brawl. After he had swung at the spectator he continued on his way to the infirmary and was having his wounds dressed when the stick-swinging reached its peak. Irvin wasn't the least pleased with the uproar because his Canadiens were about to embark on another Stanley Cup challenge, but he did say that beating the rambunctious Rangers gave him "more pleasure than anything which has happened during the season."

All eyes now turned to the final weekend of the campaign and the fight for the scoring title between Richard and Max Bentley. The Black Hawk center led the Rocket by a single point as the Canadiens took the ice against the Bruins at Boston and Bentley went up against the Rangers in New York in the last games of the regular season.

Richard assisted on Johnny Quilty's goal in the second period and added another assist late in the final period, but Bentley received an assist early in the third period at New York and then scored, himself, a few minutes later. Richard was edged by a single point, 72–71, although the Rocket finished the season with a league-leading forty-five goals.

If it was any solace to Richard, he helped his Canadiens to a 4–1 series win over the Bruins in the semifinal round while the Maple Leafs eliminated the Detroit Red Wings. Even before the final began, the rival coaches were at each other's throats with Irvin verbalizing like never before. He hadn't forgotten the Metz-Lach incident and, uniquely, introduced it as an essential factor in the eventual outcome of the Cup final.

"Irvin appeared in a strange new role when he prophesied that outcome of the series rested solely in the hands of Providence," reported a Toronto columnist. "White-faced, he told Toronto newspapermen that if the accident which Elmer Lach suffered playing against the Leafs earlier in the season was only an accident, the Leafs would win the series. If, on the other hand, the injury was deliberate, Providence would intervene and Les Canadiens would win the Stanley Cup."

Providence certainly appeared on Montreal's side in the opening game. Les Canadiens thoroughly wasted the Leafs, 6–0, commanding play in every period. From all indications Irvin was quite satisfied with the result; after all, there were only three more games for his Canadiens to win, and Don Metz was still prancing around the rink for Toronto to inspire Montreal, although Don's brother, Nick, had been injured in the first game. Irvin was reportedly urging his team to win the second game "for Elmer" and had stirred the Canadiens to the boiling point for the next match.

"Irvin apparently is anxious to incite mayhem," wrote Jim Coleman in the *Globe and Mail*. "If a riot results, it is probable that the names of a few of his own players will appear in the casualty lists and they should sue Irvin for the hospital bills."

In fact, Irvin *was* quoted rather extensively by Elmer Ferguson in the Montreal *Herald*. "I was on the air in Toronto just after Lach was knocked off," said Irvin, "and I said then that every player on the Canadien team would give every drop of blood in his body to win the National League title and the Stanley Cup for Lach."

The blood *was* spilled in the first and second periods of the second game. And it was Toronto blood. Early in the game Richard slashed Vic Lynn, sending him off the ice with a cut over the eye, and late in the second period Richard slashed Ezinicki's face with his stick, cutting the Toronto player's head wide open.

Referee Bill Chadwick banished Richard from the game with a match penalty and the Canadiens disintegrated before the angry Leafs who went on to a 4–0 win. N.H.L. president Campbell reviewed the episode and levied a one-game suspension against the Rocket as well as a $250 fine. Toronto writers immediately chastised Irvin for setting the tone of the contest and added a few choice barbs for Richard. Montreal writers were divided in their comments. Some criticized the Rocket for losing his temper; others blamed the referee for not cracking down on the Leaf players who were fouling Richard before the incident.

Writing in the French-Canadian paper *Le Canada*, Paul Parizeau noted, "Richard certainly committed a costly error in losing his temper but the incident could have been avoided had Chadwick been as strict as he should have been with Ezinicki."

As if the Canadiens didn't have enough trouble, they were now being confronted with a quote attributed to goalie Durnan, supposedly uttered after the opening game. He asked: "How did the Maple Leafs get into the play-offs?"

Selke has maintained that the normally diffident Durnan would never have uttered a remark so likely to irritate the opposition. But a Montreal writer carried the quote and it soon spread like a forest blaze across the pages of the Toronto dailies. One columnist led off his article with the following ditty:

> A goalie should eschew prediction,
> Regardless of any predilection,
> For teacup leaves or crystal balls,
> Window-tappings or psychic calls.

> Durnan—Willyum—forget that muck!
> And simply try to stop that puck!"

With each game, though, Durnan was finding it more and more difficult to stop the puck. Toronto smacked four pucks past the perennial Vézina Trophy-winner and handled the Canadiens, 4–2, in the third match. The only decision scored by Montreal all night was left to managing director Selke, who slammed the door of Les Canadiens' dressing room in the face of Canadian Press hockey writer Fraser MacDougall and refused to permit any Toronto newsmen to enter the mournful locker area.

Richard was back in the Canadiens' lineup for the fourth game of the final, but the Leafs held him in tight check as they outplayed Montreal and won the game in sudden-death overtime on a goal by captain Syl Apps. One Montreal player benefited from the game and that was Bouchard whose leg was cut and required sixteen stitches to close the wound. In those days all N.H.L. players were covered by insurance policies which provided a stipend for any stitch they incurred in action. "That came to eighty bucks for me," said Bouchard. "I'll buy a couple more hives for my bee farm."

The long-awaited Montreal resurgence finally developed on April 17 at the Forum. Led by the Rocket, who scored twice, Les Canadiens defeated Toronto, 3–1, to pull within a game of tying the series. The feeling in the Canadiens' camp was that the worst was over. They would return to Maple Leaf Gardens, mop up the Leafs, and return to Montreal for the play-off clincher.

This line of thinking appeared to be confirmed before the game was half a minute old. Buddy O'Connor of the Habitants stole the puck from a Leaf defenseman and cleanly beat Turk Broda in the Toronto net. The time was 00:25 of the first period and Les Canadiens appeared on their way to a rout. But the younger Leafs failed to crumble as one might have expected, and they battled Montreal on even terms until Vic Lynn scored for Toronto at 5:34 of the second period.

The score remained tied well into the third period when the man who was once Montreal property, Ted Kennedy, fired a long, low shot past Durnan. Montreal fought gamely for the equalizer, but the Leaf defense was virtually impenetrable and Toronto won the game, 2–1, and captured the Stanley Cup.

Oddly enough, it was Selke who deserved as much congratulations for the Leaf victory as anybody. The nucleus of the Toronto sextet was composed of youngsters whom he had help sign or discover while he was pinch-hitting for the absent Smythe. But there was no consoling the bitter Irvin. His claim that only a Montreal victory would prove Don Metz had wronged Elmer Lach boomeranged in his face and there was nothing to do but return home and brood about next year.

9

The
Crumbling Dynasty

One wouldn't have imagined that a team that had advanced to the sixth game of the Stanley Cup finals and that had finished first in the standings had any cause for concern. Certainly, Les Canadiens appeared as robust as ever despite their defeat by Toronto. They placed four players, Durnan, Richard, Bouchard, and Reardon, on the N.H.L. First All-Star Team. In addition, the Rocket captured the Hart Trophy as the league's most valuable player.

But those close to the team, especially the astute Selke, realized that Les Canadiens were in trouble. Deep trouble. True, they had four First All-Stars and some effective players of near All-Star caliber. But the Habitants were woefully weak in bench strength. The question was simple enough. Could Selke rebuild fast enough to offset the crumbling dynasty?

Because of ignorance or their own selfish interests, many outsiders insisted the Canadiens were the team to beat. "They'll be more of a powerhouse than they were last year," predicted Conn Smythe. But the Toronto overlord overlooked the fact that Durnan was being troubled by his right knee which underwent an operation during the summer. An unhealthy Durnan usually meant an unhealthy Canadiens. An added problem was a decision by Richard and Bouchard to refuse Selke's contract offer, causing dissension within the ranks. Some Montrealers were displeased with Selke's decision to deal Frankie Eddolls and Buddy O'Connor to the Rangers. It was a move that would soon stagger Les Canadiens with devastating results.

The first clue that Les Canadiens were slipping emerged

in their very first game of the 1947–1948 season at the Forum against the Rangers. After jumping into a 1–0 lead on a goal by Blake, assisted by Lach and Richard, Les Canadiens failed to score again and the Rangers went on to win, 2–1. Immediately, the wolves were on Selke's trail.

"If we didn't know that Selke and Irvin were temperate men," wrote a Toronto columnist, "we would have been forced to believe that Frankie Boucher had engineered that particular deal after the Montrealers had been entertained at Hogan's Irish House for several hours. For, in return for O'Connor and Eddolls, the Rangers gave up Joe Bell, Hal Laycoe, and George Robertson. All three of them are now languishing in the minors."

The obituary notices were a bit premature. By November, Les Canadiens appeared to be serious play-off contenders and were fighting as hard as ever. They resumed hostilities with the Leafs on November 6 when Ken Reardon and Vic Lynn slugged it out for three minutes. In that same contest Richard was hit so hard by Ezinicki that the Rocket crashed into the door to the Leafs' bench, knocking it off its hinges.

And there were laughs. One afternoon a newspaper photographer visited the Canadiens' dressing room for a gag picture of Reardon sawing at the cast covering Murph Chamberlain's injured leg. Reardon posed with the saw, the picture was snapped, but Reardon didn't stop sawing. He finally broke through the cast and threatened to continue on Chamberlain's shin bone.

The one man who wasn't laughing was Durnan. Still bothered by his ailing knee, the Vézina Trophy–winner was bombed, 9–1, by the Bruins in mid-November and began hearing catcalls from the formerly loyal Forum fans. A week later Cal Gardner of the Rangers crashed into the Montreal goalie, opening a gaping wound over Durnan's eye. He was removed from the game and replaced by young Gerry McNeil.

"The Canadiens won't finish in the first four," declared

Ranger coach Frank Boucher, in what was the most outspoken critique of the Montrealers. "The other clubs are just stronger than them; that's all." Boucher's prediction was bolstered by the performance of ex-Montrealer Buddy O'Connor, who was leading the Rangers in scoring, and Frank Eddolls, who had become a first-stringer, and a good one, on the New York defense.

Selke stunned the Montreal club in mid-December with a wholesale shake-up. He demoted Bobby Carse to Cleveland and Murdo MacKay to Buffalo. Forwards Jimmy Peters and Johnny Quilty were traded to Boston for Joe Carveth, but there were no noticeable results. Matters became so grave that by Christmastime coach Irvin kicked a Santa Claus played by a French-Canadian writer out of the dressing room! Then in early January a permanent gloom set in when Toe Blake broke his ankle in a game against the Rangers. The Canadiens had slipped to fifth place and the question was no longer whether Montreal would finish first but whether they would gain a play-off berth.

Meanwhile, Richard was absorbing trip-hammer assaults from the presiding N.H.L. hatchet men and finding it more and more difficult to maintain decorum, particularly when Bill Chadwick happened to be the referee. In a game on January 18, 1948, at Boston, Chadwick whistled off Richard for slashing Milt Schmidt. When he joined teammate Chamberlain who had been banished for roughing, Richard hurled his stick to the ice. Then he pulled himself away from the restraining Chamberlain and returned to the rink. Thereupon referee Chadwick ordered the Rocket out of action for the remainder of the game and called for a policeman to escort him to his dressing room.

N.H.L. president Campbell, who was fast becoming as much an enemy as Chadwick in Richard's eyes, fined the Rocket seventy-five dollars for the explosion and considered the incident closed. Apparently it never dawned upon the legally trained Campbell that each team was sending its most notorious agents provocateurs to inflame Richard and inspire him to violence. It was one of the gravest oversights Campbell has made in his career as hockey czar.

Apart from Les Canadiens' abrupt demise, the surprise of the season was the state of equanimity with which the usually volatile Irvin was accepting the catastrophe. Friends were astonished to find him more amiable than ever and philosophical about the whole debacle. "I'm coaching the same as I always did," Irvin explained. "I still use my left hand to open the gate for the players. When we used to be trailing by one goal I'd say to the Punch Line, 'Go out and get a goal.' And they'd go out and get a goal, maybe two goals. Now when we're trailing by one goal I say to what remains of the Punch Line, 'Go out and get us a goal.' If I'm lucky, I can get them off the ice before the other team scores again. Last year they said I was a great coach. Maybe I'd better try opening the gate with my other hand."

Impartial critics outside of Montreal wasted no time fingering the Canadien most culpable in the slump. "Richard alone is responsible for the sorry showing," said Jim Coleman of the *Globe and Mail*. "Up in Montreal they insist that he isn't giving his best for the Canadiens." Others argued that it wasn't Richard who was the culprit but rather the veteran goalie, Durnan. Late in February, following another merciless booing from the Forum fans, Durnan barged gloomily into the dressing room and said he was ready to quit. Selke immediately conferred with his brooding ace and persuaded him to remain active.

"He didn't want to accompany the team to New York," said Selke. "He asked me to get someone else. I told him there was no chance at this late hour. It would be impossible. When we talked things over, I pointed out that he had had a long and brilliant career, and an honorable record, and he should finish out the season with us like the rest of the fellows were doing and he agreed."

Even more embarrassing to Selke was the fact that the Rangers' little Buddy O'Connor who had played in the shadow of Elmer Lach for six years maintained a slim lead over the Montreal center in the scoring race. All sorts of absurd misfortune assailed the Canadiens' camp. One such episode involved Montreal defenseman Roger Leger who managed to lose a game for the Flying Frenchmen when his bridgework started down his gullet.

Les Canadiens were playing the Red Wings and led by a single goal late in the match. Leger got the puck from a faceoff. Ted Lindsay of the Wings slammed a terrific body check into the burly defenseman and in the process Lindsay's elbow caught Leger smack in the mouth. Choking, sputtering, and waving his arms like a madman, Leger disregarded the puck and skated frantically to the bench. The Wings immediately seized the chance and put the puck in the net before Leger's bridgework could be plucked from his throat!

As the schedule reached the homestretch in early March, it appeared that the Rangers who had embarked on a perilous seven-game winless streak would fold completely and allow the Canadiens to squeeze into a play-off berth. But the Montrealers couldn't regain enough momentum and the Rangers finally won a game and clinched fourth place in the final week of the season. Les Canadiens' only consolation was that Lach beat out O'Connor for the scoring championship by a single point. "The collapse of the Canadiens," said one respected analyst, "can be blamed not on Selke but on the failure of the reserves developed by his predecessor, Tommy Gorman."

The challenge now facing Selke was not *whether* he should rebuild his tottering team but *how* it should be done. "I'm convinced," said Selke, "we will gain nothing by making any trades involving established players. There were a few players, I know, who had a bad season. But I feel they more than redeemed themselves by the way the team fought out the tag end of the schedule. Any veterans who appear on their way out will be given an opportunity to show what they can do at next fall's training camp."

Two bright spots emerged. Both Lach and Richard were

named to the First Team and Blake announced he would try a comeback if his broken ankle had healed. In addition, Selke underlined his faith in Irvin by signing him to a new one-year contract.

Through the deepest slough of despond Les Canadiens never lost their will to fight. One of the most fascinating feuds involved Ken Reardon and the Rangers. Following the classic brawl in New York in March, 1947, Reardon sought to determine who had actually clobbered him. At first the culprit was thought to be Bryan Hextall, but when Hal Laycoe was traded from New York to Montreal he purportedly informed Reardon that his assailant was Cal Gardner. Meanwhile Gardner had been dealt from New York to Toronto and was wearing a Leaf uniform when he confronted Reardon during the 1948–1949 campaign. The date was January 1, 1949; the site, Maple Leaf Gardens.

Referee Chadwick had sentenced the two with minor penalties for slashing after a brief but violent clash. As Reardon turned toward the penalty box, he overheard a remark from Gardner that displeased him. What's more, Gardner's stick was raised. Reardon wheeled, stick at the battle point, and headed directly for Gardner. "They then flailed each other vigorously about the heads and shoulders," said the *Globe and Mail*. At this time burly linesman George Hayes attempted to intervene and referee Chadwick stood a few yards to the side screaming at the players to cease and desist.

His peacemaking efforts fell on deaf ears. Both players dropped their sticks and swung fists in what one observer described as "a life-and-death grapple" before they were finally pried apart by the officials. N.H.L. president Campbell fined Gardner $250 and Reardon $200 and suspended both players for the next meeting of their respective teams. Campbell's weak decision was to prove once more the fallacy of his monetary penalty system and was to result later in an even more gruesome battle between Gardner and Reardon.

In addition to fighting, Les Canadiens were winning some

hockey games in 1948–1949, but the big story of the season was an offer made to Selke by the Toronto Maple Leafs. Conn Smythe astonished the hockey world by dispatching coach Hap Day to Montreal with instructions to obtain Maurice Richard's contract.

"Maple Leaf Gardens has never been close with a buck," said Day, "and I have explicit instructions to meet any price mentioned for Richard's services. We consider Richard the greatest right wing in the major league, if not the greatest player."

The *Globe and Mail* followed suit by printing an arresting photograph of Richard, *wearing a Maple Leaf jersey*, adding a caption, "Wouldn't he look good in a sweater like this?"

Officials of Les Canadiens reacted to the story with the same brand of enthusiasm as the President of the United States might if he was asked to take up citizenship in Moscow. "All the money in Toronto wouldn't buy him," carped Selke. Irvin then underlined the point: "It's propaganda. All this is merely an attempt to upset my boys on the eve of a game."

Selke might have been tempted by the six-figure offer proferred by the Leafs but there were other considerations. "The Rocket is rooted among the predominantly French population," Selke explained. "Even if I even suggested, even in fun, that the Rocket might go, the fans would tear the Forum down, brick by brick. The only time you'll ever see Maurice in a Leaf uniform is in that artist's conception in the *Globe and Mail*."

Selke's retort provided the kind of reassurance Montreal fans needed. The Montreal *Star* then printed a picture of the Rocket under the caption "He's Still With Us, Folks." To which Selke then offered to purchase the contracts of any or all of Max Bentley, Bill Ezinicki, Harry Watson, or Garth Boesch of the Leafs.

Richard's response was to battle Ezinicki the next time the teams played. He outfought the doughty Leaf, taking the decision with an effective wrestling headlock that defused Ezinicki. A photo of the battle appeared in the Toronto *Globe and*

Mail and, surprisingly, inspired a stern lecture of criticism from a Montreal rooter who claimed to have been sitting thirty feet from the brawl.

"I notice that after the fights begin," the correspondent wrote, "several of the Canadien players remain in the background, or engage in very light fisticuffs, managing to keep an eye on the principals. Then, when the principal has his opponent winded and is in much the same condition himself, the 'gentlemen' who remain on the side climb into the brawl in a fresh condition and many times manage to 'beat' the opponent on which their teammate started to work."

Selke's success in persuading Durnan not to retire proved fruitful. The big goalie was better than ever in 1948–1949 and on March 7 scored his fourth straight shutout, for a total shutout skein of 283 minutes, as Les Canadiens defeated Boston, 1–0. The lone goal was scored by Rocket Richard!

Although Toe Blake had retired to become coach of the Valleyfield Braves of the strong Quebec Senior League, the two-thirds Punch Line still boasted the Rocket and Elmer Lach. The pair played well through the season and helped Montreal to a third-place finish and the right to face league-leading Detroit in the first round of the play-offs.

Thanks to young Gordie Howe, Ted Lindsay, Sid Abel, and a well-rounded bench, the Red Wings had become the new class team of the N.H.L. They were also rough and they proved it in the opening game when Lach left the game with a broken jaw after colliding with "Black" Jack Stewart of the Detroit defense. Once again poor Elmer had become the center of an acrimonious controversy. On the one side, Les Canadiens claimed Stewart had deliberately maimed Lach, much in the manner that Don Metz of Toronto had done so in the 1946–1947 season. On the other side, the Red Wings piously denied any foul play.

"Elmer doesn't carry the puck in his teeth," Irvin pointed out, "but that's where they've been checking him." Both Selke and a Montreal columnist tossed in their bits of fuel, charging that Stewart had deliberately injured Lach. As for Elmer himself, he declared that he had had it and would quit hockey. "I'll miss the game," he said, "and I'll have a lot of memories, both good and bad."

Even without Lach, Les Canadiens extended the Red Wings to seven games before bowing out of the Cup round. Immediately after the last game they received another blow when their colorful veteran Murph Chamberlain announced that he, too, was through. "That ice can get awfully hard," explained Murph. "Three years ago against Detroit I tumbled on my head, hard. I came back and played. I played in the next game, too. But I didn't know much of anything for four days."

Surprisingly, it was the talkative Chamberlain who stuck to his retirement prediction. But Lach returned for the 1949–1950 season and Les Habitants showed no inclination for anything less than a contending spot. Nor did they display any lack of fire, despite the departure of Chamberlain. If anything, Ken Reardon appeared to personally attempt to compensate for any loss of mustard by Chamberlain's departure and immediately got himself into deep trouble on a visit to Chicago.

The furor developed in the second period of a game on November 2 at Chicago Stadium. A rinkside fan snapped at Reardon, "You're a brave man with a hockey stick in your hand." Reardon purportedly reached over a protective fence and hit the fan with his hockey stick, opening a severe wound. Leo Gravelle and Billy Reay of the Canadiens promptly joined the battle. One of the fans jumped over the boards and chased Reardon on the ice, but referee Chadwick caught the fan and turned him back. The crowd along the rinkside fence pressed hard and threatened to overflow onto the ice in a general melee before ushers and officials rushed to the area to restore calm.

Four of the spectators brought charges of assault against Reardon, Gravelle, and Reay, who were arrested at the end of the game. They were booked in a Chicago jail and released when Black Hawk president Bill Tobin posted the bonds for the trio. That proved to be just the beginning of

Reardon's problems. A few days later he collided with Cal Gardner, and the Leaf center left the ice with a jaw broken in two places. Few observers believed it was an accident.

In January, Reardon was fined twenty-five dollars for his part in a fight with New York's Pentti Lund. Richard was similarly fined. The Rocket had been tormented by pesty Tony Leswick of the Rangers and sought revenge as the final buzzer sounded. "Perched on the rail as time ran out," said a Canadian Press dispatch, "Richard hopped to the ice, headed straight for Leswick and started swinging. . . . Pulled away several times, Richard went back to the attack. . . . At one time, close to the Ranger bench, Richard took a wild swipe at coach Lynn Patrick, who appeared to have said something to the rampaging Richard."

It was Reardon, not Richard, who immersed himself in the deepest hole with league president Campbell. Kenny collaborated with Montreal author Vince Lunny on an article that appeared in *Sport Magazine* late in February, 1950. Throughout the article Reardon referred to his feud with Cal Gardner.

"I tried to smash Gardner in the face with my stick," said Reardon, alluding to one of their eruptions, "but his stick broke in the first exchange of blows and he held the butt end in front of his face as a protector. I was going to smash him to pieces, but the other players intervened. I was so determined to swing at him full force that I never thought of jabbing the end of my stick into his mouth. I could have done it easily."

"Someday," the article went on, "the Canadiens' wild Irishman is going to carve Gardner into little pieces and it will take a brave man to restrain him." The article spoke of Reardon as a man "who intends to pursue his course of intended action even at the risk of being expelled from the league."

Reardon again was quoted: "I am going to see that Gardner gets fourteen stitches in the mouth. I may have to wait a long time, but I'm patient. Even if I have to wait until the last game I ever play, Gardner is going to get it good and plenty."

As soon as the magazine hit the stands, Campbell had a copy of it delivered to his office. He summoned Reardon to his Montreal headquarters and later revealed that Kenny acknowledged the magazine statements attributed to him. Not long after that, Campbell announced an unprecedented fine. Reardon would have to post a one-thousand-dollar cash bond with the league "for his good conduct in the future and Reardon will be entitled to petition for its refund when he retires from the league." The president added that he thought Reardon was sincere in telling him the Reardon-Gardner feud was finished.

The regular season ended on a pleasant note for Les Canadiens when they clinched second place. They defeated Chicago, 4–0, on the final weekend of the season, and Durnan had the rare delight of receiving an assist after passing the puck ahead to the Rocket who, in turn, scored a goal. At the conclusion of the game the thirty-five-year-old goaltender said he was "getting tired" and planned to retire at the end of the season.

Durnan's decision was reinforced by the Canadien's dismal effort in the first round of the play-offs against New York's fourth-place Rangers. Durnan faltered behind a weakened defense and Richard was overshadowed by Pentti Lund of the Rangers who suddenly developed into a potent scorer. The New Yorkers swept the first three games before Elmer Lach scored an overtime goal to temporarily save Les Canadiens in the fourth match. In that same contest Durnan was replaced by young Gerry McNeil who played a commendable game.

Irvin decided to go with McNeil again in the fifth game which was scoreless until the fourth minute of the third period. Then the Rangers opened the floodgates and poured three goals past McNeil, winning the game, 3–0. When it was over Durnan sat on his dressing-room bench, his eyes welled with tears. "Rangers," he kept repeating, "couldn't do anything wrong; couldn't do anything wrong."

Durnan wasn't the only member of the old guard to throw in the towel. Pugnacious Ken Reardon, bothered by an old back injury, conferred with Selke prior to the 1950–1951 season and said he was finished. "Reardon is convinced he should withdraw from active play while he is still in one piece," said Selke. Durnan was replaced by McNeil, a very efficient but somewhat nervous type while Reardon's place was taken by a baby-faced defenseman who was to become one of the greatest in N.H.L. history. His name was Doug Harvey.

In the meantime, Richard was fulfilling all the rave notices that suggested he was hockey's greatest goal scorer. "He can shoot from any angle," said goalie Frank Brimsek. "You play him for a shot to the upper corner and the Rocket wheels around and fires a backhander into the near, lower part of the net."

"When Richard breaks on one defenseman," said Boston's Murray Henderson, "there's no telling what he'll do. If he gets his body between you and the puck, you just can't get at it. He cradles the puck on the blade of his stick, steers it with one hand, and wards off his check with the other. Strong? That guy is like an ox, but he sure doesn't look it."

Even then few but his closest friends were able to understand the brooding Richard personality. True, the Rocket had learned to speak English, but when he was around the rink he rarely betrayed a smile. Once, after a game with the Maple Leafs in which he scored a three-goal hat trick, Toronto photographer Nat Turofsky asked him to smile for the camera.

"What have I to smile about?" asked Richard. "We only tied tonight."

Like the good photographer he was, Turofsky persisted. "C'mon, Rocket," he urged, "smile and kiss the stick!"

"Kiss it yourself," snapped Richard. And that was that!

At home Richard was no less ebullient. "He roams around the house muttering to himself," revealed Lucille Richard, his affable wife. "He gets mad and stays that way until he gets a goal. And even a goal, or a cluster of them, won't make him completely happy unless the Canadiens win. When he's in a surly mood, all he does is eat. He keeps me busy broiling steaks and frying pork chops."

Author Vince Lunny, who had great insight into the Rocket, added, "His nerves are as taut as trout lines. If he had to keep the tension bottled up within himself, he'd probably blow up. Luckily, hockey is a physical contact sport which provides a release for the nervous tension that twists his stomach into knots and threatens a mental breakdown."

During a game against the Red Wings, Detroit manager Jack Adams dispatched Ted Lindsay to unnerve Richard. The Rocket wound up with a five-minute major penalty and Detroit rapidly scored two goals. "Perturbed by the turn of events," said Lunny, "rivers of anger scalded the Rocket's brain. When he served his time he leaped from the bench like all hell breaking loose."

The Rocket pounced on the puck and drove it past the Detroit goaltender. He remained on the ice and, seconds later, took a pass from Lach, rounded the defense, and fired one of his patented backhanders into the twine. By now coach Irvin figured the Rocket was ready for a respite and called him to the bench. "Never mind," countered Richard, "I had my rest in the penalty box."

Lach won the next face-off and passed the puck to a teammate who relayed it to Richard. He skated straight into Lindsay, bowling him over, and thus countered the critics who said he couldn't play the game Morenz-style. He raced in for another goal. Montreal won the game, 3–2.

On another occasion he walked into the dressing room and approached Irvin. "Dick," he said, "I feel pretty bad so don't give me much ice tonight. This afternoon I moved to another apartment and I couldn't hire a truck. My brother and I carried everything on our backs."

Irvin planned to use the Rocket for spot duty that evening but once the game started, Richard asked him to take his regular turn. He scored five goals against the Red Wings! "I wonder," said Irvin, "what you'd have done if you weren't tired."

Richard's inflationary scoring did nothing to calm his temper, principally because he was still being mauled, maligned, and generally mussed up by the opposition. Early in March, 1951, the Rocket was incensed over what he believed was poor refereeing in a 2–1 loss to Detroit. The following evening the Canadiens were scheduled to play the Rangers in New York. Richard remained furious over the previous night's episode and found it difficult to sleep en route to New York or at the hotel in Manhattan. He told friends how Sid Abel, of Detroit, had grabbed him by the chin and ditched him into the goalpost where he was cut. When he pointed out the infraction to referee Hugh McLean, the official supposedly laughed in his face.

"I skated away," noted the Rocket, "saying, 'This is the damnedest thing I ever saw.'"

McLean immediately gave him a ten-minute misconduct penalty. In the penalty box Richard was needled by Detroit defenseman Leo Reise. He punched Reise and then shoved linesman Jim Primeau. For this he was handed a match penalty and an automatic fifty-dollar fine. It was while stewing over these incidents that Richard became involved in one of his most curious difficulties.

Prior to the game with the Rangers he was standing in front of New York's Picadilly Hotel and was next seen heading into the lobby. Canadian Press reporting the following: "In the lobby he saw McLean and grabbed the official by the neck. He was ready to pour on some punches when two members of the Montreal Forum staff restrained him. Meantime, linesman Primeau hove on the scene and attempted to get in a lick or two at Richard but was held off." Campbell's response was a five-hundred-dollar fine for the Rocket for "conduct prejudicial to the welfare of hockey."

Campbell emphasized that no blows were struck during the encounter, but, "Richard's action in grabbing McLean was accompanied by a lot of foul and abusive language at the official, which was continued throughout the entire incident, lasting several minutes, and during which several women were present."

There were mixed feelings about Campbell's handling of the case. Some observers believe the president erred in not prying further into the background episodes that led up to the clash, which would have caused him to be more lenient with the Rocket. But writers in Boston and New York contended that Richard should have been suspended.

"A few weeks ago," wrote James Burchard in the New York *World-Telegram*, "Richard received thousands of dollars' worth of gifts from fans in Montreal. Now they'll start a fund to pay his fine and he'll probably make several hundred dollars out of the deal."

Much of the displeasure in New York was galvanized by the Rangers who appeared to be edging Les Canadiens out of fourth place in early March only to see their lead erode with every game. When the clubs met on March 11 at Madison Square Garden, the Rangers held a three-point lead over Montreal. It was believed that a New York win would cinch a play-off spot for them, but a loss or tie would set off a panic that would enable Les Canadiens to sweep past the Rangers and into the playdowns.

The Rangers held a relatively secure 5–2 lead as the timer clock ticked past the nine-minute mark of the last period. Then, without any notice, the Canadiens struck like thunderbolts. First, defenseman Tom Johnson shot the puck past substitute goalie Emile Francis at 9:40 and then rookie Claude Robert pulled Montreal to within a goal of tying the game with only sixty-two seconds remaining. Nevertheless, it still appeared that the Rangers would be able to control the puck for the remaining minute of play.

But Les Canadiens have a way of overwhelming teams that often appear to have them on the ropes. Brilliant New York *Herald Tribune* hockey analyst Al Laney described the Ranger collapse: "It was hard to believe the Rangers could lapse into such utter confusion so quickly when the Montreal skaters turned on the pressure. They were, in fact, visited by a case of the jitters after Robert scored and it is their own fault."

Promptly after referee Chadwick dropped the puck for the last-minute face-off, coach Irvin watched the puck skim into New York territory and called goalie McNeil off the ice for an extra attacker. The Rangers frantically attempted a clearing shot down the ice at the unguarded Montreal net, but Butch Bouchard stopped the puck at the left point. His shot on goal was weak and wobbly, and Francis, who played shortstop for a crack Canadian baseball team in the off-season, appeared to have no trouble handling it. Francis *did* get his glove on the rubber, but somehow he fumbled it and the puck trickled over his mitt and into the net with forty seconds remaining. Les Canadiens tied the game, 5–5, and captured a play-off berth as the Rangers continued to panic and lose more games.

Montreal's opponents in the first round of the play-offs were the powerful Detroit Red Wings who were rated heavy favorites to bump Les Canadiens out in short shrift. The opening game in Detroit on March 28 was tied, 2–2, after three periods of regulation time, thus setting the stage for sudden death. After the first twenty minutes of extra time neither team scored. Another twenty minutes were played and still no decision. Unbelievably, it was past midnight when the third sudden death was completed and the score remained the same. By now the leg-weary athletes were having trouble racing up and down the ice and it appeared that the game would last until morning without a score.

Irvin sent his bread-and-butter scorer, the Rocket, onto the ice for the start of the fourth overtime and a minute went by without any decisive thrust. It was almost 1:10 A.M. when the Red Wing defense attempted to launch an attack. Richard saw the pass coming and pounced on the puck like a leopard spotting an antelope. "He sped past the Detroit defense," said the Canadian Press, "with a blazing burst of speed. Alone in front of the net, he paused before lining a ten-footer past Terry Sawchuk."

Amazingly, the second game of the series, also at Detroit's Olympia Stadium, was a virtual duplicate of the first. The teams were tied this time 0–0, at the end of regulation time. They struggled without success through two scoreless sudden-death periods and were on the brink of collapse when defenseman Bud MacPherson of the Canadiens commanded the puck at 2:10 of the third sudden death. MacPherson spotted Billy Reay near the Detroit goal and delivered him a crisp pass. Reay tempted Sawchuk with a feint but, instead, skimmed the puck to Richard who was zooming in from the left. Richard's shot was so hard it nearly tore a hole in the mesh, and Les Canadiens were now ahead two games to none. "He is as great an opportunist as the game has ever known," said Baz O'Meara in the Montreal *Star*. "His great adversary, Gordie Howe, was a spent force. The Rocket has taken up the challenge to the pretender to his crown and has thrown it back in his flaunting face and emerged again as not only the man of the moment but the man of momentum. Richard may be the most maligned man in hockey. He may be the most unpredictable, temperamental cuss that ever laced on a skate, but he is the special delivery kid."

The Rocket himself described the shot this way: "I went only five feet after I got the puck. Sawchuk was standing in the middle of the net. He had the angle cut down so I backhanded it for the far corner. I meant to shoot it right along the ice. But it raised off the ice about five inches. Sawchuk didn't move. It came at him so fast I caught him with his stick still on the ice."

Detroit rebounded to win the next two games in Montreal but it was the Rocket again in the fifth game, scoring the winning goal in the third period as Les Canadiens prevailed, 5–2. The sixth game of the series was described by Toronto Hall of Famer King Clancy as "the greatest game I ever saw in my life."

Neither team scored a goal until six minutes of the third

period when Montreal went ahead on a shot by Reay. The Red Wings tied it less than a minute later but the Rocket and then Ken Mosdell each beat Sawchuk to put the contest out of Detroit's reach. Montreal finished on top, 3–2, and when it was over the Rocket was still the unpredictable Rocket in the dressing room. "He was the quietest of the winners," observed Montreal writer Vic Morris, Jr. "He changed his uniform without saying a word."

Others were more excited about Richard's stunning performance in the sudden-death games. "Twenty years from now—in April, 1971—we will edge our rocker up next to some crony on the porch of an old folks' home," said Detroit *Times* columnist Bob Murphy, "and say, 'Do you remember when the Rocket won those two big overtime games at Olympia in 51?' The Rocket is made to watch and write about."

But Richard alone couldn't cope with the Toronto Maple Leafs in the 1951 Stanley Cup final in which every game went into sudden-death overtime. The Leafs won the opener, 3–2, on a goal by Sid Smith at 5:51 of the first extra period. Then it was the Rocket's turn and he saved the Canadiens in the second game with his third sudden-death winner of the 1951 series. Richard then went on to break Toe Blake's record for points scored in the play-offs, but it was the Leafs who took the Cup, and they did it with a remarkable win in the fifth game.

Les Canadiens were leading, 2–1, with less than a minute left in the third period when Toronto's Ted Kennedy and Max Bentley combined to feed a pass to Tod Sloan. Goalie McNeil couldn't cope with Sloan's shot and the game, once more, went into sudden death.

Irvin hoped the Rocket would come through for him as he had earlier in the game when he scored the opening goal in classic Richard fashion. "He had only Jim Thomson between him and the goal," recalled Dink Carroll, of the Montreal *Gazette*. "Thomson may have been an All-Star defenseman, but they all looked alike to the Rocket in those circumstances. He went around Thomson like a hoop around a barrel, pulled goalie Al Rollins out, and fired the puck into the empty net."

That, however, wasn't enough, and when the first overtime began, the Richard line lost the puck to Harry Watson of the Leafs. He passed the puck to Howie Meeker inside the Canadiens' zone and the crew-cut right wing cut behind the Montreal net before sliding a crisp pass toward the blue line. Bill Barilko, the bushy-haired Leaf defenseman, saw it coming and dived headfirst at the puck, swinging his stick in the same motion. While Barilko was still hanging in midair the puck sailed over McNeil's right elbow and into the net.

"There's only one thing to do" was the murmuring in the Montreal dressing room, "and that is wait till next year."

This, of course, was an old refrain except that under Selke's deft maneuvering, "next years" were becoming more and more attractive to Montreal fans. The essential reason was that Les Canadiens' farm system had begun to transport several excellent prospects to the big club and there was more help on the way. One of the first arrivals was Bernard Geoffrion, a brash young man with a stunning shot who had learned his hockey within trotting distance of the Forum. Even more promising was Jean Béliveau, a huge skater who was playing amateur hockey in Quebec City. With Geoffrion and Béliveau in the fold, there would be lusty and lively days ahead.

10

Another Dynasty
on the Horizon

Selke looked confidently at the prospects of the 1950's because of Richard, the promise of his kids, and the strength McNeil displayed in goal. He described his goalie as "the best in the business," despite some excellent work by Al Rollins in Toronto and Terry Sawchuk in Detroit, and argued that McNeil proved his mettle in the play-offs.

"He outgoaled Sawchuk, Rollins, and Turk Broda at every turn," saild Selke. "Losing out in our bid for the Stanley Cup was a bitter pill to swallow, but we think that we've found something more valuable than the Stanley Cup. That something is an outstanding goaltender."

Selke's fondness for McNeil would prove to be somewhat overenthusiastic in the years to come, but there were other sources of jubilation, not the least of which was the development of junior hockey in the city of Montreal, not to mention the province of Quebec. Since most of the young players were French-Canadian, their progress helped insure the French fact on Les Canadiens for years to come. In 1965, for example, four members of the Canadiens were natives of Montreal and six others from different parts of Quebec. But in 1951 there was one French-Canadien above all who captured Selke's imagination and tantalized the people who ran the Forum. His name was Jean Marc Béliveau. As centermen go, he was a behemoth, standing six feet two inches and weighing 192 pounds, but he had uncanny speed and maneuverability for a man his size, and, most of all, he could score goals.

Normally, one would have imagined that Les Canadiens

could have obtained Béliveau merely by snapping their fingers. Not so. Jean Marc was something very special and the citizens of Quebec City were quick to recognize this. By 1951 Béliveau virtually owned the town. If he went into a clothing store to buy a couple of suits the proprietor would forget the bill. Having "Le Gros Bill" (Big Bill) drop in was honor enough. That same situation prevailed wherever Béliveau turned.

Béliveau's team, the Quebec (Junior) Citadelles, were technically considered "amateur." But Béliveau grossed more than twenty thousand dollars in the 1950–1951 season, including a new car presented him by admiring fans. Jean Marc, however, seemed equally impressed by a ring which was given him the same night by his teammates. "Beautiful ring they gave me," he remarked proudly. Had he chosen politics Le Gros Bill could have easily become the mayor of Quebec City or the premier of Le Province de Quebec.

"Jean Béliveau in Quebec," remarked author Leonard Shecter, "is like Mickey Mantle and Joe DiMaggio in the United States. When Jean Béliveau walks down the street in Quebec the women smile, the men shake his hand, and the little boys follow him."

With this background in mind it was understandable that Jean Marc was reluctant to leave Quebec City, no matter what Les Canadiens had to offer. In addition there is a certain sociological element not generally known: The less urbane citizens of Quebec resent the Montreal sophisticates, and they were determined to keep Béliveau, who had put Quebec City back on the map, nice and comfortable in their *ville*.

Such a coup was not impossible because when Béliveau became too old to play junior hockey for the Citadelles he would easily move into the Quebec Senior League and do the same wonderful things for the Quebec Aces. But the ramifications of Le Gros Bill remaining in Quebec ran as deep as the black well of politics. Several Quebec City businessmen had backed construction of the handsome Colisée, which was the equal in size of many N.H.L. rinks. Without Béliveau to fill the seats either as a junior or as a member of the Aces, Le

Colisée and its backers would lose money. They had a very relevant issue to put before young Jean when he got the urge to go south to Montreal.

It was freely noted that these same Quebec businessmen-politicos were pressuring Les Canadiens to lay off Béliveau, or else such economic sanctions as the loss of The Montreal Forum's beer license would be imposed by the provincial government in Quebec City. All of this was becoming terribly relevant as August, 1951, approached because Jean Marc was about to turn twenty and would be too old for the juniors.

In those days an amateur player was allowed to play five "trial" games with the professionals without losing his amateur status. So, while Béliveau was still nineteen, Les Canadiens invited him for a couple of N.H.L. games. After watching Le Gros Bill in one turn on the ice, coach Irvin waxed ecstatic and told the world Béliveau would be a big-league star the moment he signed an N.H.L. contract. "He's the closest thing to Lester Patrick that I've seen," said Irvin. "He didn't make one mistake in the two games with us."

The Aces made no mistakes either. They managed to sign Béliveau prior to the 1951–1952 season to another "amateur" contract, this time in the fast Quebec Senior League. Without question Béliveau became the dominant force in the circuit from his very first game with the Aces. Crowds that had previously filled Le Colisée to watch the Citadelles were now coming to see the Aces and it is safe to say that Béliveau might still have been enjoying life in Quebec were it not for the irresistible pressures on him from Montreal and Quebec City itself. The two seemingly opposing forces united to form an interesting *entente cordiale* that eventually squeezed Béliveau out of his Quebec cocoon and into a Canadiens uniform.

The most obvious lobbying was done by Selke and his Montreal colleagues. More subtle efforts were launched by backers of Quebec's other junior team, the Frontenacs, who were losing money now that Béliveau was drawing all the crowds to the senior games. They allied with Les Canadiens to get Béliveau out of their hair and the device was a curious but effective one.

By exerting pressure in the proper places Les Canadiens hoped to persuade most members of the Quebec Senior League to abandon the "amateur" label and become out-and-out professionals. Were this to happen, Les Canadiens would then have the rights to sign Béliveau and there would be no way he could avoid coming to Montreal. At the time, George "Punch" Imlach was coaching the Aces, and he employed all the know-how at his command, which was plentiful, to thwart the move. He succeeded for two years, until the summer of 1953, when the representatives of the Quebec Senior League teams, with the exception of Imlach, voted to turn the league professional. It was then that Les Canadiens finally annexed Béliveau, but meanwhile they had to make do without him. This was not really that hard because of the continued excellence of the Rocket and the coming of age of Bernard Geoffrion.

Nicknamed "Boom-Boom" because of the reverberation of his stick hitting the puck and the puck hitting the end boards (although it often went directly into the net), Geoffrion had many of the incendiary qualities of Richard. "Remember," the Boomer would say, "the Rocket always was my idol when I was a kid in Montreal. When Maurice doesn't score he's not happy and he doesn't want to speak to anyone. I'm the same way."

But the Geoffrion character had one ingredient that was missing in the Richard psyche, a flamboyant sense of humor. For the most part the Rocket was a quiet, introverted sort even when life was agreeable, but when Geoffrion was scoring easily he became an opera-singing clown who led the Canadiens' laugh parade. He began delighting teammates late in the 1950–1951 season after scoring 103 goals in fifty-seven Montreal Junior League games. Like Béliveau, Geoffrion was under great pressure to turn pro with Les Canadiens and he resisted until there were only eighteen games remaining in the 1950–

1951 schedule. His reasoning was different from Béliveau's. Geoffrion realized that the Calder Trophy for rookie of the year was given to players who had skated in twenty or more games. By waiting until there were fewer than twenty games in the 1950–1951 schedule he thus became eligible to win it the following season.

When approached by Selke, Geoffrion laid the facts on the line: "I'll lose my chance for the Calder. It's too late in the season to catch up with the other guys."

The Boomer was no fool. He opened the 1951–1952 season with two goals, including the winner, against Chicago in a 4–2 Montreal victory and immediately established himself as the newest Canadiens hero. For Geoffrion it was relatively easy. Not only was he an excellent young prospect but he had recently married Marlene Morenz, the attractive blonde daughter of the late Howie Morenz.

"I was a figure skater at the time," Marlene remembered, "and was practicing at the Forum for an ice carnival. While I was doing a spin I missed a piece of cardboard on the ice and took a bad spill. As I looked up, deeply embarrassed, I noticed this fellow laughing his head off. I was furious and was still furious after the show when a knock sounded on the dressing-room door. It was my brother (Howie Morenz, Jr.) who wanted me to meet a friend of his from junior hockey. It turned out to be the same fellow who had been laughing at me. And that's how I met Boomer. Soon we were all laughing."

Not long after Geoffrion's opening scoring burst, Les Canadiens visited New York and Geoffrion was interviewed by New York *Daily News* sports columnist Jimmy Powers. The writer observed that the N.H.L. had a prize crop of rookies and wondered just who the Boomer thought would win the prize.

"Me," said Geoffrion, in as candid a reply as Powers could hope for.

The Boomer then set about the business of proving himself correct, while the Montreal brass attempted to thwart a revolt between Irvin and his veteran defenseman Butch Bouchard. The thirty-one-year-old Bouchard had just opened a lavish new restaurant in Montreal and was apparently eating some of the tasty dishes. Irvin claimed Butch was overweight and Bouchard demanded that Dick apologize—or else he'd quit.

Irvin and Bouchard quickly came to terms and everything seemed about normal in the Canadiens' camp. On October 31 the Habitants visited Toronto, lost the game, 1–0, and the Rocket clashed with a few Leaf fans as well as the team physician, Dr. Jim Murray. The Rocket had been frustrated in his attempt to score his three-hundredth N.H.L. goal and took exception to a remark tossed by the doctor.

The episode lit the fuse for the explosion that would take place the following night at the Forum when the same teams clashed. It began sputtering in earnest when the Rocket and Fern Flaman of the Leafs exchanged blows in the second period. Referee Chadwick sent Flaman to the dressing room and Richard to the penalty box. As the Rocket was about to take his seat, defenseman Bill Juzda, of the Leafs, delivered a few indiscreet remarks to Richard, who left the box and skated straight for Juzda.

"Richard lashed a jolting right from behind one of the officials," said Gord Walker of the *Globe and Mail*, "and it found a target on Juzda's left eye. Juzda dropped heavily and lay on the ice for almost a full minute." The Rocket had scored another TKO!

A few miles away, at a local Montreal rink, another Richard was also exploding. This one was fifteen-year-old Henri Richard, the Rocket's kid brother, who had betrayed signs of becoming a star just like Maurice. Some critics cautioned that it was premature to foresee the N.H.L. for Henri. Unlike Maurice, Henri was small and showed no signs of filling out. Besides, another of the Richard brothers, Jacques, had failed after suggesting some of the Rocket's ability. "Jacques," said Baz O'Meara of the Montreal *Star*, "didn't have the same drive as his famous brother, nor the tenacity to make the bigtime. On the other hand, Henri has hockey players' legs, a very good shift, and if he listens to his older brother he might become a star."

In time Henri would join the Rocket on the same line. In the meantime Irvin sought a left wing to round out the abridged Punch Line. Both Maurice and Elmer Lach had sprung ahead in the scoring race, first with Bert Olmstead on left wing and later with Dickie Moore, another Montreal-bred youngster with all the mustard that Richard possessed. But there was something else in the Rocket's system that perplexed doctors early in 1952. Several examinations produced nothing but an announcement that Richard was suffering from a "stomach ailment" and would be sidelined indefinitely while Les Canadiens struggled for a play-off berth.

"Richard," said a Toronto writer, "owns the most famous bellyache in sports since Babe Ruth's burps." In New York, Ranger manager Frank Boucher charged that the Canadiens, and especially coach Irvin, were a bunch of "crybabies." Irvin took the charge seriously and replied that if Ranger coach Bill Cook would play for the Rangers in their game against the Canadiens on January 13, he (Irvin) would take the Rocket's place on right wing for Les Canadiens. Boucher immediately accepted the challenge on behalf of Cook.

"I'll guarantee," said Boucher, "that if Irvin takes the ice, Cook will skate out and make him look sick—just as he always made Irvin look sick when they played against each other."

Needless to say, neither Irvin nor Cook dressed for the game because Richard, of all people, returned to action the previous night and merely scored a three-goal hat trick as Montreal routed Chicago, 8–3, at the Forum. "Irvin," commented Jim Vipond, sports editor of the *Globe and Mail*, "hit a new low in childishness and he should be taken to task for it." Irvin couldn't care less about the bleats from Toronto as long as his club stayed in play-off contention, and now that the kids were producing he dismissed his critics with a wave of the hand.

As he had so candidly predicted, Geoffrion had become

the foremost rookie-of-the-year candidate but it was more the manner in which he was scoring that was meaningful than merely the fact that he was scoring at an amazing clip. Geoffrion, although he may not have realized it at the time, had become a hockey revolutionary. Instead of using the traditional forehand wrist shot or the backhand shot for his tries at the goal, Geoffrion would draw his stick back like a golfer and slap the puck. The result was the "slapshot" that would eventually be adopted by most of the leading scorers in the N.H.L. and would dramatically change the face of the game.

The essential forte of the slapshot was the extraordinary speed Geoffrion generated, harder than anything the league had seen, including the bullet-shooting Charlie Conacher of the early thirties. Toronto coach Hap Day, who had played with Conacher on the Maple Leafs, had no qualms about putting the Geoffrion shot in proper perspective.

"It's definitely harder than anything Conacher shot," said Day. "I watched Geoffrion closely on one play. I saw him draw the stick back, but I never saw the puck until it bounced off the goalpost. It's the first time I never saw the shot I was looking at."

Geoffrion, alone, wasn't galvanizing Les Canadiens, nor was Dickie Moore. A speedy youngster named Paul Meger was shining on the forward line along with Dick Gamble. Young Tom Johnson and Doug Harvey offered goalie McNeil formidable protection on defense. "We like Moore," said Jim Vipond in his *Globe* and *Mail* column. "He's a chippy operator who mixes with the toughest and still knows how to stick-handle and skate his way to the opposition net. He's not unmindful of Milt Schmidt as he leans far forward in gaining top speed. These Montreal kids are making the customers forget Maurice Richard."

But the Rocket wouldn't let anyone forget him. Recovered from his stomach ailment after a Florida vacation, he returned to Maple Leaf Gardens on March 19, 1952, to aid Les Canadiens in their second-place battle with Toronto.

Montreal won the game, 3–0, which enabled them to beat

out Toronto for second place and it was the Rocket who proved the catalyst with one of his displays of pure fury on ice. "The Rocket's goal was typical," wrote Gord Walker in the *Globe and Mail.* "On a two-man break in the second period, Lach was covered by Jimmy Thomson. He still got over a perfect pass to Richard who appeared to be blanketed by Jimmy Morrison. Yet the Rocket somehow got his stick around and zipped the puck into the net."

Richard's histrionics had already become too numerous for most fans to remember. Some rooters preferred to recall the goals he scored. Others remembered the fights, and still others pointed to the obscure episodes that marked Maurice so unique.

"The impact Richard had on the Canadiens," said Peter Gzowski, "and through them on the rest of the league, seems to me beautifully summed up in one incident that occurred in Toronto. It was the time that, soaring head over heels as the result of an artful Maple Leaf check, Richard shattered the 'unbreakable' Herculite glass that had just been installed in Maple Leaf Gardens around the top of the boards. No one had nicked it before, and only Eddie Shack has broken it since, which was unfair, since Shack hit a faulty piece. Richard put the *heel of his skate* through it, and there was something perfect about its being the Rocket, the epitome of recklessness, of untrammeled fire and fury and abandon on the ice, who did it."

Few players ever upstaged Richard. One of those who did was Gordie Howe, and the Red Wing immortal managed to pull the surprise on "Maurice Richard Night" at the Forum. As the presentation was coming to an end, Richard headed for the sideboards when Howe called out, "Hey, Rocket!" As Richard turned, Howe pulled off his leather gauntlet and extended his hand. For a brief second the Forum crowd hushed as the two archfoes shook hands at center ice. "It was a sort of genuinely unrehearsed spontaneous gesture that caught the big crowd completely by surprise," said Elmer Ferguson.

The crowd remained silent for another moment and then

burst into a thunderous ovation that gave veteran press-box viewers a case of goose pimples. Howe then went out and scored a big goal for the Red Wings.

Les Canadiens finished in second place during the 1951–1952 season and went up against the fourth-place Boston Bruins in the opening Stanley Cup round. Those who still held reservations about Richard's health were put at ease in the very first game when he scored twice as Montreal romped to a 5–1 win. The Rocket was held scoreless in the second match, but Geoffrion, who was to win the rookie-of-the-year award, helped Montreal to a 4–0 victory with a three-goal hat trick.

Les Canadiens received a stunning surprise as the Boston sextet swept the next three games and put Les Canadiens squarely on the ropes. In the sixth game Boston virtually completed the upset, scoring twice in the first period while they blanketed Montreal with severe checking.

When Les Canadiens skated out on the ice for the second period, they pecked away at the staunch Bruin blue-line corps and finally found an opening at 4:53. Eddie "Spider" Mazur shot the puck past goalie Jim Henry, and now Montreal was alive. Still, Boston held the lead and continued to nurse the one-goal margin well into the third period.

At the eleven-minute mark captain Milt Schmidt of the Bruins allowed the puck to slip off the blade of his stick. The Rocket, hovering nearby, seized the opportunity and dashed straight down the middle of the ice. His thirty-foot shot fooled Henry, and the teams went into the sudden-death overtime tied, 2–2.

Neither team scored in the first extra period, but early in the second session Doug Harvey organized a rush at the Bruin net. His shot was blocked by Henry, but rookie Paul Masnick, who had been recalled from the American League, snared the rebound and beat Henry at 7:49 of the second overtime.

The seventh and final game of the semifinal was played at the Forum on April 8, 1952, and there are those who consider it the most exciting hockey match ever played. This, of course, is debatable, but there was no disputing the assertion that it *was* Maurice Richard's most courageous display of hockey playing.

Each team managed a goal in the first period and then settled down to vigorous exchanges of end-to-end rushes that gave the ice the look of an endless stream of downhill ski racers. With one *major* exception the game was, as one reporter noted, "clean, hard-fought, and played with fine spirit." But that one exception played a vital role in the game's ultimate evolution.

With the score tied, 1–1, in the second period, Leo Labine, a Bruin forward with scant acquaintance with the rule book, took a dead aim at Richard as the Rocket knifed through the Boston defense. Richard had tripped and already fallen to his knees when Labine ruthlessly charged into the Rocket. Labine's stick thudded against Richard's head and his knees rammed into Richard's stomach with the impact of a battering ram.

Already down, the Rocket keeled over on his back and, from all appearances, seemed to be dead. His legs spread out in an inverted V formation as trainer Hector Dubois, physiotherapist Bill Head, and teammate Bert Olmstead hovered over Richard's limp body, searching for some signs of life. In time he responded to the waft of smelling salts and, with his face smeared with blood, Richard clambered to his feet and groggily skated to the Forum first-aid room where the deep cut over his left eye was stitched and repaired. That completed, he returned to the bench and imbibed the action with the special kind of reflex that only the very unusual athlete possesses.

"My legs felt fine," Richard recalled after the game, "but my head . . . was I dizzy! I didn't remember anything after I got hit. They told me it was Labine. I don't know. I didn't even know the score when I went back to the bench."

Toe Blake, the retired member of the Punch Line, was standing in the press box, high in the Forum rafters, when Richard returned to the bench. Blake immediately spotted his old buddy, and turned to one of the reporters. "You watch," Blake said, "the Rocket will get one in the last five minutes of the game."

It became apparent as the third period moved along without a score that the next goal would decide the series. It also was obvious to most observers that Richard, of all people, would *not* score that goal. "After receiving his stitches," commented one Montreal newspaperman "he was in a partial coma for a while, his head fuzzed up from pain, his eyesight impaired, with dull noises ringing in his ears."

More than sixteen minutes had elapsed in the third period when Bruin veteran Woody Dumart carried the puck toward the Canadiens' zone. Butch Bouchard thrust out his stick with rapier-like speed, jabbing the puck away from Dumart. The Montreal defenseman looked up for a moment and spotted Richard near the blue line. The Rocket captured the pass as Dumart futilely tried to bat down the puck. Richard wheeled around Dumart like a speeding car skirting a disabled auto on the highway. First he reeled to center and then cut sharply to the right, jabbing the puck ahead of him with short pokes from his black-taped blade.

Blond Bill Quackenbush, one of the most experienced and intelligent defensemen in the N.H.L., skated backward on the Bruin defense, prepared to meet the ominous challenge, for Richard was now in full flight, his eyes blazing madly, his destination known to all. Quackenbush was traveling at about ten miles per hour in reverse as Richard bore down on him with more than twice that speed. Quackenbush hurled his black-shirted body at the Canadien ace, but it was as if he were checking a phantom.

Nevertheless, Quackenbush had done his job quite well, for he had forced Richard to take so circuitous a route along the right side that the Rocket appeared to have taken himself right out of the play. "He looked to be too deep for a shot," said Baz O'Meara of the Montreal *Star*, "but then he suddenly did a deft cut to the left."

A right-handed shot playing right wing would have been

cradling the puck too far to his right to release a threatening drive, but Richard, the anamoly, was a left-handed shot. Thus, the puck was on his left side, closer to the net, as he barreled past the flailing Quackenbush. "Sugar" Jim Henry, both eyes blackened from previous injuries and barely recovered from a broken nose, guarded the right corner of the net, allowing Richard nothing but the "impossible" angle shot to the far left corner.

Almost atop Henry's bulky goal pads, Richard finally released his drive. It was low and hard and Henry never managed to touch, let alone see, the puck. "One minute I was facing him," said the Boston goalie, "waiting for the shot, the next he had whizzed by and the puck was in the net."

The ovations that have traditionally greeted Richard goals have had the impact of a thunderclap. This time, however, the din shook the very foundations of the ancient Forum. "Richard has received ovations in his day," said O'Meara, "the likes of which have never been seen in the Forum, but the ensuing roar, which lasted fully four minutes followed by a paper shower, left all others in the also-ran class."

Reactions to the goal were as surprising as the score itself. Elmer Lach, who was sitting on the bench watching the Rocket in orbit, leaned forward onto the sideboards and fainted. Art Chapman, manager of the Buffalo hockey club, was watching from the press box and simply stood mouth agape after the red light flashed. "Only Richard could score like that," he said later.

"He is like Babe Ruth was," said Irvin. "He adds that little extra flourish to everything."

"That little flourish" provided Les Canadiens with the winning goal, although Billy Reay added another score into the open net with less than a minute remaining and Montreal won the game, 3–1. When the final siren wailed, signaling game's end at the Forum, reporters searched their mind for the proper adjectives with which to describe Richard's feat. Baz O'Meara, who had seen more hockey games than nearly every member of the press corps, summed it up this way:

"In all his storied, starry career, Richard has scored some of the most spectacular goals of hockey history. No player has ever matched him as a thrill-producer. No one has come close to him for versatility of execution. Of all the goals credited to him, none ever excelled that game-winner against Boston. . . . None ever drew a greater ovation, more gasps of admiration, because it was scored under the pressure of pain."

The pain had not entirely dissipated when the Rocket fell onto the bench in Montreal's joy-filled dressing room. His father, Onésime Richard, walked in and put his right arm around the Rocket's shoulder and hugged his son. No longer able to control the emotion that welled within his battered frame, the Rocket broke down and cried.

Decimated by injuries, Les Canadiens were no match for the Red Wings, who were well rested after their four-game sweep of the Maple Leafs. The Detroit sextet swept the Canadiens in four consecutive games to win the Stanley Cup, although some observers argued that Detroit benefited from the officiating throughout the play-offs. "The Wings can put the best seven men on the ice of any team in the league," said Toronto's managing director, Conn Smythe. To which Irvin added: "And the referee must be one of them!" Bitter to the end, Irvin refused to congratulate the winners and slammed the dressing-room door in the face of Detroit reporters.

Irvin's grumpiness and the general depression in the Montreal dressing room was not reflected by the even-tempered Selke. He realized that his plans were jelling and that only a few more years were required before his rebuilding job would be complete. In the meantime, he bathed in the fading sunlight generated by such veterans as Bouchard and Lach. Although Elmer had vowed to retire a few seasons earlier, he appeared at the 1952–1953 training camp with the same vim and vigor he had displayed as a rookie, and he continued to excel as the campaign got under way.

On Saturday night, November 8, 1952, the Black Hawks were playing Les Canadiens at the Forum when Lach scored his two-hundredth N.H.L. goal. Not surprisingly it was the

Rocket who had fed him the lead pass and it was Richard who was the first to congratulate his old buddy. "Keep piling up the points," kidded Maurice, "but keep away from those fractures."

The partisan crowd lustily cheered the pair but they were more anxious to see the Rocket score because his *next* goal would be number 325 and would break the N.H.L. record held by Nels Stewart. Only thirty seconds after Lach's historic score the Rocket throttled past the Black Hawk defense and reached his newest plateau. This time it was Lach who did the congratulating and the needling. "Nice going, Rocket," he laughed, "and no more broken bones, please!"

Paced by Lach, Richard, and the energetic youngsters, Montreal finished second behind Detroit and went into the play-off semifinal a heavy favorite to defeat the fourth-place Black Hawks. But Chicago was not the traditional doormat of yesteryear. They presented a creative coach in Sid Abel and a superb but underrated goaltender named Al Rollins. This still should not have presented a problem for Les Canadiens, except for an unexpected development—goalie Gerry McNeil had become overwrought with nervousness and suffered an awesome letdown in the series.

Before Irvin could grasp hold of the situation Chicago had advanced to the lip of victory in the semifinal round with a 3–2 advantage in the best-of-seven series. With an ironic twist of strategy, Irvin suddenly benched McNeil—much in the manner that he had replaced Durnan years previous—and inserted Jacques Plante, an unusual goaltender if ever there was one.

In his spare time, Plante had a hobby of knitting *toques*, the French-Canadian wool caps worn by his ancestors. He was confident to the point of being cocky and betrayed a bizarre goaltending style that would soon be copied by other netminders around the league. It was Plante's idea that he would be aiding his defensemen by roaming out of his cage, formerly a strict taboo, and behind the net when the pucks

were caromed off the boards and skidded behind his cage.
By so doing, Plante was able to control the puck and pass it
off to a teammate, while scrambling back to his goal crease
before any shots were taken.

All this was well and good and terribly fascinating, but
for the adventurous and unconventional Plante to experiment
with the Canadiens in the play-offs and on the brink of elimination was something else! But Irvin had made a commitment,
and Plante was his goalie. Jacques the Roamer immediately
went into the cage and stopped the Black Hawks cold. He
foiled a breakaway early in the fifth game, and with that
impetus Les Canadiens won two straight games and captured
the first round.

Meanwhile, the Bruins had stunned the league-leading
Red Wings with a four-games-to-two upset in the other semifinal round, and qualified to meet Montreal for the Stanley Cup.
After building up a 3–1 lead in games, Les Canadiens clinched
the Cup when the Rocket passed the puck to Lach in a sudden-death overtime with the score tied, 0–0, and Elmer converted the pass for a goal.

The success of Les Canadiens, as well as the Maple Leafs
and Red Wings, was soon to boomerang on them in a rather
perverse manner. In the early fifties it had become apparent
that the Bruins, Rangers, and Black Hawks were suffering attendance setbacks that were also complemented by great
deficiencies in player personnel, although the Rangers, under
the guidance of Frank Boucher, were building a formidable
farm system.

Pressure from the three losing cities was finally felt in the
N.H.L. hirearchy, which responded by creating a draft system.
Selke contended, and rightly so, that the new draft was aimed
at diluting his dynasty. He fought the draft on the grounds
that Montreal should reap the rewards of its hard-earned success. In a significant display of altruism, Selke sold highly
regarded young Ed Litzenberger to the Black Hawks for only
fifteen thousand dollars, although the crack forward was

worth more than four times that amount. It was that same Litzenberger who spearheaded Chicago's march to the Stanley Cup in 1961.

One of the prime reasons for the "Curb-the-Canadiens" movement was Selke's own triumph in signing Jean Béliveau for the 1953–1954 season. Unlike previous contract agreements, the Béliveau negotiations were conducted in the same atmosphere of excitement that might have greeted the signing of the North Atlantic Treaty. Le Gros Bill was accompanied by an accountant and an attorney and came away with one of the largest salaries in hockey history, as opposed to the Rocket who entered the league earning coolie wages and with virtually no fuss or fanfare.

Béliveau's premiere was widely trumpeted throughout the league. His decision to stay in Quebec had merely served to whet the interest of hockey fans throughout the N.H.L., and they came out in extraordinary numbers to see what he was all about. At first glance, he suggested that he would be the most overrated flop since the aluminum hockey stick!

Béliveau was the antithesis of Richard, Geoffrion, and Moore. His long strides indicated that he was not really trying very hard and his phlegmatic disposition was in hard contrast to the volcanic teammates surrounding him. Even worse, Béliveau displayed no thirst for fighting and that would prove to be his downfall in his rookie year.

Every low-salaried skater from New York to Chicago was determined to get a piece of Le Gros Bill and many of them succeeded. He suffered a cracked fibula after being heavily checked in Chicago shortly after the start of the season and was sidelined a total of twenty-six games for assorted injuries during the season. But Béliveau had a good sense for history and realized that his teammate, Richard, had endured a similar spate of injuries when he broke into the N.H.L. "If my career turns out like the Rocket's," he said, "all of this will really be worthwhile."

Occasionally, Béliveau offered cause for favorable comment. His stick-handling ability suggested that he had an invisible string linking the puck to his stick blade, and his shot was hard and accurate. "The playing of Béliveau," commented Canadian novelist Hugh MacLennan, "is poetry in action."

But Béliveau's production left him overshadowed by his teammates' histrionics, which were abundant in 1953–1954 and not all that positive either. Clearly established as a star, Geoffrion found himself assailed and assaulted just like the Rocket. The Boomer's boiling point was equally low and in November, 1953, he was fined $250 for charging referee Frank Udvari. A month later Boom Boom immersed himself even deeper in hot water during a game against the Rangers at Madison Square Garden. The rivalry between New York and Montreal had remained keen ever since the classic 1947 brawl and was no less sharp on this night when several players piled up along the sideboards in a high-sticking joust. One of them was Geoffrion and another was Ron Murphy, a crew-cut Ranger rookie not known for his truculence.

At the time of the collision Geoffrion had lost his stick. Murphy, who had been standing at the perimeter of the general melee, still had his stick and appeared to massage and cut Geoffrion with the shaft of his stick. Press-box observers took it for granted that the trouble would soon be calmed and nobody expected Geoffrion to retaliate with anything more than a countershove. But the stickless Boomer felt the blood on his head and without notice bolted from the bout and frantically searched for his "lost" stick.

From the grandstands it appeared that he had gone temporarily berserk as he regained his stick and moved menacingly at Murphy. The young Ranger perceived trouble and conducted a disorderly retreat toward center ice where he finally stopped himself, alone, with fifteen thousand spectators looking on with expectant horror. What they saw was Geoffrion advancing on his foe, stick over his shoulder in a swinging position. Up until then it appeared that the Boomer was merely taunting Murphy as players are wont to do, and was goading him to drop his stick and engage him in a bare-fisted fight. But Murphy merely stood transfixed at the center-ice circle with his stick in hand.

When Geoffrion had skated to within arm's length of Murphy, the Boomer pulled his stick even farther back and took a complete cut at the Ranger's head. Somehow, he missed completely but quickly drew back his stick and, this time, felled Murphy with a direct clout on the side of his head. The Ranger fell to the ice in a pool of blood while Geoffrion stood over him, his eyes on the other Rangers who advanced to the scene. Except for an exchange of words and some idle pushing, no further blows were struck, and Geoffrion was led away from the scene by teammates. Murphy was taken to the hospital, disabled by a fractured jaw. The incident was thoroughly reviewed by President Campbell who suspended Geoffrion for eight games against the Rangers while Murphy was suspended for five games.

"L'Affaire Geoffrion" did nothing to cool New York's enthusiasm for the Flying Frenchmen. Some observers marveled at veterans like the Rocket and Lach. Others raved over the kids, and still others marveled at the raw intensity with which the Habitants approached the game.

"Before every game," said television commentator Bud Palmer, "they must put in thirty minutes of silence. They just sit there, backs to the wall, and their heads are down, as if in prayer."

Nevertheless, the Red Wings remained the class of the league and proved it in a stirring Stanley Cup final with Les Canadiens. The teams went down to a seventh and final game that was decided on a rather innocent long, soft shot by Tony Leswick, of Detroit. Goalie McNeil, who had made a brief comeback with the Canadiens, appeared to have it in hand when defenseman Doug Harvey attempted to deflect it out of danger. Harvey managed to get only a piece of the puck and it caromed off his left gauntlet and into the net behind the startled McNeil.

That was enough for McNeil. He permanently retired after four full seasons in the N.H.L. and never fulfilled the promise

Selke had held for him when he hired McNeil to replace Durnan. The great Lach also retired, but neither of the older players would be terribly missed. Plante would be an excellent replacement in goal, and the front line was fortified with the likes of Richard, Béliveau, Moore, Olmstead, and Floyd Curry.

"One of the most remarkable facts about the team—and a tribute to Frank Selke's talent-seeking abilities—has been the way it has been able to refresh its strength from new, young players whenever a group of older ones begin to disintegrate," wrote Peter Gzowski.

Yet the balance wheel of the dynamo that was Les Canadiens remained the galvanic Richard. Consequently, he continued to be the target of incessant abuse from the rank-and-file among his opponents. During the 1954–1955 season the Maple Leafs owned Bob Bailey, a third-rate player who had a habit of wielding his stick as a weapon.

Bailey and Richard battled several times, but one of the most severe clashes caused referee Red Storey to dispatch the Rocket to the dressing room. According to Frank Selke, Irvin leaned over the boards as Richard was heading for the showers and said something to his star. The Rocket wheeled in his tracks and accosted Storey with an assortment of epithets before retiring to the dressing room once and for all.

The dispute would have ended there were it not for Conn Smythe who happened to have had movies taken of the game. Armed with the films, Smythe showed them to Campbell and N.H.L. governors from Boston, Chicago, and New York. "All of the gentlemen demanded that something be done to curb Maurice Richard," said Selke, "whose greatest fault was defeating their teams and filling their arenas to capacity."

Campbell then summoned Richard and Selke to his office and presented the filmed evidence. Selke properly countered that it was unjust for Campbell to have held a kangaroo court with the three governors without permitting the Rocket to defend his action. Selke later asserted that Campbell was "ashamed" of the governors' meeting, "but an ugly black mark was placed alongside Richard's name."

Richard was more concerned with the scoring race than anything else. For the first time in his long career it appeared that Maurice was going to lead the league in points, while teammates Geoffrion and Béliveau followed behind. With only a week remaining in the schedule nobody doubted that the Rocket was home-free as Les Canadiens faced the Boston Bruins at Boston Gardens.

The Bruins were not a very good team in those days but they knew how to hit and they tormented Les Canadiens with an assortment of body blows in the first and second periods. This rankled Irvin who had become more and more irritable as the season progressed. Part of the problem was the fact that Irvin was uneasy about his future.

Sometime late in December, 1954, he had conferred with Conn Smythe, his former boss, and mentioned to Smythe that he, Irvin, wouldn't mind coaching the lowly Black Hawks *if the price was right.* Surprised by Irvin's remark, Smythe later called Selke and mentioned the conversation to him. Since Selke had no idea of Irvin's thinking, he was both surprised and vexed. Later, when Selke confronted Irvin with the information, the coach replied that he wasn't really interested in Chicago, and the two left it at that. It has been Selke's conviction not only that Irvin was becoming a changed man but that his vitriolic temperament was having an unfortunate effect on Richard. The Bailey incident was one example and the late-season game in Boston was to be even more significant—and damaging—to all concerned.

By the end of the second period in Boston Garden, Irvin had become dismayed with the abuse his team was absorbing from the Bruins. He urged them to come out fighting in the last period, and some of them, notably the Rocket, emerged from the dressing room lusting for combat. The Bruins, supported by a fanatic crowd, provided plenty of cause for trouble, but the chief culprit turned out to be an ex-teammate, Hal Laycoe. The bespectacled defenseman crashed into Richard and opened a bloody cut in the Rocket's scalp. Maurice responded by challenging Laycoe to fight and the

Bruin executed an orderly retreat. The Rocket continued in pursuit but was intercepted by both teammates and linesman Cliff Thompson, a former defenseman who had played for the Bruins and lived in the Boston area. Instead of calmly buffeting Richard from Laycoe, the linesman used an assortment of antagonizing holds that merely exacerbated a worsening situation, and inevitably Richard and Thompson fell to the ice. The Rocket was suitably penalized for his outburst and the episode should have ended there, except that a subjective and thoroughly biased Boston press demanded that sterner action be taken against Richard. Campbell responded by ordering Richard, Irvin, and Ken Reardon to his office for a hearing along with a contingent from the Bruins.

After studying the testimony, Campbell shocked the hockey world with an extraordinary announcement. Richard was suspended for the remainder of the regular season *and* the play-offs! Based on the ill-handling of the situation by Thompson and the provocation delivered by Laycoe, the Rocket's penalty was unfair in the extreme and a classic example of Campbell's negative treatment of Richard. But there was no appealing his decision. It was upheld by the other teams, who envisioned a Richard-less Montreal team as a siting duck in the play-offs. Les Canadiens had to make do without him.

Montreal had three remaining games on its schedule: Thursday night at the Forum against the Red Wings, Saturday night at the Forum against the Rangers, and Sunday night at Detroit against the Red Wings. Up until the suspension, the Canadiens were expected to nose out Detroit and win the league championship. "Without Richard," said Selke in his book, *Behind the Cheering*, "the team had lost its soul. Our boys were certain that, in one fell stroke, they had lost both the league championship and the Stanley Cup."

The same feeling permeated among the devoted Montreal fans who became increasingly enraged over Campbell's decision. By game time on St. Patrick's Day, 1955, the city was in a veritable uproar. Several fans had phoned threats against

Campbell's life and warned him to stay away from the Forum when the Red Wings played Les Canadiens. Undaunted by the challenge, Campbell had made up *his* mind to attend, although there was mounting evidence that potentially violent protests would be staged on Ste. Catherine Street West, outside the arena. By early evening the evidence proved correct. Placard-carrying fans marched along the sidewalk calling for Campbell's dismissal, if not execution, in several variations of French and English. However, none of the demonstrations had an effect on the start of the game.

Without the Rocket, Les Canadiens were a shade of their former selves and the Red Wings knew it. They seized the opportunity and quickly took the lead as their traumatized opponents skated as if dazed. Campbell had not yet arrived. He reached the Forum well after the opening face-off. Since his presidential box was well known to most Montreal fans, it was not difficult to discern his arrival, along with his secretary, and a resentful murmur spread across the building as Campbell climbed the steps to his seat.

Officials of the Canadian Arena Company contend that the audience was unusual in one respect. There was a covey of leather-jacketed toughs lining the standing-room area not far from Campbell's seat. Not long after the president had arrived, one of the anti-Campbellmen stalked over to his seat and attempted to attack the league boss. Soon, a hail of debris, rotten fruit, and vegetables descended on Campbell while other patrons attempted to get in a good shot at him. One assailant managed to crush a rather large tomato on Campbell's head.

Police moved in to protect the president but the mood of the crowd was so surly that by this time it appeared that the police would have difficulty preventing an attempt on his life. Precisely at this moment Campbell was saved by a mysterious and completely unexpected incident. Somewhere, someone in the audience of fourteen thousand exploded a tear-gas bomb directly in front of Selke's box. The rising fumes and acrid odor completely distracted the fans from the destruction of Campbell, and a state of temporary chaos ensued as spectators made their way to the exits. The public-address announcer attempted to restore calm and succeeded to a point, since no deaths resulted from the panic. Soon the fire chief ordered the building cleared and the game was called off, forfeited to the Red Wings. As the teams repaired to their dressing rooms and the fans groped their way out to the street, it seemed that the worst was over. But, actually, it was only beginning.

Campbell managed to escape through the rear of the Forum after first finding a sanctuary in the first-aid room. But when the spectators emerged from the rink and onto Ste. Catherine Street West, they were confronted by a huge crowd that had gathered in the park directly across the street from the Forum lobby. The combination of coughing, distressed spectators and the unruly protestors in the park detonated an even more calamitous scene.

Bands of vandals tossed every available item, from bricks to vegetables, at the Forum, at passing trolley cars and automobiles. Newspaper kiosks were set afire and burned down, and roving bands soon proceeded east along Ste. Catherine Street smashing store windows and looting at every turn. The rioting continued on into the night until it finally dissipated of its own accord. When the final tally was in, damage was estimated at more than $100,000.

By next morning the Richard Riot was headline news around the world. *The New York Times,* in an unprecedented move for a "hockey story," played it on page one as did other distinguished dailies. Everyone from the police chief to the mayor deplored the affair and everybody appeared to blame everybody else for letting it develop. First, Campbell came under attack for showing up in the first place. His retort was legitimate enough: he was only doing his duty as league president and he wasn't about to be intimidated by any fans or hoodlums. Secondly, the police chief was accused of not having provided adequate protection. Finally, there were those who charged that the Forum could have done a better job of preserving order.

In an editorial, the Montreal *Star* indicted the citizens of the city. "Montreal," said the *Star*, "stands convicted of emotional instability and lack of discipline. . . ."

Ironically, one of the most calming agents was the Rocket, who went on radio and television pleading with the community to accept Campbell's decision and to look forward to his return next season.

The Rocket's plea became a balm to all, and fans turned once again to the business of the pennant race. Les Canadiens regained enough equilibrium to defeat the Rangers on Saturday night, but they were beaten by Detroit in the final game and had to settle for second place. That, however, was the lesser of the two tragedies in the eyes of Montreal fans.

The major catastrophe developed when Boom Boom Geoffrion made a determined bid to score goals and assists in the final two games. The Boomer was in the most difficult position of his career. On the one hand, he preferred that his idol, Richard, win the scoring championship, but on the other, there was the matter of helping Les Candiens annex first place. The best way to do that was to score goals or at least set up goals for his teammates. By the time the third period of the final game had ended at Detroit, Geoffrion had passed the Rocket and won the scoring championship. Richard was runner-up and Béliveau finished third.

Les Canadiens pulled themselves together and routed Boston in five games of the Stanley Cup semifinal while Detroit took the measure of Toronto in four games. Montreal then extended the Red Wings to seven games before bowing out in the final match, 3–1. More than ever, the defeat was hard for both Selke and Irvin to swallow. The coach placed the blame directly with Campbell for not curbing Richard's assailants and for suspending the Rocket. The manager, surprisingly, considered Irvin at least partially at fault for the tragedy. He reasoned that Irvin had goaded Richard above

and beyond the call of duty and this goading, in turn, had
led to his squabbles and ultimate suspension.

Unknown to Selke at the time, Irvin was suffering through
the first stages of a bone cancer that would cost him his life
two years later. Soon after the final game Selke summoned
his old friend, Irvin, into his office and informed him he could
remain with Les Canadiens in "another job" but not as coach.
He also made it clear he would have no objections to his
moving to the coaching job in Chicago.

Irvin, a tough Irishman whom many regard as the greatest
coach hockey has known, considered Selke's proposal and
said he would move to the Windy City. Selke had inherited
Irvin when he made the switch from Toronto to Montreal in
1946 and never had to face the problem of selecting a new
coach for Les Canadiens. Now he had a most difficult decision to make.

Surely, there was an abundance of qualified coaches to
choose from, but the task of controlling Les Canadiens was
something special. No team in the N.H.L. had the distillation
of French- and English-Canadians that the Montreal sextet
possessed. Selke would have to find a man who, like Irvin,
would be able to maintain harmony in the club. On top of
that, he required a personality who could command the
respect of aces such as Richard, Béliveau, and Geoffrion and
who could follow in Irvin's difficult footsteps as a winner. A
big winner.

One rumor had it that Selke would be obliged to select a
French Canadian. One suggestion was Butch Bouchard; another was Roger Leger, both former players and both well
respected in the French-speaking community. Others specu-
lated that Billy Reay, though not a French Canadian, would
wind up with the job. Several of the Forum directors were
partial to Reay and he was the only choice seriously in the
running for the job along with the favorite, Hector "Toe"
Blake.

"The Old Lamplighter" had studied coaching well in the
Quebec Senior League. He was partially French Canadian

and he was admired by all the players, particularly Richard. Kenny Reardon, who had moved up to a key front-office position with the Canadiens, was a strong advocate of Blake, and ultimately the opinions of Selke and Reardon prevailed. On June 8 the signing of Blake was officially announced before a standing-room crowd at the Forum, and Les Canadiens were ready to become the greatest team in hockey history.

11

The Greatest
of Them All

*T*oe Blake wielded a dictator's baton over Les Canadiens, but at first he ruled them like a benevolent despot. This was easy because the players, to a man, respected Blake, and vice versa. The pivotal personality on the team was the Rocket. He went out of his way to assure the Canadiens' hierarchy that he backed Blake to the hilt, and he meant every word of it.

Now it was up to the Old Lamplighter to produce. All the ingredients were there: a young competent goaltender, a strong, intelligent defense, and the most explosive collection of scorers in history. It was simply a matter of stirring them to the proper boil without creating the fire hazard of previous years. Richard Riots were to be avoided at all costs.

"Blake and Selke were trying to give the Rocket all they had by way of a tranquilizing program," says Josh Greenfeld. "They started giving him de-pep talks long before the season began. They pointed out to him that he was thirty-five years old, that he did not have to carry the emotional burden of victory alone, that he still would be treated with sufficient respect by the other players around the league even if he went a little easier on the roughhouse, and that the important thing was not one game, not one fight, but to lead the team to a Stanley Cup victory."

The Canadiens' organization, not to mention the city of Montreal, was still smarting from the black eye it had received from the St. Patrick's Day disaster. A unique community spirit seemed to engulf the team right from the start of training camp in nearby Verdun, Quebec. "I could see immediately," said Blake, "that we would have good harmony in the club. The boys were greatly disappointed with the way they'd finished the last two years. One year a bad goal beat them, the next year a bad fuss. They were determined they were not going to let anything beat them this time, least of all themselves."

The major roadblock would be provided by the Red Wings. Fortified by the Production Line of Sid Abel, Alex Delvecchio, and Gordie Howe, an excellent bench, and good goaltending, Detroit seemed as powerful as ever. To dethrone them would be a major accomplishment and would require adroit manipulation of lines—right down to the third unit. And that was as much a key to the success as anything. When the Béliveau line or the Richard line was exhausted, Blake had the good fortune to call upon Floyd "Busher" Curry, one of the essential unsung heroes, Claude Provost, and a very capable rookie, Don Marshall.

His scrubs, such as defenseman Jean-Guy Talbot and Bob Turner, were good enough to be first-liners on almost any other team, which was a credit to Selke's superb farm system. It was, indeed, a galaxy that dazzled nobody more than it did Blake. "I couldn't help be amazed once we started holding our first workouts," said Toe. "I was glad I was as young as I was. Otherwise I would have been killed. All those great shots. The puck was flying around with such speed I thought I was in a shooting gallery."

It is impossible to project just how the 1955–1956 Canadiens would have reacted to Dick Irvin, but one can surmise the results would not have been as positive as they were with Blake. Irvin was confounded with a ramshackle Black Hawk team in October, 1955, but he managed to give them an aura of respectability although they failed to make the play-offs. The condition of his health was worsening and by the start of the 1956–1957 season he had deteriorated to a point where he had to be given a sabbatical. Irvin died in May, 1957.

The memory of Irvin had lingered on when Blake took

over as Montreal coach. His success at Valleyfield in the Quebec Senior League was well known to management, but it hardly made an impression on the rank-and-file fan who had as many doubts about Blake as Toe himself. "I was nervous," the rookie coach allowed. "I felt I had to produce with a club like that. So much potential. And it was a big test for me. But the Rocket went out of his way to help me. So did Kenny Mosdell and Floyd Curry and Butch Bouchard.

"Sometimes it's tough to coach players you once had as teammates. But these fellas went out of their way to make it easy for me. Even from the beginning we were like one big happy family."

This was virtually a miracle because Blake's Canadiens boasted a number of extroverts who bordered on egomaniacs. One of them was Plante who regarded himself as a Most-Holy-Blessed-Be-He and eventually collided with Blake one time too many. But that was later. Geoffrion was very much a team player but also a clown, given to renditions of Pagliacci in the dressing room, television singing appearances, and occasional dashes of braggadocio. The Rocket remained basically an introvert and a loner while Béliveau exuded a princely humility that endeared him to practically everyone. "Jean is so modest," said Selke, "he blushes when anybody says anything nice about him."

To that, Béliveau would reply: "If people are saying I am good, it is nice to hear. But to play good hockey you must be lucky to be born with ability. Then you work hard at it the rest of the time. I work hard for my job and I think this team is a good one. We are one big happy family here."

The "happy family" theme would be a recurring one with people dissecting Les Canadiens. Normally, a hockey team splinters into small groups of players after each game. With the exception of Richard and Plante, Les Canadiens would travel *en masse* to the movies, a tavern, or a restaurant.

One might have suspected that the Rocket would be jealous of the Young Turks grabbing the spotlight from him, but the opposite was true. The Rocket went out of his way to make life comfortable for Le Gros Bill and was quick to praise the big youngster. "He gets along with everyone," said Richard, "and he's the best center I've seen since I've been in the league."

Still another young center captured the Rocket's attention as much as Béliveau. Henri Richard, only nineteen years old, was invited to training camp for an audition. This was a rudimentary procedure with the Canadiens. After a week or so of scanning the youngsters the high command would then distribute them to any one of several farm teams. Certainly a kid straight out of junior hockey and as small as Henri was not going to crack the varsity.

At first Henri was named "Flash" but this was soon changed to "the Pocket Rocket" as he displayed less and less inclination to be dropped from the varsity. This disturbed management because everyone agreed that at least a year in the minors would be most beneficial to young Richard.

Merely for experimental purposes Blake inserted Henri at center with his brother and Dickie Moore at left wing. Whenever he stepped on the ice Henri controlled the play, dashing around the rink with his lilting hop-steps. The appearance of his kid brother seemed to galvanize thirty-five-year-old Maurice while Moore complemented the line perfectly with his tough checking and superb shooting. It was no contest. Henri Richard made the team in his first try.

"He's a little small yet," said Blake, "but with his speed we keep telling him not to try to go through the big opposition defensemen, just go around them."

Henri's arrival enabled Blake to compose a second line of Béliveau, Geoffrion, and Olmstead while mixing Mosdell, Curry, Marshall, Provost, and Jackie Leclair in varying combinations for his third unit. "I'm lucky I was a member of that team," recalled Béliveau. "We had everything. We had great scoring, we had great checking, we had great goaltending. And we had great blending, the ideal combination of experienced veterans and good young rookies. And also great team spirit."

Experts varied in their opinions of the final standings for 1955–1956, but Dick Irvin had no qualms about rating his former team: "They should win the championship by ten games!"

To which Blake agreed: "If we finish anywhere but first I'll feel I've done a very bad job. If things go right, yes, we should win by ten games. But any hockey man will tell you that in hockey things don't always go right."

The gears didn't mesh perfectly for Blake. His club was baffled by an uncommon number of injuries. Yet whenever one ace was sidelined another filled the breach to play just as well. As Les Canadiens approached the midpoint in the season, they were already six games in front of the pack. The Rocket was having another splendid season and just about everyone hoped that *this* time he would win his long-coveted scoring championship. But he would be deprived of this honor by a changing Béliveau who, ironically, was adapting some of Richard's old belligerence.

Up until 1955–1956 Béliveau had become known as "Gentleman Jean" because of his abhorrence of rough and dirty play. As a result, the league bullies punished him severely. Just before Irvin left Montreal, he persuaded Béliveau that he had better fight back if he wanted to survive in the N.H.L. jungle. Béliveau began retaliating in 1955–1956. His penalty minutes mounted alarmingly but his scoring totals jumped just as fast.

"Like the other great players Jean smartened up when he saw the opposition getting the better of him," said Irvin. "He'll never be the type to go around looking for trouble, but now he can be as tough as anybody."

Blake had one more worry. By placing the two Richards on the same line he was inviting trouble. "We figured," he explained, "that if they were together they'd always be looking for each other or if the Pocket got into a scrape, the Rocket would be over in a second and explode." Blake kept his fingers crossed and played *Les Fréres Richard* with Moore, and, sure enough, there was trouble.

When Les Canadiens played the Rangers at Madison Square Garden, the Pocket Rocket rammed the much bigger Lou Fontinato into the boards and the Ranger defenseman retaliated by pushing both gauntlets into Richard's face. In a trice the Rocket arrived on the scene and did battle with Fontinato. The scene was repeated in other arenas until it soon became clear to Maurice that Henri could handle his dukes better than most players in the N.H.L and the Pocket Rocket was afraid of absolutely nobody.

Selke was a very happy man at the start of 1956. There was no longer any doubt that he had chosen wisely in Blake. The Rocket was turbulent, to be sure, but managed to maintain decorum at the right time, and his prize catch, Béliveau, had become the talk of hockey.

"Big Jean is great," said Black Hawk manager Tommy Ivan, "because he takes the direct route. No long way around for him. He has the size and the weight to hold his own. He's tremendously strong, a beautiful skater, a superb stick-handler, strictly a team man and with a perfect sense of playmaking. He'd be a star on any hockey club."

He was, significantly, different from Maurice Richard in one area. "Jean doesn't have the desire to score that Maurice has," said Blake.

This was meant more as an analysis than criticism. "With Maurice," said Selke, taking the issue a step further, "his moves are powered by instinctive reflexes. Maurice can't learn from lectures. He does everything by instinct and with sheer power. Béliveau, on the other hand, is probably the classiest player I've ever seen. He has a flair for giving you his hockey as a master showman. He is a perfect coach's hockey player because he studies and learns. He's moving and planning all the time, thinking out the play required for each situation. The difference between the two best players in the game today is simply this: Béliveau is a perfectionist, Richard is an opportunist."

The Rocket and Le Gros Bill formed two fifths of the most devastating power play, the five-man charge when the enemy is shorthanded, in hockey history. Doug Harvey and Boom Boom Geoffrion were stationed at the left and right "points" near the blue line. Béliveau, Richard, and Bert Olmstead played up front with Olmstead doing the major digging in the corners for the puck. "Of all the players, Blake once observed, "I don't think Olmstead received all the credit he deserved."

More often than not, Olmstead would head for the boards to fetch the puck. If he fed it to Harvey, the hyperrelaxed defenseman would calmly look around and thread-needle a pass to someone near the net. Or, if everyone was covered, he'd skim it across the ice to Geoffrion whose potent shot was the fright of every goalie. For purposes of variety or deception the Boomer might feed the puck to Béliveau or Richard stationed closer to the net.

Statistics underlined the potency of Montreal's power play. Les Canadiens scored 25 *per cent* of their goals on it, a fact that terribly distressed their five opponents. At a meeting convened after the season, the N.H.L. voted against Montreal's opposition to change a rule terminating a minor penalty at the scoring of a goal. The rule was specifically aimed at curbing Les Canadiens' awesome power. "When they're playing that power play right," said the oft-critical Blake, "it is a beautiful picture to watch."

Finding a flaw in this armament was virtually impossible. The best the critics could do was charge that Selke's dreadnought was too old a club to last long. "They can say what they want," the manager replied. "When our old men stop producing we'll bring up younger fellows who will start producing." He would then unveil charts indicating that Les Canadiens had strings on some ten thousand players on 750 teams across the continent. Launched in 1946, Selke's farm system was bigger than the farm systems of all other N.H.L. clubs combined.

There was no need for replacements in 1955–1956. By the end of January, Montreal's lead was substantial, but three games with the hated Red Wings loomed on January 29,

February 2, and February 4. The loss of all three or even two of the three games could have induced a panic, a slump, and loss of first place.

The teams played a 1–1 tie in the first game at Detroit. The Rocket and Béliveau scored in the second match, giving Montreal a 2–0 win. Le Gros Bill scored twice in the rubber game and Les Canadiens came from behind to win, 2–1. They now sported a fifteen-point lead and, for all intents and purposes, the battle for first place was over.

Blake nevertheless continued to run a tight ship while allowing for healthy injections of humor here and there. Once, Blake reminded his players that he had imposed an eleven o'clock curfew. "Gee, coach," said Harvey with a straight face, "does that mean we have to wait until eleven to go to bed?"

Even the Rocket got in on the banter. Andy O'Brien, sports editor of _Weekend Magazine_, was accompanying the team on a trip to New York when he noticed most of the players posing for a photographer, kissing their wives goodbye at the railroad station. The Rocket stood by, biting on a long stogie and looking not at all amused by the scene. O'Brien sauntered over and wondered whether Maurice objected to kissing his wife good-bye. "Not on short trips," quipped the Rocket.

By this time the Pocket and the Rocket had jelled perfectly with Moore. Despite the Rocket's age he managed to keep pace with his younger cronies, although one afternoon he nearly regretted it. The Canadiens were in the midst of a workout when Henri rounded the net at full speed from one side and Maurice approached on the same track from the other direction. They collided violently and both fell to the ice unconsicous. When they were finally revived, both were escorted to the first-aid room where Maurice needed twelve stitches to close his wound and his kid brother, six stitches.

Then, in a masterful understatement, Maurice intoned: "You'd better watch yourself, Henri. You might get hurt."

Only once did the Rocket nearly approach the fury that

engulfed him in previous seasons. The Canadiens were playing the Rangers at Madison Square Garden in a game that
was so wild and turbulent that columnist Red Smith likened
it to a Roman circus. Late in the second period the Rocket
and New York's Lou Fontinato clashed. Fontinato connected
with a hard right that opened a wound over Richard's left
eye. The bloodthirsty New York crowd went into transports
of joy at the sight of the bleeding bear. Richard seethed with
contempt for Fontinato and continued stewing in his quiet
rage as the Canadiens trooped into the dressing room for
the break between the second and third periods.

Ken Reardon, by that time a major executive with the
team, dashed down to the dressing room from his press-box
seat. Reardon had more than a passing knowledge of temper
tantrums and had played with the Rocket long enough to
know how to deal with him. As soon as he opened the locker-
room door, Reardon went straight to Richard's bench and
talked hard but calmly to him. He stressed the obvious.
Fontinato had hit him a lucky punch and it would be better
for all concerned—Maurice and Les Canadiens—if he cooled
it this time.

The Rocket listened impassively like a boxer more intent
on getting back into the ring than listening to the ministrations
of his trainer. For a few seconds it appeared that all hell
would break loose again and the Rocket would be in the
middle of it. Without notice, Doug Harvey came up with a
droll remark and the sullen dressing room erupted with
laughter. An almost embarrassed smile crossed the Rocket's
face. Then he was laughing with the rest of them and he was
never in real trouble again.

"Sometimes," said Blake, "I had to cool the Rocket on the
bench. He'd glare at me, but he took it from me, too."

A year after his suspension the Rocket was virtually
canonized in Montreal. A French-Canadian record company
pressed a disk in his honor, as well as one for Geoffrion,
and an English outfit came up with a hillbilly version of the
St. Patrick's Day riot called "The Saga of Rocket Richard."

His goals received as thunderous a response as ever, and from time to time, when Gordie Howe visited the Forum, the crowd would boo whenever Howe carried the puck.

Conversely, the Forum faithful took a dim view of Geoffrion, as good as he was. They resented the fact that he had wrested the scoring championship away from Maurice while the Rocket was under suspension, and they generally made life miserable for the normally ebullient Boomer. Geoffrion was so despondent about the negative reaction that he seriously considered retiring before the 1955–1956 campaign.

"It was not my fault the Rocket was suspended," Geoffrion would say in defense of his position. "I couldn't deliberately *not* score. So I was sick of the whole thing. Even thinking about hockey made me throw up. I wanted to get away from hockey. But then before practices began Béliveau and Richard visited me. And they urged me to stay in the game."

Plante was another eccentric, and not only because he knitted *toques* or traveled far and wide from his goal crease. Some people contend that he was a hypochondriac. Others noted that he did, in fact, suffer from asthma and in cities such as Toronto he would divorce himself from the team and stay at a select "nonasthmatic" hotel. At the time, Blake didn't mind that. "Starting that season," said the coach, "and for five years he was the greatest goalie the league has ever seen."

Interestingly, the Habitants' defense was not all that tough in the Murder, Inc., sense of the word. They didn't have to be. With the forwards outskating the opposition at every turn, the defensemen were mobile enough to outwit the enemy with brainpower and speed without resorting to violence. That is, unless suitably provoked.

Once, during a game with the Rangers in New York, Harvey planted the pointed blade of his stick in Red Sullivan's gut and sent the Ranger center to the hospital with a ruptured spleen. For a time Sullivan's condition was so grave he was given the last rites of the Catholic Church. Fortunately, he recovered completely and returned to play out his career in the N.H.L. Honest to a fault, Harvey never denied the attack, but he pointed out that Sullivan had developed an obnoxious, not to mention dangerous, habit of "kicking skates," so that when the two went into the corner of the rink Sullivan would kick Harvey's skates out from under him, making it very easy for the Montrealer to fall on his head. According to Doug, he warned Sullivan about his unfortunate proclivity and when the warning went unheeded the stick was plunged into Sullivan's stomach.

Harvey had one "flaw" as a defenseman. He was so laconic in style, so calmly sure of himself, that he executed plays of extreme complication with consummate ease. Lacking the flamboyance of Eddie Shore or other Hall of Fame defensemen, Harvey was slow to receive the acclaim he deserved. But by 1955–1956 it had become apparent that he was superior to Shore in many ways. "Doug Harvey was the greatest defenseman who ever played hockey—bar none," said Blake. "Usually a defenseman specializes in one thing and builds a reputation on that, but Doug could do everything well."

Inevitably, Harvey has been compared with the contemporary defensive star, Bobby Orr of the Bruins. In all fairness to both athletes, Orr has not been in the league long enough to merit a judgment with Harvey. On specific performance, Orr has yet to match Harvey *defensively*. "Often Harvey's cool was mistaken for disinterest," said Josh Greenfeld. "Actually it was the result of an always calculating concentration." By contrast, Orr often appears to make outrageously obtuse plays in his own defensive zone and occasionally betrays moves that suggest a quasi-panic.

Harvey was a superb rusher but lacked the blazing shot that characterizes Orr's arsenal. There is little doubt that Orr has the advantage offensively but not as much as current statistics would suggest. "Harvey," wrote Greenfeld, "could inaugurate a play from farther back and carry it farther than any other defenseman."

Not far behind Harvey in all-round ability was Tom Johnson, himself a well-coordinated puck-carrier and a solid man behind the blue line. "It took everybody a long time to know that Johnson was as good as we knew he was," said Blake. In 1970 Johnson was inducted into the Hockey Hall of Fame.

With this abundance of stars Blake was careful not to introduce any bizarre stratagem that would disrupt the team. Under Irvin, Les Canadiens had become renowned for what was known as "Firewagon Hockey," which, as the name implies, accented the rush, rush, rush until the enemy was run through the ice with exhaustion. Peter Gzowski said he preferred to describe the Canadiens' trademark as élan. "On the ice," he wrote, "the Canadiens swoop and gambol, skating like fury and burning with zeal; they are somehow romantic, like Scaramouche or Cyrano or Jean Gascon."

Blake was acutely aware of this quality. All he did was improve on Irvin's failing psychology. Everything else then fell perfectly into place. "Your style of coaching has to depend upon the players you have," said Blake, "because if you try to change the styles of your players, you're in trouble.

"If you're connected with so many superstars as I was, then you've got to let them go all out and let the defense look after itself. And, fortunately, I had a defense that could look after itself. But I told my team that four or five stars don't make a team. Everyone in uniform is important."

With Blake orchestrating his club to perfection, Les Canadiens romped home first with ease—twenty-four points, or twelve games, ahead of Detroit. Four of the top seven scorers were Canadiens. Béliveau led the league with eighty-eight points while the Rocket was third with seventy-one, followed by Olmstead's seventy and Geoffrion with sixty-two. Béliveau, Richard, Harvey, and Plante were named to the First All-Star Team. Plante's 1.86 goals against average gave him the Vézina Trophy. Harvey captured the James Norris Trophy as the league's best defenseman and Béliveau was voted the Hart Trophy as the most valuable player in the N.H.L. The club set a record by winning forty-five games, losing only fifteen, and tying ten for one hundred points.

This, however, was quickly forgotten once the play-offs began. To hockey fans, the Stanley Cup round is a completely new season and all the triumphs and achievements of the season gone by are as old as ancient history. For a change the Rangers had won a play-off berth and, having finished third, were slated to meet Montreal in the opening round. New York was coached by the onetime Canadien Phil Watson, and from time to time the New Yorkers generated enough power to be considered a threat to any team.

The Rocket's three-goal hat trick defused the Rangers in the opening game at the Forum and Les Canadiens romped to an easy 7–1 victory. Everyone in Montreal expected the second game to be just as easy, if not easier. Gump Worsley, the Rangers' regular goalkeeper, was injured, and Watson was compelled to use thirty-one-year-old Gordie Bell, a weather-beaten minor-league goaltender with virtually no N.H.L. experience. Somehow, the Rangers rallied around Bell and defeated Montreal, 4–2. Heartened by the upset, the Rangers returned to New York, hopeful to win the next two matches on Madison Square Garden ice.

The Rangers fought gamely but Les Canadiens were not fooling around either. Montreal won both games in Manhattan and eliminated New York with a 7–0 victory in the fifth game at the Forum. Once more, the Rocket starred, setting up five of the seven goals. "Now," he kidded in the dressing room after the game, "I've become a playmaker."

Only the Red Wings stood between Les Canadiens and the Stanley Cup. Detroit had moved into the finals on the strength of a four-games-to-one sweep of the Maple Leafs and impressed Toronto's King Clancy enough to persuade him to predict that Montreal would lose to the Detroiters. For a couple of periods in the first game at Montreal it appeared that Clancy might have something there. Les Canadiens fell behind, 4–2, and appeared to be in a state of inertia.

"Sometimes," said Blake, "your aces get heavily checked in the play-offs. When that happens you have to hope that your lesser lights can come up with a couple of goals and bail you out."

Jackie Leclair did the spade work on Montreal's third goal, and Jean-Guy Talbot spearheaded the fourth and tying goal. Then big Jean Béliveau came through with the tie-breaker, followed by an insurance score from the stick of Claude Provost. Before the Red Wings could turn around, they had been swept off the ice, 6–4.

Demoralized, the Red Wings were no match in the second game and bowed easily, 5–1. Only once, in the third game, was the Detroit club to perform respectably. The Wings prevailed, 3–1, but they lost their next home game, 3–0, and returned to the Forum for what 14,151 fans expected would be "the kill." They were disappointed throughout the scoreless first period and waited expectantly, but forlornly, as the second period moved along without either team getting a goal. But late in the session Harvey spotted Floyd Curry breaking toward the Detroit goal. His pass was radar-perfect, and Curry moved swiftly, with Béliveau flanking him on the other side. Curry's pass was true and Béliveau's shot beat Glenn Hall in the Red Wing goal.

The second period had still not ended when the Rocket detonated another explosive roar as *he* beat Hall. Boomer Geoffrion made it three for Montreal in the third period and Alex Delvecchio scored for Detroit. Meanwhile, the clock ticked closer and closer to the twenty-minute mark and the crowd launched into a crescendo roar that reached new heights in decibel counts when the siren wailed, signaling the end of the game. Les Canadiens had regained the Stanley Cup. Butch Bouchard, the tall captain, who was on the verge of retirement, accepted the trophy at center ice and then the champagne flowed. A day later, the citizens who a year ago were the shame of the N.H.L., proudly toasted their heroes with a thirty-mile parade through the city of Montreal.

"Perhaps to some Montrealers it was as if Bonnie Prince

Charlie had become king," said Josh Greenfeld, "perhaps to others it was like the restoration of the Bourbon dynasty. But all of hockey-mad Montreal was happy—in any language."

It was more than that. The deafening cheers were an expression of retribution for the previous year's "crime" against the Rocket as well as a feeling of jubilation about the rosy future; what Canadiens' publicist Camil Desroches called "those wonderful five years."

Armed with basically the same lineup as they had iced in 1955–1956, Les Canadiens won an unparalleled five Stanley Cups in succession and finished in first place in six out of seven years! "I saw the old Canadiens with Morenz and Joliat," said Muzz Patrick, the Rangers' manager. "There's no comparing that team with this one. This Montreal outfit is many, many times better."

"Nobody seems able to skate with them, to shoot with them," said New York columnist Jimmy Powers, "and if, as happens, they have a bad night and get licked, it is an event." Such was the case until 1960, although Les Canadiens were experiencing an inner upheaval of major proportions which would affect the team right up to the present.

12

The Coming
of the Molsons

While Les Canadiens overran the N.H.L., Selke had surrounded himself with a loyal high command that included Ken Reardon, Toe Blake, and such minor-league operatives as Mickey Hennessy, Del Wilson, Frank Carlin, Sam Pollock, and Mike Kartusch. They were to Montreal hockey what the Supreme Allied Command was to General Dwight D. Eisenhower at the time of D-day.

At the top of the pyramid was Senator Donat Raymond, who scrupulously avoided interference with Selke's day-to-day manipulation of Les Canadiens' empire. Both Selke and Raymond were getting on in years, and it was believed that sooner or later successors would have to be chosen. The obvious heir to Selke's throne was the popular cigar-smoking Reardon who was related to Senator Raymond through marriage. Reardon traveled extensively with the Montreal sextet and was often called upon as club spokesman in Selke's absence. He was a hockey man with insight and the same respectful legacy as a player that Blake possessed.

Finding someone to follow Senator Raymond's footsteps would be another story. The Senator was a wealthy and distinguished French-Canadian with a genuine love for hockey and a passionate interest in Les Canadiens. When Senator Raymond began suffering from ill health, he confided to Selke that he preferred the next boss of Les Canadiens come from the Molson family, one of the most respected and oldest in the province of Quebec. Selke acted as unofficial liason between Raymond and Senator Hartland de Montigny Molson, who headed the Molson Brewery, one of Canada's largest makers of beer and ale.

Prior to the 1957–1958 season the Molson family acquired the Canadian Arena Company with Senator Molson at the helm. Like Raymond, Molson had the respect of both the French- and the English-speaking communities of Montreal. He was an avid sportsman and had served as a fighter pilot during the Battle of Britain.

It didn't take very long for Senator Molson to establish his loyalty to the Canadiens. While attending a Stanley Cup game in Detroit, the Senator found himself sitting disturbingly close to a Red Wing rooter who noticed Molson and proceeded to hurl various forms of abuse on him and Canadians generally. The Senator absorbed about as much as a dozen men could endure and finally challenged his tormentor to fight. Selke and another friend quickly intervened before any blows were struck; but there was no mistaking Molson's interest after that.

Having a powerful organization such as Molson's Brewery behind the N.H.L. club was rather unprecedented and it raised conjecture about whether the character of Les Canadiens would change. At first there was no perceptible alteration in the team's image and structure. Selke remained at the controls, flanked by his trusted lieutenants. Undisturbed, Blake ran the team with his usual efficiency, although there were occasional signs that he was feeling more pressure as a winner than most coaches do as losers.

Conversely, the Rocket appeared more relaxed than ever and he, in turn, became almost beloved, if that's possible, in alien arenas throughout the league. When he scored a three-goal hat trick at Olympia Stadium in Detroit in October, 1957, Richard received a standing ovation. "It took sixteen years," said Detroit writer Marshall Dann, "but the time finally came when Rocket Richard drew more cheers than jeers in Detroit." The Rocket soon scored his five-hundredth N.H.L. goal and said, "I'm dedicating it to Dick Irvin. He taught me everything I know about hockey."

Richard had leaped ahead of the scoring race in 1957–1958 like a Kentucky Derby sprinter. By the second week in November it appeared that, at last, he would go on to win that elusive scoring championship. Then tragedy struck again. While playing against the Maple Leafs at Toronto on November 13, the Rocket tangled with defenseman Marc Reaume of the Leafs. It was an innocent collision, ironically different from so many of Richard's clashes with his foes.

As Reaume scrambled to his feet, his razor-sharp skate blade sliced between Richard's tendon guard and his stocking. Reaume pressed forward and, in so doing, his blade cut into Richard's tendon, almost snapping it in half. The Rocket was carried into the Maple Leaf Gardens' hospital where Dr. Jim Murray administered fifteen stitches to the wound. "He was lucky," said Dr. Murray. "Just a shade more and the tendon would have snapped. Had this happened it could very well have meant the end of his career."

Richard was thirty-six years old at the time of the mishap and it was freely predicted that this would be the end of the line for him, whether he recovered completely or not. But by February 20, 1958, Richard was back in the lineup and celebrated his return with two goals and two near-misses.

Meanwhile, Boom Boom Geoffrion was in the throes of one of his own near tragedies, which were to pockmark his long and successful career. On January 28 Blake was running his team through a routine practice when Geoffrion collided with young André Pronovost. When the Boomer fell to the ice his teammates reacted as if Geoffrion were perpetrating one of his numerous japes. "We didn't do a thing," said Tom Johnson, "because we thought he was joking."

As the players gathered around the fallen right wing they heard him moan, "*J'étouffe, J'étouffe*" (I can't breathe). Forum physiotherapist Bill Head was summoned and ordered Geoffrion transported to the hospital. A day later the Montreal *Gazette* ran a banner headline: "HOCKEY STAR BERNIE GEOFFRION FIGHTS FOR HIS LIFE IN HOSPITAL."

What had seemed at first to be a gag turned into a near

disaster. Geoffrion had suffered a ruptured bowel, and only the quick work of Head at the Forum and surgeons at the hospital saved his life. But the Rocket soon returned, took Geoffrion's place, and led Les Canadiens to first place. His teammate, Dickie Moore, played for five weeks wearing a cumbersome cast on his right wrist yet still managed to win the scoring championship.

In the fourth game of the semifinal play-off round against Detroit, the Rocket celebrated his one-thousandth N.H.L. game by scoring a three-goal hat trick. It pulled Les Canadiens up from what appeared to be a 3–1 loss and guided them to a 4–1 series victory over the Red Wings. By now Geoffrion had returned to the lineup, and between the Boomer and the Rocket, Montreal defeated Boston four games to two to win the Stanley Cup once more.

Selke's only concern for the future related to the 1958 N.H.L. draft. Toronto did the most significant raiding and came away with Bert Olmstead, the tenacious and pestiferous digger who had lent so much support to Béliveau and Geoffrion. Any suggestions that Olmstead was over the hill were dissipated in future seasons, but neither Blake nor Selke appeared terribly concerned. They had designated tall, husky Ab McDonald to replace Olmstead and also promoted speedy Ralph Backstrom from their farm system to operate at center.

Over the years Backstrom would prove to be an effective big-leaguer but never the star his early press notices suggested. He won the Calder Trophy as rookie of the year in 1958–1959 with eighteen goals and twenty-two assists, but he symbolized something about Montreal rookies that would plague the Canadiens to the present. By an unfortunate (although some may debate the term) stroke of fate, some of the finest youngsters to ripen on the Canadiens' player tree happened to be of small stature and disinclined to the brutal warfare of hockey. Players like André Boudrias, Yvan Cournoyer, and Bobby Rousseau were among them—all worthies and stars in junior hockey but lacking that extra beef so often needed in the N.H.L. Backstrom was among the first and he managed to dazzle with his footwork in the early years although he never became a star. But by the spring of 1959 Backstrom's promise was so enormous that Chicago Black Hawks' owner Jim Norris offered Selke $135,000 for the young center. Selke's reply was an unequivocal "no."

Such affluence began to have an interesting effect on Montreal's crowds. They still reserved hoarse cheers for the beloved Rocket but success turned them, once more, into vocal critics. Perfection was expected at every turn, and when it wasn't accomplished, scapegoats were quickly found. One of the first was goalie Jacques Plante. Still the best in the league, "Jake the Snake" occasionally enraged spectators with his scrambles behind the net for the puck. Once, the play backfired on him. He missed the disk; an opponent retrieved it and shoved the rubber into the yawning cage before Plante could return to guard it. In November, 1958, Plante's goals against average began climbing, matched by Blake's temper.

"Worse than that is Plante's nervousness," snapped Blake. "Our home fans have been riding him and he's let it get his goat. It's affecting his work. He's got to get over it; after all he is a professional. . . . The only way to shut up a guy who boos you is to play better. If you have a bad year, he'll boo all the more. This ought to make Plante fight back. Instead, he's getting worse. I realize that as a French-Canadian, Jacques is more emotional than a lot of guys. But Bill Durnan wasn't a French-Canadian and it got him. Same with Wilf Cude. Same with Gerry McNeil."

"I know what Plante is going through," said Durnan. "The only thing Jacques can do is hitch up his pants and let them boo."

The Blake-Plante repartée was, perhaps, even more ominous than it sounded. Severe to a fault, the coach was down on his goaltender and was to become more and more disenchanted with Plante's behavior as the seasons progressed. Ultimately, it resulted in a rupture that never healed and Plante, not Blake, was sent on his way. Blake would have preferred it if Plante displayed an uncompromising attitude toward the game that marked the personality of his buddy, the Rocket. Now, there was a man! The elder Richard kept steaming along, completely recovered from his tendon mishap and as dedicated as ever. "He lives for only one thing in life," said Blake, "to score goals!"

On November 26, 1958, the Rocket underlined Blake's point with the six-hundredth goal of his N.H.L. career. Needless to say, it was another classic from the Richard mold, spectacular to the nth degree. He swooped around his nemesis, Lou Fontinato, along the right side of the Ranger defensive zone but found himself too deep to release a shot on goalie Gump Worsley. With blinding speed, Richard swerved around behind the net and emerged at the left side to fling the puck into the unguarded corner before Worsley could make a move! In the process Richard fell to the ice as Rangers fell over him. Once more, the thirty-seven-year-old veteran was hailed with a standing ovation in a normally hostile rink. It was a glorious event, except that the Rangers rallied to win, 5–3, and reporters were afterward greeted with Blake's inimitable "wrath of God."

The Montreal mentor had completely forgotten about the Rocket's noteworthy score. All that mattered was the defeat. When approached by the press at the entrance to the Canadiens' dressing room, he slammed the steel door with such force that the impact seemed to shake the very foundations of the huge Garden.

Richard himself was shaken in January, 1959, when he suffered a broken ankle that sidelined him for three months. Even without the Rocket, Les Canadiens finished on top. They edged Chicago four games to two in the semifinal that teetered between tremulous and turbulent throughout. Referee Red Storey was attacked by an irate Chicago fan who disapproved of his failure to call a penalty in the sixth game, yet he finished the match. Shortly thereafter, President Clarence Campbell was quoted in an Ottawa paper to the effect that the veteran referee had "choked" on the play that led to the fan's attack. Storey refused to continue working the play-offs and resigned on April 7 with a scathing attack on Campbell.

The Rocket returned to the lineup in time for the 1959 Cup final against Toronto. The Leafs managed just one victory, despite numerous perorations by Toronto general manager–coach Punch Imlach, and Les Canadiens walked off with an unprecedented fourth straight Stanley Cup victory. What's more, they owned a collection of starry minor-leaguers —Red Berenson, Wayne Connelly, Bill Hicke, and Bill Sutherland—who appeared capable of cracking the varsity lineup if an opening developed.

Perhaps the most significant opportunity would be in goal, if the Blake-Plante feud ignited again. From time to time Les Canadiens would elevate a brilliant little netminder named Charlie Hodge from their minor-league affiliate and Hodge would play like a champion. Plante still had all the ability in the world but he had been hit in the face by an Andy Bathgate slapshot during a game in New York and, for the first time in modern hockey, donned a protective face mask. Once again Plante offered a portent of things to come, but Blake was not the least enamored of the mask idea, although he publicly asserted that as long as it helped Plante keep the pucks out of the net it would be all right. For 1959–1960 the mask proved effective enough to enable Plante to win the Vézina Trophy.

The Rocket signed his eighteenth N.H.L. contract with Les Canadiens that season, but in November a flying puck smacked into his face, smashing a cheekbone, and deactivated him for a month. Montreal managed without him, and when Richard returned, the Habitants staged another successful assault on first place. Ab McDonald had not been an adequate replacement for Bert Olmstead, so Selke tried the French-Canadian Marcel Bonin whose claims to fame, apart from hockey playing, were that he wrestled bears and ate glass. Another interesting newcomer was Bill Hicke, a right wing with an extraordinary burst of speed and a wide repertoire of stick-handling maneuvers. Unfortunately for the youngster, some reporter tabbed him "the next Rocket Rich-

ard" and Hicke had to bear that onus for the rest of his
playing career in Montreal.

Hicke and Bonin were among the young Canadiens to
lead the team to a four-game sweep of Chicago in the semifinals. They then proceeded to do the same thing to Toronto,
only the second time that an N.H.L. club has swept to the
Stanley Cup in eight consecutive games and remained undis-
puted kings of hockey.

Never one to stand pat, Selke was acutely aware of one
problem—the Rocket was fast approaching the end of the line.
If he decided to retire, a new captain would have to be
selected and some way had to be found to replace Richard's
extraordinary effect on his teammates and fans alike. This
would prove to be an impossible chore. There would never
be another quite like Maurice Richard; not Jean Béliveau, not
Bernie Geoffrion, and not Henri Richard. And nobody knew
that better than Selke.

The Rocket dropped his bomb on September 15, 1960, and
announced he was through as a hockey player. Selke
promptly revealed that Maurice would become a "vice-
president" of the team and its goodwill ambassador. Later, in
his memoirs, Selke was to recall that Richard did as much
good for hockey by speaking to youths across Canada in his
new job as he had as a hockey player. This, perhaps, was
something of an exaggeration since the Rocket had set
seventeen records as a player. He participated in 978 regular
season games and 133 play-off matches. He was selected to
one of the N.H.L.'s two All-Star Teams for sixteen straight
seasons. Both the Lady Byng Trophy and the league scoring
championship eluded him; and the latter would remain the
tragedy of Richard's career.

Now the Canadiens turned to the itchy job of picking a
new captain to succeed the Rocket. The logical choices were
Doug Harvey, Jean Béliveau, and Boom Boom Geoffrion.
Harvey, who had seniority over the others, got the nod and
led Montreal to still another first-place finish. They went into
the play-offs favored to win their sixth straight Stanley Cup

and found themselves confronted by a tough Chicago sextet that finally had found a formula for routing Les Canadiens.

Montreal won the first match, 6–3, but the big, tough Hawks battered the smaller Canadiens at every turn. One by one, Hicke, Marshall, and Béliveau were sent to the hospital with injuries. Blake denounced the Hawks for their back-alley tactics but it was too late. Former Montrealer Ed Litzenberg came up with the winning goal for Chicago in the second game at the Forum, putting Les Canadiens behind the eight ball.

By Chicago's standards, the third game of the series in cavernous Chicago Stadium was a classic. Three overtime sessions were required before Murray Balfour, once Montreal property, scored for the Black Hawks. Blake, who had been seething over the officiating since the second game, raged when the red light signaled Balfour's score. The traumatized coach headed for referee Dalton McArthur and swung at the official. Blake was fined two thousand dollars for his behavior and McArthur became a marked man as a result of the incident. Les Canadiens recovered briefly in the fourth game, but Chicago goalie Glenn Hall blanked them in the fifth and sixth contests and Montreal found itself in the unusual position of not hosting a Stanley Cup final for the first time in eleven years!

Now that the unthinkable had actually taken place, it was time for housecleaning. Les Canadiens' lack of a policeman to protect the smaller forwards was an albatross that hovered over Selke for years. A deal was in order, and Selke obtained the oft-hated Lou Fontinato from the Rangers in return for Doug Harvey. To say the least it was a very controversial deal. Big and strong, Fontinato was nevertheless a clumsy defenseman, the antithesis of the smooth-skating, sharp-passing Harvey. Even Fontinato's fighting ability was debatable ever since Gordie Howe had plastered him with a broken nose during a notorious battle in New York. But Louie still liked to hit and that was what mattered most to Selke; besides he was considerably younger than the thirty-six-year-old

Harvey who was *mistakenly* believed to be in the twilight of his career.

In a related deal, Selke peddled young defenseman Al "Junior" Langlois to New York for John Hanna, another stocky and rough defenseman. Thus, Montreal sacrificed ability for brawn and hoped for the best. Harvey was named player-coach of the Rangers and immediately went about the business of embarrassing his former employers. He scored six goals and twenty-four assists and won the James Norris Trophy as the league's best defenseman. While he was at it, Harvey led the Rangers to a play-off berth.

Finding an heir to Harvey's throne as team captain was an even more difficult task for Selke than it was replacing the Rocket. For now the choice narrowed down to a pair of worthies—Boom Boom Geoffrion and Jean Béliveau. The electrifying Boomer had seniority over Béliveau and appeared a slight favorite in the balloting. On the other hand, Béliveau was admired as a virtuoso and a gentleman. He won the captaincy on the second ballot and that might have been a bigger mistake than the Canadiens imagined.

Geoffrion was crushed by the decision. When Béliveau learned of his teammate's depression, he went directly to management and offered, unsuccessfully, to step aside. Several observers wondered whether the diffident, mild-mannered Béliveau was psychologically equipped to be the new Canadiens' leader. They suggested that he could never galvanize the team to action like the volcanic Rocket or the lighthearted but determined Harvey. In a sense, they were to be proved wrong. Montreal finished first by thirteen points, and Plante won the Vézina Trophy again. In addition, fleet Bobby Rousseau won the Calder Trophy as rookie of the year. "Rousseau," said Peter Gzowski, "makes up in zest and recklessness (he always seems to be shooting from his knees, or lying down, or leaping high in the air) what he lacks in size." But Rousseau had that characteristic fragility that so many of the Canadiens' youngsters had, and although Rousseau developed into a superb artist, he always had difficulty when

the checking became overly rough. The Canadiens finally unloaded him to Minnesota in 1970.

The easy conquest of the regular schedule proved to be
a deception. Chicago lost the opening pair of games of the
semifinal in Montreal, then breezed to victory in the remaining
four contests. It was a fate both Montreal rooters and Captain
Béliveau found difficult to accept.

"We began to feel the pressure of losing," said Béliveau.
"We had been winning for so long we did not know what it
was like to lose. The people started to talk."

They continued talking when Montreal finished third the
following season and Béliveau scored only eighteen goals
for the second year in a row. "By that time," said Le Gros
Bill, "I was ready to quit. If Senator Molson had told me to
leave, I would have gone."

A patient man, Molson realized that Béliveau had been
tormented by injuries and personal problems that affected his
play on ice. "Jean," Molson comforted him, "you've given us
so many good years you could have some bad ones and we'd
still owe you a lot. We need you now more than ever."

Molson persuaded Béliveau to return, which was a good
move all around. Béliveau went on to play several seasons
of superb hockey for Les Canadiens and became a vice-
president with Molson's Brewery. Nevertheless, his lyrical
style never captured the imagination of Montrealers the way
Morenz, Richard, or Geoffrion did and nobody was more
keenly aware of it than Le Gros Bill himself.

"I have heard people talk about me," he said. "I have
been asked why I have not scored more goals. It is something that has been with me for a long time. You live with it,
but it is not easy. 'What do they want? What do I have to do?'
I would ask myself. But I suppose it goes back to all that
publicity I had. It was easy in those days playing amateur
hockey. It was easier to get five goals in senior hockey than
one in the N.H.L. Everybody expected it would be easy in the
N.H.L. But it wasn't. Always it was the pressure. People would

come to the rinks and if I would score only one goal the people would be unhappy."

Béliveau's uncertainty about his future was but one of several dilemmas disturbing Selke. Plante was assailed by more frequent asthmatic attacks and became more and more estranged in his relationship with Blake. In addition, Plante's defense literally crumbled in front of him. A fractured cheekbone sent Tom Johnson to the hospital and a freak accident to Fontinato shocked Forum onlookers almost as much as the Morenz mishap.

In a game against the Rangers, Vic Hadfield of New York pursued Fontinato, who was skating close to the end boards, behind the net. The Montreal defenseman detected the onrushing Ranger and employed one of his favorite checking devices. Fontinato crouched low in the expectation that Hadfield, upon hitting him, would sail over his body and into the boards. But the impact was such that Hadfield's body caught Fontinato in the shoulders and neck. As the Montreal strongboy hit the hard wooden boards, his neck broke. The combined dislocation and fracture of the neck permanently injured Fontinato, and he never played for Les Canadiens again, although he was later able to regain some mobility in his neck.

Fortunately for Selke, the vast farm system was still dispatching players to the big team. Eager but clumsy, Terry Harper, almost a replica of Fontinato, was called to Montreal along with tall, stylish Jacques Laperriere. The Canadiens, symbolically, gave Laperriere Harvey's number two, and for a while he appeared to be almost as accomplished as his predecessor.

Left wing Gilles Tremblay was another with great potential. He scored thirty-two goals in 1961–1962, and the Rocket said he was capable of scoring fifty goals in a season. But Tremblay was soon afflicted with an asthmatic condition, even worse than Plante's, and had to retire permanently in the 1969–1970 campaign at the age of thirty. Thus, with all these woes, it was not surprising that Toronto bounced Les Canadiens out of the 1963 Stanley Cup semifinal in five games.

That was as humiliating a situation as Selke could absorb. "Too many chiefs and not enough braves," was Ken Reardon's explanation. Plante's behavior, for one thing, had grated both Blake and the front office. He had to go, and he did. A major trade was concluded with New York in which Plante, Don Marshall, and Phil Goyette were transplanted to the Rangers for goalie Gump Worsley and forwards Dave Balon, Leon Rochefort, and Len Ronson.

"I really believe it was all for the best," said an enthused Blake who finally had Plante off his back. "I think the players involved as well as the clubs are going to benefit. I also feel we're going to benefit more in the long run because we gained a big edge in youth as well as getting an extra player.

"There simply had to be changes made. You can't stand pat after being eliminated from the play-offs like we were. As for Plante, I always said, when he played for our club, that he was the best goalie in the league. But last season I found a big change in Jacques. He was nervous—very nervous. I don't know who made him nervous, whether it was the club, or the people in the stands, or what, but something was bothering him. He wasn't sure whether he'd be able to play or not play. I think he needed a change, and I think the trade will help him."

Blake commended Marshall but noted that in the "last couple of years I thought Donnie hadn't been extending himself—with us he just didn't seem to be going all out anymore." He also lauded Goyette but pointed out that Montreal was strong at center and Phil, therefore, was expendable.

Just which team benefited most from the trade can be debated to this day. Only Worsley was good enough to stick with Montreal for a substantial length of time. Plante failed, despite occasional histrionics, in New York, but Goyette and Marshall became rejuvenated as Rangers and Marshall remained with the team through the 1969–1970 season.

When Dickie Moore announced his retirement after twelve years with the club, Les Canadiens redoubled their efforts to find a hard-checking forward. A tip from former Montreal ace Floyd Curry resulted in the signing of John Ferguson, a muscleman with the Cleveland Barons, of the American League. "Fergie" was an awkward skater with limited ability, but his addition to the squad would turn out to be of utmost importance in years to come. In some ways it was the most important decision made by Les Canadiens in the 1960s.

No player since Rocket Richard exuded so much raw fire as Ferguson. As a matter of personal policy he never talked to the opposition either on or off the ice, and he would resort to any means available to score a goal or stop an enemy. He was complimented by another, although smaller, hitter named Bryan Watson whose career in Montreal was considerably less extensive than Ferguson's.

Worsley, the great new and corpulent goaltending hope, was lauded by Blake as a notable replacement for Plante. "With the Rangers," said Blake, "he was going nowhere. Maybe, just maybe, he got to feel that it didn't matter too much whether the team won or lost. There was no future. But it'll be different now. It's bound to be. He's got an opportunity for his talents now that he never had before in his career."

The blimpish Gunp responded by getting injured early in the season. Little Charlie Hodge stepped in and played brilliantly for sixty-two games, winning the Vézina Trophy. Thanks to Hodge, Montreal went on to fool the experts and finished in first place, but Toronto came on strong and beat them, four games to three, in the semifinal play-off round.

Ever since he had become owner of Les Canadiens, Senator Molson remained unobtrusively behind the scenes as Selke diligently put together the pieces of the Montreal hockey empire. That Selke was succeeding was evident by the first-place finish in March, 1964, but the Canadiens' elimination in the play-offs underscored the fact that there still was work to be done. Selke acknowledged this just as he had realized there was a formidable task ahead of him in the late forties when he first arrived in Montreal.

Selke had reached the age of seventy-one by the spring of 1964 but he had the attitude and energy of men thirty years his junior. He loved hockey as passionately as he had as a kid in Berlin, Ontario, and saw no reason for not continuing in his position. Flanked by the dynamic Reardon and clever Sam Pollock, Selke could see the Stanley Cup only about a season away.

However, behind the scenes a big-business power play was under way that would ultimately reshape the entire structure and character of Les Canadiens. Hints of a shake-up were heard during the 1964 Stanley Cup finals after Montreal was eliminated. Word was out that instead of the traditional player shake-up that follows defeat it would be the high command that would face the inquisition. Early in May, the first signs of trouble bubbled to the surface. Ken Reardon, who had served so loyally under Selke and who was expected to succeed him as managing director, resigned as vice-president of Les Canadiens. Since Reardon had been closely aligned with Selke, the move startled the hockey world and set off even more speculation as to the Habitants' palace revolution.

On Friday, May 15, the cat was out of the bag, and all hell broke loose in the front office. Senator Molson announced that sweeping changes were being made in the Canadiens' organization from Selke to Rocket Richard to Sam Pollock!

Big business had finally extended its tentacles and completely engulfed Le Club de Hockey Canadien. What had once been a rather homey operation run by Leo Dandurand and later by Senator Raymond and Selke had now become a high-pressure outfit with a new president and a new managing director.

To begin with, Selke "resigned," although the circumstances and remarks he made to newsmen suggest that the veteran hockey man had been ceremoniously pushed out of his job. "I'm disappointed," he said soon after he stepped out. "I'd have liked at least one more year to finish reconstructing the team. We're almost there, but not quite."

The sop profferred to Selke was an obscure title, "vice-chairman of the board of the Canadien Arena Company." "I'll help with the selection of new players," Selke said with an overdose of wishful thinking. "If the new fellows want that kind of help, they're going to get it. If they don't . . . if they don't, it's so long. . . . Those who ask your advice really want your support of their opinion and will be content with nothing less. . . . I feel lost."

And well he might have. His successor was thirty-eight-year-old Sam Pollock, who had been director of the Canadiens' farm system since 1958 and was now the youngest club manager in the N.H.L. Pollock's appointment immediately clarified the meaning behind Reardon's departure a week earlier. Sam had outfought Kenny, somehow, in the behind-the-scenes infighting for Selke's job.

Pollock's credentials were quite sound. He had devoted nineteen of his years to hockey management, seventeen of them as a full-time employee of the Forum. He was instrumental in developing the Junior Canadiens and led them to the Memorial Cup, emblematic of national supremacy, in 1950. In more recent years Pollock took a more active role in the actual manipulating of players on the N.H.L. Canadiens and helped negotiate the famed Worsley-Plante deal.

Pollock knew what he wanted, and he was going to run Les Canadiens his way. Thus, having Selke around would soon prove to be an embarrassment and an irrelevancy until the elder statesman finally moved gracefully to the background. But there were others crowding Pollock for the limelight.

In another interesting move Rocket Richard was appointed "assistant to the president of the Canadiens" with emphasis on public relations. The front-office communiqué also said he would aid in the development of hockey personnel. At first, Richard was overjoyed to be back with the club on a full-time basis. It appeared, at least superficially, that the New Order would rely on Richard's hockey wisdom instead of merely trading on his good name. This, however, would prove to be untrue and Richard eventually detected the deception and left the organization.

Frank Selke, Jr., son of the former managing director, was named vice-president for sales and publicity of the Canadian Arena Company. This was expected because of a desire to keep the Selke name affiliated with the team and also because the thirty-four-year-old had been master of ceremonies of the between-periods shows of the hockey telecasts.

Zeroing in on the target with the same flair he displayed as a player with the Montreal Junior Royals was dashing, blond thirty-five-year-old David Molson, who succeeded his cousin, the Senator, as president of Les Canadiens and the arena company. David had become increasingly active in the Canadiens' hockey business and was to become even more active in future years than his cousin had been during his term.

Just about the only key member of the organization to survive the upheaval was coach Toe Blake. Following Montreal's elimination from the play-offs, Blake expressed a certain disenchantment with the status quo. The pressure and general wear-and-tear of nine years behind the bench had frayed his nerves. "I want to live the way Toe Blake *used* to live," he said. Retirement was very much on his mind.

That, significantly, was at the close of the season. Hockey people always talk about retiring at that time. Blake carefully added a rider to his remarks: "I want a month or so to think about it."

A pincer movement of pressure from the Molsons, Pollock, and Selke was enough to persuade Blake to try one more year. Toe's only problem was the fact that referee Eddie Powers was suing him for remarks he had allegedly made following a Montreal-Toronto game. Aside from the rehiring of Blake, which won almost unanimous approval, there were mixed reactions to the Canadiens' upheaval. Some observers believed that an infusion of youth was both necessary and beneficial to the organization. Others pointed out that Pollock was a man of unimpeachable integrity as an organization man, a tireless worker, and a hockey brain without peer. Still others remarked that young Molson would be a better choice than the Senator because of his increased involvement with the team's affairs, not to mention his elaborate background as a player.

Critics, on the other hand, experienced annoying pangs of dispair over the handling of Selke who had no intentions of stepping down. "Considering Selke's performance," said Dick Beddoes in the Toronto *Globe and Mail*, "it is not agreed that Senator Molson had valid reason for detaching him from the managing director's chair. The age of seventy-one is beyond the biblical milestone of three score and ten, but it doesn't necessarily disqualify a man, except perhaps from the Olympic high jump. There is absolutely no evidence that he could not have continued to operate the Canadiens with the shrewd skill and unrivaled success that he exhibited when the team won five successive Stanley Cups. Moreover, he had earned the right to continue or retire as he preferred. . . . But some in the Molson family are in a hurry with what James Russell Lowell called 'the elbowing self-conceit of youth.' . . . Ken Reardon, a worthy vice-president, was flung into discard."

It was time for the New Order.

13

Sam Pollock
and the Contemporary Canadiens

Selke and Reardon weren't the only members of the alumni association dispairing of the new regime. The Rocket was soon to join them and then there was Bernie Geoffrion whose on-ice performance had slipped in recent years. When a coaching job opened at Quebec City, the Boomer announced his retirement from the N.H.L. and became coach of the American League Aces. Geoffrion hoped that with a couple of good years under his belt in Quebec he might—just might—get Blake's job when Toe decided to quit Les Canadiens.

The Rocket was provided with a small office in the Forum and awaited his assignment with the enthusiasm of a rookie. Unfortunately, the work never came. One afternoon, early in the 1964–1965 season, Peter Gzowski paid a visit to the Rocket. He came away with this report:

"However executive Maurice Richard's manner has become, a visitor to his vice-presidential office at the Forum can still see the fire in his eyes has only been banked; through an interview he twists and fiddles restlessly, as if wishing he could start just one more explosive rush down the boards, and hear 'vas-y Maurice' once more."

Nobody had come along to fill the Rocket's boots on the ice. Bill Hicke was a failure and now Les Canadiens turned to another small, chunky forward, Yvan Cournoyer, who had been promoted from the junior ranks. The handsome slick-haired skater betrayed brilliant flashes of speed and an enormously dynamic shot for his size. Cournoyer would prove to be an asset as a scorer but owned nothing like the tough fiber that Maurice displayed, and Yvan would be, at best, a very efficient but not a great hockey player. Another significant addition was tall, gangly Ted Harris, a raw-boned defenseman who would, in time, aid John Ferguson as the team tough guy. Goaltending was shared by Charlie Hodge and Gump Worsley, and the scoring, surprisingly, was paced by hard-checking Claude Provost, who skated with an abnormally wide stance.

Blake's decision to continue was a wise one for both himself and the hockey club, even though Les Canadiens finished second to a surprisingly strong Detroit sextet in March, 1965. This placed Montreal against Toronto in the first round of the play-offs and they disposed of the Leafs in six games with Provost and young Bobby Rousseau leading the attack. They had even less trouble with Chicago in the final, winning it in five games and the Stanley Cup. A new award, the Conn Smythe Trophy, for the most valuable player in the play-offs was won by captain Béliveau.

The success formula devised by Blake was interpreted in various ways by different analysts of the game. One theory had it that Toe was the ultimate tyrant who frightened his players by slamming doors, shouting at them on the bench, and doing sardonic dances in the dressing room. Selke, who was admittedly closer to Irvin than Blake, insisted that Toe was not a martinet. He contended that Blake empathized with his skaters more than most coaches and was a master psychologist. There was no question that when the times were right, Blake was an amiable chap who could go along with a jape.

Once, after Montreal had won the league championship the players were celebrating at a banquet in downtown Montreal. When they reached the banquet hall, somebody remarked, "This is room six. Does that mean number six [Ralph Backstrom] is paying the bill?"

Backstrom laughed. "It means the guy who wore it before me [Floyd Curry] can take care of it. But he's not here, so whoever had it before Curry and that's the coach."

Blake was standing there at the time. "Not me," he shot back with a leer. "Who wore number six before me?"

"Before you," chided Backstrom, "they used Roman numerals."

Blake was less amiable during a losing streak but, then again, so was Irvin and so many of the other excellent N.H.L. coaches.

"The Canadiens consistently deliver a greater percentage of their capabilities than any other team in hockey because of their respect for Blake," said Jim Proudfoot, Toronto *Daily Star* columnist. "Blake is the best coach in the National Hockey League."

Goalie Gump Worsley, who was playing the best goal of his life for Les Canadiens, put it another way: "There isn't a man on this club so important that the coach won't bench him if he doesn't move his butt. We all know that. Toe doesn't humiliate you or mouth off to the press. A guy just finds himself sitting the next one out and he sees some kid skating like the wind in his spot."

This was not a unanimous opinion. One who later rose to stardom under a different coaching technique was Gordon "Red" Berenson, whom the Canadiens signed after he had completed his studies at the University of Michigan. Berenson, a tall, rangy center, would have been a superb replacement for Béliveau had Blake managed to nurse him along properly, but the two never quite got along.

"I was a different kind of player compared to the ones Blake was accustomed to," Berenson once said. "He knew I was a college man and I don't think he believed I could make it. When your coach is thinking that way your chances are not too good."

Berenson's problem, aside from his college diploma, was that he shied away from heavy physical combat. By contrast, little Henri Richard seemed to enjoy mixing it with the musclemen and endeared himself to Blake right from the start. The coach liked to kid about the Pocket Rocket's diffidence. One day a magazine writer approached Blake and asked the coach whether young Richard spoke English. "The guy's so quiet," Blake replied, "I don't even know it he talks French."

Henri measured his words as carefully as he doled out passes. The first time he appeared on an English telecast of an N.H.L. game he was asked about his summer plans for keeping in shape. "I'm going to get married," he said, and left it at that.

Henri and Maurice Richard began drifting apart as the kid brother came into his own around the league. The Rocket was like the maternal lioness, watching over her cub at first but leaving it to fight for its place in the world once it reached maturity. For Henri, maturity came fast. He fought on even terms with his tormentors. He would not be run out of the league and he would be a very accomplished hockey player although never the electrifying personality that the Rocket was.

By contrast, the Pocket was determined but not explosive, strong but not overpowering. If the Rocket was the home-run hitter, the Pocket was more the base stealer and opposite-field hitter. He also had the Rocket's touch of the brooder in him. One season he invested twenty thousand dollars in a garage and renamed it Henri Richard's Automobiles. The venture failed and the experience had a very obvious effect on his play—all negative. "What bothered me more than losing the money," he confessed, "was that my name was in the business and it folded. I wouldn't admit it to myself, but it affected my play. I couldn't sleep and I couldn't get myself up for the games."

The Pocket Rocket was an essential cog in Selke's rebuilding plan, and he was an asset to Pollock, too, in Sam's first years in Montreal. Les Canadiens finished first in 1965–1966, breezed past Toronto in the first round of the play-offs with four straight wins, and appeared capable of disposing of the Detroit Red Wings at will in the Cup finals, especially since the series opened with two games at the Forum. But Detroit's hot hand, goalie Roger Crozier, was sizzling, and the Red Wings upset Les Canadiens in the first two games. They became favorites as the series shifted to Olympia Stadium. But Blake rallied his crew and Montreal didn't lose again. The Cup-winning goal was scored by the Pocket Rocket in sudden-death overtime as he slid feet-first toward the net. Crozier appeared to have the puck in hand but both the puck and the Pocket got past him. Richard crashed into the end boards and the puck slid into the goal.

While all this was going on, Boom Boom Geoffrion was leading the Quebec Aces to first place in the American League and casting an eye on Montreal where it was assumed that, sooner or later, Toe Blake would retire. Naturally, Geoffrion was hopeful that it would be sooner than later, but when Toe announced he would return to the Habitants' bench for the 1966–1967 season, Geoffrion figured that Blake's retirement would never come. That, as well as disenchantment with the Quebec situation, inspired Geoffrion to try a comeback, but not with Les Canadiens. He was acquired by the New York Rangers and went on to prove there was still life in his old legs and plenty or radar in his stick.

It was a strange and near-tragic year for the Flying Frenchmen. Béliveau nearly lost the sight of one eye after being hit by a stick, and Worsley was hospitalized following a curious accident at Madison Square Garden—he was hit in the head by an egg. Pollock surprised the N.H.L. when he imported a green goaltender named Rogatien Vachon from the minors to replace Worsley. Toronto's vocal Punch Imlach said Vachon was nothing but "a junior B goalie," but little Rogo managed to play capably if not frequently with a spectacular flair.

Despite the injuries, Les Canadiens finished second and confronted the Rangers in the opening round for the Stanley Cup. Coached by crafty Emile Francis, the Rangers had emerged as a budding new power in the league. Francis had hoped to take the play away from Montreal in the series' premiere at the Forum by outhitting Les Canadiens. The strategy seemed to be working splendidly as New York flabbergasted the Montreal crowd by running up a 4–1 lead midway in the third period. Even coach Blake was prepared to concede the game and was waiting for an opportunity to yank Vachon and replace him with Worsley. Then, with 10:48 remaining in the period, Claude Provost beat Ranger goalie Ed Giacomin from in close and reduced the margin to 4–2. From that point until the end of the game Montreal gave a vivid demonstration of its awesome power.

Les Canadiens pounced on the puck following the center-ice face-off and carried it directly into the Ranger zone. A pass was skimmed to defenseman J. C. Tremblay near the blue line. He wound up, cracked the puck, and it was past Giacomin only twenty-two seconds after Provost's goal. "From the minute they got their second goal to the end of the game we hardly seemed to touch the puck," said Francis. "I was wishing I could call a time-out."

The entire Ranger team turned impotent, and the Montreal skaters buzzed through the defenses until they won the game, 6–4. "It was," said Pete Axthelm, *Newsweek*'s sports editor, "as demoralizing a loss as any team could suffer."

Even Francis admitted it was difficult to hem in the speedy Montreal skaters. "Rugged-checking teams used to bother our fast skaters," added Blake. "But no more. Since we got some big guys ourselves—Ferguson, Terry Harper, and Ted Harris —we can hold our own in any brawls."

Nobody reinforced Blake's point more than the Pocket Rocket who tangled with tall Orland Kurtenbach, who was regarded as one of the best fighters in the league. "The body checks keep me in the game," said Henri. "I don't mind mixing it up with those big guys. But I wasn't looking to fight Kurtenbach although I looked good holding him back, anyway."

Rejuvinated by their come-from-behind win in the first game, Les Canadiens ousted the Rangers in four consecutive games, although each of them was relatively close. Players like defenseman J. C. Tremblay, who had skated lethargically during the season, appeared to have sipped a tonic as they sprinted past New York. "The money is here, big money," said Tremblay, explaining the motivation. "And it seems that I play better when the money is on the line."

For others the inspiration came from the seemingly prosaic influence of tradition, a factor no other team could match with the Flying Frenchmen. Béliveau, the distinguished captain and spokesman, expressed this feeling the way Georges Vézina might have said it decades earlier.

"There is no doubt that this team is very proud," said Béliveau. "We represent all of French Canada, and we know that a lot of people are counting on us. And we are very conscious of the tradition we must keep up. There were some good men here before us, you know. When I first came up Butch Bouchard was captain. Then it was the Rocket, then Doug Harvey and then myself. I'm following some great men and I want to be a service to the team. Being the oldest, I know that all the other players will keep going at top speed as long as they see me doing my best."

In a sense Béliveau fulfilled the most realistic expectations of management when he was named captain. His calm assurances proved to be a balm to the younger Canadiens and his deportment on ice was a tacit encouragement to the team as a whole. But the volcanic essence of the Rocket was nowhere to be found in Béliveau, so the natural reaction was to turn to the other Richard for fire and brimstone. Henri resented these demands as much as Béliveau.

"What do they expect from me?" the Pocket said. "I am me, not my brother. Maurice is the best hockey player of all time. I do not try to imitate him. I just try to do my best. All I can say is that I try to play my best."

Henri's best was quite good. Within five seasons of big-league hockey he had helped win five Stanley Cups; he made the All-Star Team twice; he led the league in assists; he finished second in scoring; and he was called the fastest skater of all time. "The Pocket," said Blake, "became a better all-round player than Rocket was. But it's asking an awful lot of any man to be the scorer that Rocket was. He was the greatest scorer under pressure that I've ever seen."

Selke defined their differences in another but equally cogent way: "Henri is mechanically better than Rocket was. But he doesn't have the killer instinct to be the great scorer that Rocket was."

Henri himself once elaborated on that theme. "My brother's biggest thrills came when he scored many goals. I am most satisfied when I play in a close game and do not have any goals scored against me. Sometimes people have asked me whether it helped or hurt having Maurice as an older brother.

"Sometimes it was not easy, because many people expected me to be as spectacular as Maurice. But I believe it helped me more than it hurt me. Don't forget, Maurice was a great scorer, and he could get goals that many other players could not get. That helped my passing because I knew that he would always be near the net waiting for a shot. But Maurice never gave me any advice. I never asked him for it and he never offered it. Except for a few fundamentals, it is hard to teach anyone how to play hockey. It is a game that you must learn yourself."

When Les Canadiens entered the 1967 Cup final against Toronto, of the stars of the Montreal team that had won the Stanley Cup in 1960 only Henri Richard and Béliveau remained. The total power of the fifties' dynasty was missing, and the goaltending of Worsley and Vachon could not match the perfection of vintage Jacques Plante. As a result, Toronto bumped Montreal out of the finals in six games.

In a sense the defeat marked the end of an era for Montreal as it did for the other five N.H.L. clubs. Expansion had finally come to hockey, and in June, 1967, representatives from Pittsburgh, Los Angeles, Oakland–San Francisco, Minneapolis–St. Paul, Philadelphia, and St. Louis participated in the draft to stock the six new teams of the West Division. The Canadiens were on the spot because they owned the most abundant stockpile of young talent in the N.H.L. and figured to be riddled by the hungry new clubs. But that was where the genius of Sam Pollock intervened to protect the glittering herd. Wheeling and dealing with expansion teams, Pollock peddled off enough fringe talent to enable Les Canadiens to retain the nucleus of a future winner and they entered the 1967–1968 season as strong as possible under the circumstances.

This time it required more than the usual time for Les Canadiens to get going. They were in last place in December, 1967, but soon achieved a relentless climb to the top that placed them first in the newly created East Division of the N.H.L. They then wiped out the Bruins and Black Hawks in short order and proceeded to the East-West final against the St. Louis Blues for the Stanley Cup.

The expansion sextet extended Montreal in each of the four games, but Les Canadiens gave the impression of a German shepherd toying with a kitten. At any given time the Montrealers suggested they could devour the Blues whole. It was merely a question of how much energy they wanted to generate. The next question was, How much talent would Pollock relinquish in the 1968 draft?

By West Division standards it was considerable. Los Angeles came up with Gerry Desjardins, who had starred in the Canadiens' farm system. Danny Grant, who was ultimately voted rookie of the year, went to Minnesota, and Norm Ferguson, runner-up for the rookie prize, was picked up by Oakland. That was for starters. Other Montrealers dotted the enemy rosters. Claude Larose became a star in Minnesota as did Danny O'Shea. The North Stars' manager, Wren Blair, did a low bow in the direction of Montreal to honor Pollock. "Look at it this way," said Blair. "Sam's big club made the final, and two of his farm clubs fought it out to meet the big club."

Pollock was appreciative. "I'm glad to see the teams we dealt with got their money's worth," he said.

In a matter of four years Pollock, at forty-three, had completely overshadowed his predecessor, Selke. The former managing director was forgotten as Pollock accepted the compliments as big-league hockey's presiding genius. "Sam," wrote Dick Beddoes in the *Globe and Mail,* "is the smartest man now connected with hockey in any front-office job." The words were kind, but Pollock would now have to reinforce them as he prepared to face the biggest challenge of his career.

14

Exit Toe Blake,
Enter Claude Ruel

"*T*his could be the last dynasty in professional sport," Wren Blair said of the 1968–1969 edition of Les Canadiens. "But it's one dynasty that may last a long time. It's going to be much harder to pull down the Canadiens than either the Yankees or the Green Bay Packers."

Blair's opinion was not unanimous for one very good reason: The pilot of Les Canadiens dynasty, coach Toe Blake, had finally given in to his better judgment and his nerves and retired after the 1968 championship sweep. In his thirteen years as coach, Blake had finished first nine times and won eight Stanley Cups. Few would argue that he was the finest all-round coach the N.H.L. has known.

"Under Toe's stabling influence," said Jim Proudfoot, "the Rocket earned the stature he surely would have missed otherwise. This might have been Blake's finest achievement as a coach. Another would be the rehabilitation of the Montreal club after it came apart in 1961 and 1962. In two years, Canadiens were back in first place and, a year after that, they won the Stanley Cup again."

Now it was up to Pollock to replace the great man. His choice was a superb touch of understatement, a man virtually unknown to but a choice few insiders, a man who had no major-league coaching experience and unlike Irvin or Blake had never played a game in the N.H.L. He was short (five foot five), fat (223 pounds), crew-cut, and so Santa Claus–like that you laughed when you saw him in spite of yourself. He was thirty-year-old Claude Ruel—not Rocket Richard and not

Floyd Curry, those most prominently mentioned for the job.

Delving beyond the superficialities of the appointment, one found elements of logic. Before he lost the sight of one eye in a hockey accident, Ruel had been one of the best junior defensemen in Canada. He later coached the Junior Canadiens and, in time, became the director of player development for the N.H.L. club. Perhaps more important, Ruel was the way Blake wasn't; he was Pollock's first handpicked choice to coach Les Canadiens. "Claude is the coach—the best man we had for the job," said Pollock in defending his choice against critics who charged that Sam would do the coaching from the sidelines.

Following Blake and Irvin was about as easy as a team of trained seals following Frank Sinatra and Barbra Streisand at the Copacabana. "Me, I can only go down," said Claude in his fractured English. "I can't go up."

"If the Canadiens finish first this season," said Paul Rimstead, ex–sports editor of *The Canadian* magazine, "and again win the Stanley Cup, people will say the players have done it again. But if Montreal slips, they'll say it's all Ruel's fault."

Montreal slipped all right! Les Canadiens appeared destined for third or fourth place by midseason, and there were rumblings that Ruel wasn't getting through to his men the way Blake had. But devoted Canadiens-watchers were quick to realize that the Flying Frenchmen often slumped in December (they had done it under Blake only a year earlier) and climbed to the top by March.

"I like the fundamentals of hockey," said the new pudgy mentor. "Skate, play position, and move that puck ahead. You got to be tough and honest for success."

Success came in the homestretch of the season. Les Canadiens moved ahead of the Rangers and the big, tough Bruins and remained in first place by a couple of points as they prepared to meet Boston twice on the final weekend of the season. The first match was at the Forum, the second in Boston. All the Canadiens needed was a win in the series opener and they would have first place all wrapped up.

Boston already had a well-earned reputation as the bully-boys of hockey, but when it came down to the sweat-inducing clutch game Montreal prevailed. It was the Bruins who won the Sunday night game, the one that didn't matter at all. In his first Stanley Cup round Ruel masterfully directed Montreal to a four-game rout of New York while Boston was doing the same to Toronto. As a result the archrivals, Montreal and Boston, met in the East Division final. It was Ruel's second major test against the bashing Bruins.

To many seasoned critics the Boston-Montreal East Division final of 1969 ranked as one of the best-played and most exciting of all hockey tournaments. It was the classic confrontation of the artists and the bullies, and Boston's Bruins bashed the Canadiens at every turn. Somehow the Montreal skaters managed to stay within striking distance of the Bruins despite being outplayed in the first two games. Les Canadiens rallied in the final minutes of both contests and won each in sudden-death overtime. Veteran Ralph Backstrom was the hero of the opening game and young Mickey Redmond was the sharpshooter in the second.

Boston finally asserted its mastery in the next two games played on Bruin ice and tied the series. At that point it appeared that the Canadiens would be knocked out of the series, but a key check thrown by John Ferguson against Boston's effective Derek Sanderson neutralized the Bruin center. Montreal won the fifth game with special help from another veteran, Claude Provost, and eliminated Boston in the sixth match when Jean Béliveau converted Provost's pass in sudden-death overtime.

Once again Les Canadiens were catapulted into the East-West finals against St. Louis amid loud assertions from the Blues' front office that the West Division representatives would not be humiliated in four straight games. However, the outcome was even more embarrassing than that of the previous spring. Montreal swept past the beleaguered and outclassed Blues in four games and presented coach Claude Ruel with a first-place championship, an East Division play-off win, *and* the Stanley Cup—all in his rookie year. Minutes after the final game Toe Blake walked down to the Canadiens' dressing room to congratulate his successor.

"He's done a terrific job," said Blake. "I've been through it all myself. I took over from a coach [Dick Irvin] who I always thought was the greatest. There was pressure on me from the start, but I think there was greater pressure on Ruel. Everybody sat back and waited for him to break down. He knew it. Nobody wanted to take into account that the team had a lot of troublesome injuries.

"The goaltenders were hurt. Other guys were hurt. Ruel, he knew everybody was waiting for him to fall on his face, but the team won it all and what more is there to say? I couldn't have my old job back now even if I wanted it."

In his joy, Sam Pollock impetuously added that Ruel "is with the team for life." He then toasted his personal choice—one who was considered too young and too inexperienced for the job eight months earlier—and accepted the compliments himself. "Nobody really knows how big a job he did for us," Pollock said.

The man who counted most, David Molson, joined the Ruel bandwagon, at least for 1969. "Let's face it," said Molson, "he was in a terrible position right from the start. If he failed to win, he would be severely criticized. If he did win, people would say he had nothing to do with it. That is just not so. He has done the job and he has done it well."

As the team dispersed, pundits around the N.H.L. again wondered what special formula Les Canadiens distilled to achieve such eminence, to conduct themselves, as Montreal *Star* sports editor Red Fisher noted, "like so many great Canadiens teams of other years."

Fisher had followed Les Canadiens closely throughout the Blake era. Probing at the contemporary champions, he came up with this conclusion: "Some of it is the coaching and a lot of it is the system and what all of it comes down to is that nobody really can be certain when a big game will be forthcoming from any one of the athletes dressed for a game.

"When Lorne Worsley was injured midway through the Boston series, there were strong doubts that Rogatien Vachon could do the job. He did. On some nights Jean Béliveau was the large-sized talent and on others Serge Savard controlled the play. And in the grand finale the goals came from Ted Harris and John Ferguson, and it is sufficient to mention that Harris's goal was his first in play-off competition."

The glow of victory in Montreal completely obscured some ominous storm clouds which were relentlessly gathering over the horizon. They were, however, visible to many hockey men in Boston and other parts of the N.H.L. It was pointed out that the mainstay of Les Canadiens, captain Béliveau, was aging rapidly and would be less and less effective. It was also noted that goalie Worsley was getting older and Henri Richard was no longer young. The Bruins, by contrast, would ice a strong, young team, led by the irrepressible Bobby Orr, and the Montreal dynasty would surely end in 1969–1970.

Perhaps Ruel had that in the back of his mind as he returned home to relax through the summer of 1969. "Just wait until next year," he warned. "They will write that I had nothing to do with this. They will write this, I know."

It is possible that Ruel had no idea how prophetic he would be. The world champion Canadiens entered the 1969–1970 campaign odds-on-favorites to sweep all the prizes—and promptly fell on their collective faces. Injuries disabled key men with the same frequency as they had in the previous season. Béliveau and Ferguson were the hardest hit. Gilles Tremblay, unable to shake his chronic asthma, retired completely, and other stars were sidelined for long periods.

Through typically clever manipulation, Pollock managed to retain the bulk of his championship roster despite the intense N.H.L. draft. But he made one crucial mistake. He chose to leave sub-goaltender Tony Esposito unprotected in the draft and decided that his "Big Three" netminders would be Worsley, Vachon, and young Phillipe Myre, a tall French-Canadian with enormous promise. Esposito had played twelve games for Les Canadiens in 1968–1969 and displayed an unorthodox but effective style of puck-blocking. He was claimed in the 1969 draft by Chicago and emerged in the new season as the most spectacular and effective goaltender in either division. By contrast, both Worsley and Vachon were playing mediocre hockey.

Even worse was the fact that loud grumblings of dissension were detected inside the Canadiens' dressing room; something that was never noticeable during Blake's regime. Béliveau had spent a good part of the summer cultivating a significant and apparently successful public-relations business. He arrived at camp exhausted and never regained his old-time form. In time, his injuries caught up with him.

Dick Duff, the experienced left wing who had played so vital a role in the 1969 Stanley Cup triumph, became saddled with personal problems as well as nonhockey physical woes. He, too, was hospitalized. Worsley, meanwhile, was having his problems with Ruel and wound up on the bench. When Pollock suggested that Gump spend some time with Les Voyageurs, Montreal's new farm team in the American League, Worsley adamantly refused. Now the feud was in the open. Duff recuperated from his ailment but angered Ruel by missing several practices.

That did it. Worsley was suspended without pay and was finished with Les Canadiens. Duff was given additional time to work out his dilemma, but Pollock saw no signs of reform. The Canadiens' manager traded him to the Los Angeles Kings. A month later Worsley was dealt to the Minnesota North Stars.

While all this was going on, Les Canadiens moved up and down like a Yo-Yo between second and third place, never quite able to reorganize for the assault on the top. The return of Béliveau and Ferguson was expected to rejuvenate the team but then Ferguson was hospitalized a second time when a puck accidentally struck him in the face, painfully breaking a cheekbone.

The dismissal of Duff and Worsley was expected to glue the club together and restore the old élan that characterized the Canadiens of yesteryear, but Ruel looked on with more and more concern as the team continued to falter. Finally, in late February, 1970, the coach himself betrayed signs of cracking. In so many words, he offered to hand in his resignation.

"I had a talk with Sam Pollock and Mr. Molson," Ruel revealed. "I told them if they felt someone else could get more out of the team, not to be afraid to make the move. It's going to be tough to make first place now. They can't do it by changing eighteen players from the Voyageurs but they can replace one man. I think enough of the team to want that if it will help. With someone else behind the bench, the players that are not working now may decide to prove something.

"This thought has been with me for many weeks. I don't want to put myself in a box worrying. When you push and push your players and there's no improvement something must be wrong. I'm no detective but I know something is wrong when some fellows feel like playing one night and leave it up to the other guys in the next game."

Pollock refused to panic into a coaching change. He pointed out that injuries had crippled the club, that Béliveau might be at the end of his career, and that Montreal fans, of all people, had hurt the team as much as any factor. "They've become spoiled by success," said Pollock. "Sometimes it seems they're rooting harder for the visiting club than they are for us. This has to have an effect on our club and it might explain why we've done so poorly at the Forum and so well on the road."

On March 5 the Montreal *Star* told the depressing story of the Habitants with a simple headline: "FIFTH PLACE LOOMS LARGE FOR WOBBLING CANADIENS."

The Montrealers had lost, 2–1, to the Pittsburgh Penguins, and players like Mickey Redmond began wondering how the club was supposed to win a game. "We never stopped working," said Redmond. "We outshot them. The puck just wouldn't go in."

Explanations for the Canadiens' demise were a dime a dozen among hockey men, but it took Pierre Leblanc, a Montreal bellhop and a student of the Canadiens, to isolate the problem. "It is wrong to blame the coaching or any other reason but one," said Leblanc. "When the Canadiens were successful it was always because they had three excellent centers, Béliveau, Richard, and Backstrom. That is the key in hockey. Now Béliveau is thirty-nine, the Pocket Rocket is thirty-four, and Backstrom is a very old thirty-two. It means that they are no longer able to skate as fast as before and that they get hurt more often. That is the story this year and forget about everything else."

By March 10 the Canadiens had plummeted to fifth place. They had lost on successive days to Detroit and Boston and there were more and more frequent demands for Ruel's scalp. "It's ridiculous to criticize the coach," Béliveau insisted. "He is the same coach we had last season. The players themselves are to blame. We know what has to be done. We've done it before. We don't need to be told. And it is a fact—I haven't been producing."

The agonizing question of what to do about Ruel was finally resolved when Pollock announced that the rotund coach had been signed to a new contract for the 1970–1971 season with an increase in pay and the usual vote of confidence from management. "If we're in trouble," said Pollock, "it's because a few of the hockey players haven't been playing as well as they should."

Béliveau, of course, was one of the prime culprits, but Pollock went out of his way to exonerate the Canadiens' distinguished captain. "That man has carried the team for so many years . . . carried players . . . put money in their pockets . . . now that he's having troubles on the ice, nobody is helping him. That's where the problem is."

What emerged as one of the most fascinating aspects of the Canadiens' downfall was the effect it was having on the players themselves. For most of the varsity members it was unthinkable, not to mention insulting, to be groping for a play-off berth. If the Canadiens fought for anything, it was first place.

"This is a new experience for us," said Béliveau. "In other years the pressure would be on us because of our fight for first place. Last year we went to the seventy-fifth game. At least we knew that if we did not finish first we would finish second. Now we are fighting to stay alive. It's an experience I would have enjoyed missing."

On March 11 the Canadiens played what, for them, was the most important game of the season. It was at the Forum against the Rangers who entered the game with a seven-point lead over the Canadiens. A win for New York would have almost surely sealed Montreal's doom. But if the Canadiens prevailed, they would have pulled themselves to within three points of the Rangers with more than two weeks left in the schedule.

This time the Canadiens rose nobly to the occasion. They built up a 3–0 lead and cruised home to a 5–3 win over the Rangers. Several explanations were advanced for the turnabout. One had it that the re-signing of Ruel inspired the players to put out, or else. Another was a handwritten letter that had been posted in the Canadiens' dressing room prior to the game. It was from a distraught mother whose six-year-old son was dying of leukemia. The woman urged the Canadiens to come up with a win for her son, who had a great love for the Montreal sextet but had only a short time to live. "And to think we've been feeling sorry for ourselves," said Backstrom. "A letter like that has to have an effect on you."

But by the time the game had ended some of the Canadiens were still feeling sorry for themselves, and perhaps they had good reason. Serge Savard, Montreal's versatile defenseman, broke his leg during the game and would be lost to the team for the rest of the season. "My best guy gone," moaned Ruel. "It's the worst man we could possibly lose now. He did two jobs for me, played defense and killed penalties. But those other guys owe him something. Okay, in pro sport you say there isn't sentiment. But Serge put money in their pockets and they owe him something. Remember last year? Serge hooked the puck from Phil Esposito and took it all the way down ice to score and we came off with a big play-off win."

With Savard gone, Ruel turned to John Ferguson for support. "In the dressing room, before the game, and between periods that Fergy makes a difference," said Ruel. "He talks and yells. He makes them listen and he makes them mad. He's the key in this run."

Ferguson responded with an electrifying effort on the weekend of March 14 and 15 as the Canadiens whipped the Blues at St. Louis and tied Toronto at Maple Leaf Gardens. But Ferguson wasn't alone in sparking the Habitants; a surprise plus was Peter Mahovlich, the huge kid-brother of Detroit's Frank Mahovlich.

The six-foot-four-inch 215-pound Mahovlich had played most of the season on the Canadiens' farm team, Les Voyageurs, but he was elevated to the big team when left wing Jacques Lemaire was injured. A pep talk by the voluble Ferguson helped energize Mahovlich. "You're the biggest player in the league," said Ferguson. "Why are you playing so politely? You should be skating over the top of people. Go after them!"

On March 21 the Canadiens defeated Philadelphia, 2–0, and a day later they edged Pittsburgh, 5–4. Suddenly they had climbed over the slumping Rangers and were back in fourth place. Mahovlich was the star in each game.

"Mahovlich has been moving," said his linemate Henri Richard. "He's been busting from behind and getting in position. That's why the line has been going well."

"It's also a matter of confidence," said the fun-loving Mahovlich. "It's difficult to explain, but it's important. You find you're making plays with assurance instead of hesitating like before when you were scared of making a mistake. I knew the Canadiens originally got me to play for the Voyageurs. Injuries gave me the chance to make the Canadiens. And now I feel I belong up here in the N.H.L."

The Canadiens defeated Toronto, 5–2, on March 25, giving them an unbeaten string of six wins and two ties and lifting them to third place. But they were still not out of danger of losing the coveted play-off berth. A home-and-home series with the Rangers confronted them on the weekend of March 28 and 29. A double victory or even one win would help keep them well ahead of the Rangers, and for a time it appeared that the Canadiens would preserve their margin.

The teams were deadlocked in a scoreless tie on March 28 when Mahovlich scored on a power play for the Canadiens at 11:27 of the third period. This appeared to be enough to insure the Canadiens of a victory, but with less than three minutes remaining, Béliveau lost a face-off to Walt Tkaczuk of the Rangers. The puck skittered to New York's Dave Balon who returned the puck to Tkaczuk. Having eluded Béliveau, Tkaczuk fired the puck between goalie Rogatien Vachon's legs and the teams left the ice with a 1–1 tie.

On the following night the Rangers outplayed Montreal for a 4–1 win, and suddenly the Canadiens appeared to be in trouble again. Only three more games remained in the regular schedule, but the Rangers were revived and apparently capable of finishing the season with a flourish. Les Canadiens had three games remaining on their schedule. Wednesday night at home against Boston, Saturday night at home against Chicago, and Sunday night against the Black Hawks at Chicago.

Facing the Bruins was hardly an appealing prospect for the Canadiens. Boston was trying to maintain its hold on first place, and the Bruins' defenseman, Bobby Orr, was on the verge of being the first backliner to win the league's scoring championship. "We've got to keep the puck away from Orr," Ruel said. "He controls the game; he can win it by himself, so try to keep it away from him."

Before Orr had a chance to organize an attack, Béliveau had struck for the Canadiens. Phil Esposito tied the game for Boston but Béliveau scored again and then Orr finally broke through. But this time the Canadiens didn't crack. They responded with another goal before the end of the first period and two more in the second. The teams exchanged scores in the last period and Montreal skated off the ice with a surprisingly one-sided 6–3 victory over Boston.

It was a remarkable turn of events from the Canadiens' point of view because the supposedly jaded Béliveau and the oft-injured Ferguson towered above the other skaters to lead their team to victory. Once again, the renowned Montreal élan had surfaced and helped them overwhelm the Bruins.

"The way the Canadiens in general," said Boston writer D. Leo Monahan, "and the ageless Béliveau in particular, were skating through and around the Boston defense, this writer wonders if the Bruins could have won that game if they had *both* their goalies out there at the same time."

Boston players agreed that the suddenly rejuvenated Béliveau called the shots in the game. "We let him control the puck," said Ken Hodge, "and he controlled the game."

Béliveau added: "I felt good and we were skating. The chances were there. They gave them to us and we had to take them. This was a game we had to win."

Coach Ruel bubbled like a child who had just opened his Christmas presents and got everything he had hoped for. "Early in the night," said Ruel, "we knew we could play our game and make Boston play it, too. They did not hit. They did not skate. We played good. We have spirit. We have pride. We want to win more than they do; so we win!"

The Canadiens entered the final weekend of the season nestled in third place, just three points behind Boston and Chicago, who were tied for the top, and just one point ahead of fourth-place Detroit and two points ahead of fifth-place New York. In this, the closest pennant race in National Hockey League history, the Canadiens were confronted with their final two games knowing that they could either finish as high as first place or as low as fifth and out of the play-offs for the first time since 1948.

The Canadiens by now had lowered their target. Retaining the Prince of Wales Trophy was out of the question, barring a miracle. Second and third place were possible, but the realists in the Montreal front office admitted privately that they would be delighted enough with fourth place and a Stanley Cup berth.

To most observers, particularly the younger ones, the idea of the Canadiens finishing out of the play-offs was incomprehensible. After all, Montreal had been competing regularly in the Stanley Cup round since the 1948–1949 season. Even more alarming to Canadian hockey fans was the prospect of Montreal finishing fifth and Toronto sixth. This would mark the first season since Stanley Cup play began in 1893 that a team from Canada had failed to make the play-offs.

The burden of responsibility lay with Béliveau. "Against Boston," the captain explained, "I felt I was going to play my best game and when I get that feeling I know we're going to win."

What perplexed Montreal rooters prior to the opening face-off against Chicago on April 4 was whether or not Jean Béliveau was getting "that feeling." Their opponents were the Black Hawks, paced by high-scoring Bobby Hull and Stan Mikita, and ex-Canadiens goalie Tony Esposito, who had already broken the N.H.L.'s shutout record. It was an awesome challenge for the Canadiens.

The pressure on the Canadiens kept building as the final weekend series with the Black Hawks approached. Nonpartisan visitors to the Montreal dressing room were able to detect the tension. "For the first time in the careers of every man on this team there is danger," said John Ahern of the Boston *Globe*. "In this locker room joy has been replaced by apprehension and the situation is strange to them. No one knows for sure whether the team can cope with it."

Veteran defenseman Terry Harper put it another way: "I was hoping that somebody would walk in the room and tell me to wake up and stop dreaming. I hope I'm dreaming bad dreams."

Saturday night, April 4, was like a nightmare for the

Canadiens. Try as they might, they could not cope with an overbearing Chicago attack and the Black Hawks stout defense, commanded by Tony Esposito. Before the game was twelve minutes old the visitors had a 2–0 lead. Dennis Hull and Bryan Campbell made it 4–0 for Chicago in the second period before John Ferguson scored for Montreal. The Canadiens lost the game, 4–1, but they still held a commanding edge in the race with New York for the fourth and final playoff berth.

The Rangers had cooperated by losing, 6–2, to the Red Wings at Detroit. Thus, Les Canadiens still held a two-point lead over New York. All Montreal required was a win or a tie at Chicago on Sunday night, April 5, or a Ranger loss or a tie when the New Yorkers played Detroit on Sunday afternoon at Madison Square Garden.

But should New York win and Montreal lose, the teams would be tied for fourth in points. Then the decision would rest with the goals-scored column, based on a league rule to handle such deadlocks. According to National Hockey League policy, the team with the most goals scored would be the winner. Since Les Canadiens held a five-point lead in this column, they were overwhelming favorites to retain fourth place, whether the Rangers won or lost.

Then the utterly impossible happened. The Rangers, who played in the afternoon, five and a half hours before the Canadiens, *scored nine goals*—something they had not done all season—and routed the Red Wings, 9–5.

The contest, which was carried on the C.B.S. television network, was viewed by the Montreal players as they prepared for their game against Chicago. What perplexed the Canadiens—and for good reason—was the strategy of the Red Wings, which, to say the least, did not appear designed for victory.

Detroit's general manager–coach, Sid Abel, used his ace, Gordie Howe, for only three shifts in the first two periods and limited the use of some of his other stars. He started his spare goaltender, Roger Crozier, rather than his regular goalie,

Roy Edwards, and he opened the game with a mediocre starting line of Gary Croteau, Al Karlander, and Ron Harris, the latter normally a defenseman. The Rangers scored within thirty-six seconds of the opening face-off against the inept Red Wing line.

Montreal players were startled by what they saw on their hotel television screens. "Their effort isn't up to N.H.L. standards," said defenseman Jacques Laperriere. "Those guys have no pride," added Yvan Cournoyer. "They don't have to lay down and die," snapped Mickey Redmond.

Newsmen surrounded Abel immediately after the game, demanding an accounting of his team's performance, not to mention his dubious strategy. "I wanted to rest several of my older players," said Abel. "This is my prerogative. I can rest players if I want to. The fact is, I didn't rest some of them as much as I had hoped."

The Detroit boss argued that the Ranger game represented the fourth in five nights for his team and that his older players had usually been weary in similar situations. "I couldn't tell my men to go out and butt the Rangers all over the place. We'd been through a very rough week and it was just asking too much to play some of the men."

Abel defended his use of Crozier on the grounds that Edwards had been suffering from nervous attacks and he commended Crozier's performance. "I did not concede second place before the game," said Abel. "And I don't think the game was a farce. The Rangers really turned it on and we couldn't turn it off."

The more Abel defended his masterminding, the less convincing he became. He pointed out that the Rangers were going for as many goals as possible, which was true, but his concluding remark raised grave doubts about his intentions. "I told my guys before the thing ever started that this would be something like a 9–8 game!"

Fidgety in Chicago, the Canadiens had little choice now but to go out and win or tie against the Black Hawks, who, in turn, required a victory to capture first place in the East

Division. Of course, the Canadiens could also lose and capture fourth, but they would have to score five goals now to do so.

For a few brief moments the Canadiens enjoyed a last romance with success. With Doug Jarrett of Chicago in the penalty box, Montreal mounted a power play which culminated in a goal from the stick of Cournoyer. The time was 9:12 and it would be the last time Les Canadiens would hold a lead for the rest of the season.

Less than seven minutes later Jim Pappin tied the score for Chicago while Ted Harris of the Canadiens sat in the penalty box. A penalty to Jacques Lemaire late in the first period sealed Montreal's doom. Pit Martin quickly scored again for the Hawks and for the rest of the game the Canadiens desperately tried to catch up—and failed.

The Hawks made it 3–1 early in the second period on a goal by Bobby Hull. In a last gasp Jean Béliveau scored for Montreal, reducing Chicago's lead to one goal. It remained that way through the early minutes of the third period as the tense Canadiens pressed for the tying score. But they were constantly frustrated by the stiffening Chicago defense and goalie Esposito. Finally, Martin broke through again for Chicago to score two quick goals and lift the Black Hawks' lead to 5–2 with 10:44 remaining in the game.

At that point coach Ruel summoned goalie Vachon to the bench and replaced him with an extra forward. The Canadiens were prepared to concede the loss but realized they could catch the Rangers by scoring three more goals. Ruel was doing exactly what Emile Francis, his New York counterpart, had done earlier in the day. He left his net wide open with several minutes remaining in the match.

The spectacle of top clubs firing at length on untended nets inspired cries of "parody, mockery, burlesque, travesty, farce, and bush" from sportswriters across Canada and the United States. "I had no choice," Ruel said later. "We were fighting for that play-off berth, and we needed goals."

Ruel, unfortunately, did not get them. The overanxious

Canadiens flubbed every opportunity and were humiliated at every turn. Chicago, though shorthanded, dominated the play, and Eric Nesterenko, Cliff Koroll, Bobby Hull, Dennis Hull, and Gerry Pinder each scored into the empty Montreal net. The Canadiens lost the game, 10–2, and skated off the Chicago Stadium ice in a veritable state of shock. For the first time in twenty-two years Montreal was not represented in the Stanley Cup play-offs!

The gloom could be cut with a knife in the solemn Canadiens' dressing room. When a newspaperman approached John Ferguson, he timidly inquired of the distressed left-winger, "Do you have a minute?"

"Do I have a minute?" Ferguson replied with mock sarcasm. "Hell, I've got all summer!"

A few seats away sat Henri Richard, who had not missed a play-off in fourteen years. "It's like a bad dream," said the Pocket Rocket.

Lantern-jawed Claude Provost, who had joined the Canadiens in the same 1955–1956 season along with Richard, allowed that the Canadiens had nobody to blame but themselves. "When we picked up only one point on the last two weekends of the schedule against teams we had to beat, we hardly deserved to be in the play-offs."

One of the team's most significant disappointments was the inferior play of defenseman Ted Harris, who had been an All-Star the previous season. "We kept telling ourselves we'd snap out of it in the next game," said Harris. "Today there's no next game."

Pundits explored all avenues of the Canadiens' failure in an attempt to discern exactly what had brought about the disastrous nose dive. General manager Sam Pollock was criticized for permitting Tony Esposito, Gump Worsley, and Dick Duff to leave the fold. Claude Ruel was blasted for his inability to maintain an aura of diligence and harmony on the roster. Captain Béliveau was chastised for devoting too much time to his nonhockey enterprises.

In an elaborate postmortem, the Montreal *Gazette* made

additional points: "The Canadiens didn't get the kind of goal-tending (from Rogatien Vachon) that helps to win champion-ships. The young goalie, often injured but still playing, was notably weak in the finishing fortnight of the schedule.

"Coach Ruel made some mistakes, too, especially in hurt-ing the morale of the club when he offered to quit if the players wouldn't work harder. Even now he doesn't come out sounding bright, without accepting some of the blame, himself, and for his reasoning why the Canadiens flopped."

Specifically, the *Gazette* was referring to Ruel's own post-game observations: "There's no doubt we were in trouble because of injuries. But this shouldn't be a reason why some players couldn't have doubled their efforts. A few players gave everything they had from start to finish but too many others worked only when they felt like it. There's no way to win like that. Last year I had eighteen players going all out but only half as many this season."

What Ruel failed to discuss was the reasoning behind his diatribe. Under Toe Blake there was no question that eighteen players would go all out at all times. Why couldn't they do the same for Ruel? Two reporters close to the scene had some theories. "There have been claims, too, with some evidence, that Ruel lost his rein on the team and that the thirty-one-year-old's lack of experience when the chips are down haven't helped," said Pat Curran of the *Gazette*.

John Robertson, the Montreal *Star's* incisive columnist, had been the most outspoken critic of Ruel all season. "He was failing," said Robertson, "because it is just not in him to lead with authority, to command loyalty and respect, to in-spire individuals to play together—for him—as a team.

"The ship has foundered without the firm, confident hand of a Blake or an Irvin to steer it. In their place, a nice little guy . . . turned bitter and confused and blaming the players for failing him. . . . When a team doesn't respond to a coach, you either have to change the coach or change the team. And the players, with hardly an exception, have proven they will indeed respond, under a leader they respect."

Dink Carroll, a veteran columnist, who had covered some of the more famous Montreal teams, looked at it another way. "Prolonged success may have made them a little fat. They lost too many games they could have won if they had all worked and played together as a team. They were waiting for George to do it, but George wasn't around. . . . The Rangers did what they had to do and the Canadiens didn't.

"The Canadiens are off the scene temporarily, but they'll be back. Suffering refines the spirit and they will suffer when they don't receive that bonus bundle that used to come their way almost automatically when the play-offs were over."

And so, explanation piled on explanation as the play-offs, for the first time in the history of hockey, were completed in their entirety in United States cities. Stung by the defeat, the Canadiens' management set about the business of rebuilding the crumbled empire.

No one questioned that the empire had crumbled. The Montreal *Gazette* played a black-bordered headline across the top of its front page, which suggested an obituary. It read:

R.I.P.—A STANLEY CUP PLAY-OFF
DYNASTY ENDS: CANADIENS (1949–1970)

All the key members of the Canadiens' family turned up at the press conference in the Forum on Tuesday, April 7. There were very few recriminations and those that were tossed inevitably zeroed in on the Red Wings and their sub-par effort against the Rangers in the essential Sunday afternoon match in New York, and Abel's decision to rest his stars.

"Maybe he [Abel] didn't do anything wrong," said Toe Blake, "but if he did, he'll have to live with his conscience for the rest of his life."

It was pointed out that the Red Wings still had a chance for second place when they went up against the Rangers, but they seemed content to settle for a play-off berth; and that was all. "I can't understand it," said Pollock. "All Toe was ever interested in was first place. Other coaches . . . all they want is to finish in the play-offs."

To which Blake added: "I don't doubt the players on the ice were doing the best they could. But why say you're resting Howe and Mahovlich and then put them on the ice later? Mahovlich scored as soon as he got on and Howe was killing penalties in the third period. Is that resting him? I wonder. I wonder if the players were fit to play their best."

But to the credit of the Canadiens' executives they dwelled not so much on the Red Wings but on their own failures. "We blame ourselves," said Pollock. "We lost. It's not just one game, it's a whole season that decides it. That's the crux of the whole bloody thing."

Club president David Molson was there. He had originally planned to discuss the Canadiens' play-off prospects. Instead, he simply apologized for his team's finish and with a minimum of grief.

"This is not a postmortem or a crying session," said Molson. "I'm just sorry we couldn't make the season longer. But we were beaten by a better club. Chicago deserved to win. We only hope that next year our team will be strong enough to win the big games. We didn't quite have it when we needed it most this season. There will be some changes but I'm not prepared to talk about them now."

The Canadiens' bid to gain a play-off berth in the 1970–1971 season was dealt a two-pronged blow in mid-October, 1970, when veteran forwards John Ferguson and Ralph Beckstrom suddenly announced their retirement at the beginning of the new campaign.

And so the Canadiens were dead—blasted from the top when they least expected it. Now they face the future with more uncertainty than at any time in their modern history. But the men at the helm believe they can steer the team to its former eminence, a challenge that will be more difficult than ever before. The onus is on Molson and Pollock, and both appear ready to accept the responsibility.

"Remember," said Pollock, "you've got to die to be born again."

PART II

*MY LIFE
WITH THE CANADIENS
by Maurice Richard*

1

My
Early Years

I first began following Les Canadiens during the Howie Morenz era. Hockey came naturally to me. My father, Onésime Richard, had been quite a good semipro hockey player and a fine baseball player, too. He encouraged me to be active in sports, and when I was only four years old he bought me my first pair of ice skates.

In those days we lived in the Bordeaux section of Montreal, which is the north end of the city. Nearly everybody who lived there was French-Canadian, like ourselves, and English was never spoken in our house. The other thing I had in common with the neighbors was a passionate love of hockey.

Winters were colder in those years, the late twenties, and there were fewer cars on the streets. So it was quite ordinary for me and my friends to skate on the streets to school and back home every day from early December to the end of February.

I didn't mind school very much, but mostly my mind was on hockey. Besides skating to school all the time, I used to skate on the frozen Back River near our house, or sometimes on our makeshift backyard rink or on the public rink run by the city. If we got tired of those places we could always pick ourselves up and go to a nearby field where there was a little lake and skate on that until we had really developed our skating technique. It was a completely different situation from what it is today. Nowadays, the city is so built up the only place where kids can play is on a public rink where they are much more regimented than we were. Our gang would play shinny on the river; that is, one guy would take the puck and defy the others—sometimes it was more than a dozen kids—to try to get it away. The only way a kid like that could retain the puck was by learning to be a good stick-handler. Which is why there were so many better stick-handlers in my day.

Much as I wanted to see a National Hockey League game at the Forum, it was next to impossible. We didn't have that much money in the house, although my father was working at the Canadian Pacific Railways' shop in Montreal. But the Depression hit Canada when I was about eight years old and things got tough and very tight from then on. To make ends meet I'd get a part-time job whenever I could. During the summer I used to go to the golf course and make seventy-five cents a day as a caddy.

The closest I came to the Forum was via the radio. Saturday-night home games were broadcast over CBF, the French-Canadian station in Montreal. By the time I was fourteen years old listening to the games every Saturday night had become a ritual with me. Up until then I really didn't have any particular favorite, although I had heard a lot about Morenz and Aurel Joliat, and pretty soon I'd get to meet and know Aurel. But once I started tuning in to the games I became more interested in the players.

It's funny the way kids develop their favorites. In my case there was no way of really knowing what the players were like because I never had the opportunity to see them play and I read very little about them in the newspapers. So my reaction had to come directly from the radio announcer's descriptions, and one player soon began appealing to me more than the others. Of course, at that time I had no idea that he would eventually play a very, very important part in my career; all I knew was that I liked the sound of his name and I liked the way the announcer described him.

That was none other than Toe Blake, who was just a youngster with the Canadiens then and who would eventually become my tutor, my linemate, and finally my coach. Hearing the announcer say, "Blake *lance, y compte!*" ("Blake shoots, he *scores!*") was the greatest thrill I could have had in those days as a young hockey fan.

Mostly, though, I was more interested in playing hockey than anything else. Being a spectator wasn't that important to me, and the proof of it is, I never went to see a game at the Forum in all the years that I played minor-league hockey in Montreal. Part of the reason was that I didn't have the money but, more than that, I didn't have that much time because whenever there was a free hour and some ice available, I was playing.

The first organized hockey I played was for our parish team. In my midget and juvenile years I played in the park leagues and then, when I went on to Montreal Technical High School, I played for them. By this time I had developed an unquenchable thirst for the ice. I played six days a week in organized games and on the seventh day I would prac-tice, sometimes with my father.

If a fellow really put his mind to it, he could play all the hockey he wanted. I put my mind to it. I met Georges Norchet at Technical High School and he asked me to play juvenile hockey with him at Parc Lafontaine. We won the city Juvenile Championship. In that same year I met his sister Lucille with whom I fell in love and later married. That same year I played with the Verdun Maple Leafs, in Junior A, and also with Bordeaux.

Of course in my early teens I had no plans for becom-ing a professional hockey player. Even though I played a lot, I wasn't really that good and I was still thinking about playing hockey for fun and learning a trade at school so that I could earn a living when I graduated. I studied to be a machinist, and during the summer I worked for a crane com-pany, which wasn't a bad job. In fact I kept at it one winter when I was also playing junior hockey. But it was becoming apparent that being a machinist was losing out to hockey. By now I was playing two games a *night*, and on weekends I played Saturday afternoon and Saturday night; then on

Sunday afternoon and Sunday night. Funny thing was, it didn't bother me a bit.

A young fellow can play a dozen games a day and it won't help him become a professional unless there is an older man around to give him directions. In my case that man was Paul Stuart, who coached my team and who took an interest in me. He phoned the Verdun coach, Art Therrien, and told him about me and arranged for me to practice with them. I didn't play regularly at first but that was okay. It was important to watch and skate with better players and I was still able to play with the other teams. Nowadays, that wouldn't be possible because if you play for one team you can't play for any others. But in the early thirties the league officials weren't strict, so I simply used a different name when I signed for each team and nobody seemed to mind it a bit.

In the second year with Verdun I began to click. They made me a regular and the goals started to come. By the end of the season I was the best goal-getter on the team.

The Canadiens Seniors were what amounted to a lower but important farm team of the Canadiens. Since the junior team was located in Montreal it was easy enough for Canadiens scouts to watch our games and if they liked any of our players there was a chance they would promote us to the Canadiens.

I had a good play-off with the Maple Leafs and the following year I got the thrill of my early career—an invitation to practice with the Canadiens Seniors. I could have played one more year of junior hockey because I was only nineteen at the time and a boy was eligible for the juniors until he was twenty. But I decided I'd benefit more if I could play with the big team, and when they said they wanted me, I leaped at the chance to go with them. Some people say it's better for a young player not to rush himself; that he should develop without too much pressure and not leave the juniors too soon. In my case they may have been right.

In my very first game with the Canadiens Seniors I was skating in front of the net when someone tripped me and the two of us fell to the ice. We were both going at full speed and when we fell we slid along the ice. I was on my stomach and all of a sudden I noticed I was heading straight for the boards like a torpedo heading for a battleship. There was a terrible crash with my foot banging the boards so hard that my ankle broke. The pain was terrible and I knew right then and there that I'd be through for the rest of the season.

This was a disastrous start for a pro hockey career. I spent the winter recuperating and wondering whether I'd ever be the same when I returned. I was very gloomy about the whole business, but by late winter, the injury had healed and I returned to the lineup in time for the play-offs.

Coming back at the end of the season was a good tonic because at least it whet my appetite for more hockey. I was quite enthused when I showed up at the Seniors' training camp the next fall. I didn't have much trouble making the team and I was off to a pretty good start this time. After ten games I felt for the first time that I really belonged and I began dreaming of making the N.H.L. sometime in the not too distant future. Then, the roof fell in on me again!

I was making a play near the net when I decided to swoop around the right side and come out on the left. Before I could actually make my move I felt a stick crack against my leg. Suddenly, I had lost my balance and extended my arm for protection. My glove hit the steel upright at the side of the net. My body went forward but my wrist rapped against the steel and I could hear that terrible sound of the bone breaking. Once again, I was badly injured and once again, I began asking myself whether this was worth all the pain and frustration.

2

At Last
Les Canadiens

*F*ortunately, I wasn't totally committed to hockey at the time. Canada had already entered World War II and there were plenty of jobs available for men who had machinists' training as I had. I went to work in a war plant that manufactured tanks which were sent to Europe.

There was another pleasant diversion in my life, my wife, Lucille. I had met her through her brother, Georges, who had been my coach when I was playing juvenile hockey. We had become very close friends and it was quite usual for me to stay overnight at his house after a late game. After two or three years of doing this I suddenly discovered that he had a very attractive sister. Lucille and I were married in October, 1942, before I turned pro and before I had any idea I'd be anything much in the N.H.L.

Thanks to her brother, Lucille was well versed in hockey and loved every aspect of the game. This made life a lot easier for me because she encouraged me to stick with the sport at a time when I was feeling very sorry for myself and very pessimistic about making a career of it. I don't think I could be blamed for my pessimism. After all, I had broken my ankle and my wrist in two seasons with the Senior Canadiens and had very few goals to show for it. On top of that, I was rapidly developing an image of an injury-prone athlete, the kind that the major-league scouts usually ignore.

That's why I was so astonished when the N.H.L. Canadiens invited me to their training camp for the 1942–1943 season. In one sense I was lucky. The war was in full swing and many of the regular Canadiens players had gone off to the armed forces so there weren't too many guys at training camp. I have to thank Dick Irvin, the Montreal coach, for inviting me to camp. He must have seen something in me that others didn't because he acted as if I was going to make the team. I suspect he was influenced more by my play in juniors, when I was scoring goals, than by what I did for the Canadiens Seniors.

In October, 1942, Les Canadiens held their training camp in Ste. Hyacinthe, Quebec. It was a crazy kind of camp because we had to come back to Montreal and work out either in Verdun or at the Forum. Another reason it was so bizarre was that most of the players were working in war plants as well as playing for the big team. As a result, we had to practice late at night, sometimes starting workouts after midnight.

A lot of people thought that it was a great accomplishment for me to make the team on the first shot at a regular's job, but actually it wasn't such a big deal. I made the team because there was nobody else around. I admit I had to work hard because that's the only way I knew how to do anything, but the competition wasn't that stiff and I wound up as the best of two prospects in camp!

Tommy Gorman was the manager of the Canadiens at the time. He was a grand, jovial Irishman who had done a lot of promoting and managing all over the N.H.L. before he wound up in Montreal. He signed me to my first N.H.L. contract and I was raring to go. It was quite a thrill because not only was I on top but I was playing with my former idol, Toe Blake. There were some good men on the team. Butch Bouchard was a young, tough defenseman, and Joe Benoît was a fine forward. Mike McMahon was a huge defenseman, and our goalie was Paul Bibeault, who had his good nights and his bad nights. Overall, it was a pretty fair hockey team with a very good coach, Irvin.

At first, Irvin and I didn't hit it off very well. He had one habit that bothered me and some of the others a great deal. Whenever he criticized a particular player, he would do it in front of the entire team, which was very embarrassing to the individual and frightening to the rest of the club. Each player felt that it could happen to him next. My feeling has always been that if a coach wants to give somebody hell he should do it privately.

On the other hand, Irvin certainly knew his hockey, and for the most part he was good for the players. He believed his team should think hockey morning, noon, and night, and he never let us forget it.

I had other difficulties with Irvin that weren't his fault at all. By the time I had signed with the Canadiens I was still unable to speak English. Where I came from, there was no reason to learn it because Montreal was divided in half, east and west, and nearly all the French-Canadians lived in the East End. As a result, all their business was conducted in French and that was the atmosphere in which I grew up.

By the time I made my first entrance into the Canadiens' dressing room the only things I could say in English were "yes" and "no." That's all. After a while I began to understand a little more. My teammates were both French- and English-Canadian, and I naturally gravitated toward the French-speaking players at first. Still, I was deathly afraid to even try to say anything in English for fear of making a mistake and looking foolish. I'd just sit there silently. That's one reason I got a reputation early in my career for being silent and sullen. Actually, it was more shyness than anything else and I'm sure many of the English-speaking players would feel the same way if the situation was reversed. I know that many of the English-speaking players who've lived in Montreal all their lives can't speak a word of French. At least most of the French-Canadians would *try* to speak English.

In time, though, I gained a little more confidence and, with the help of my older teammates, I began to understand everything that Irvin was saying, especially when it came to hockey. But, once again, I didn't spend much time in the dressing room or on the ice because still another tragedy was on its way.

The seeds of a riot! Loyal Montreal Canadiens fans parade outside the **Forum** to protest my suspension by National Hockey League president Clarence Campbell. The demonstrators gathered on the afternoon of March 17, 1955, prior to a Detroit-Montreal game. By nightfall the riot had erupted.

Campbell's in the soup! Everything from soup to nuts was thrown at N.H.L. president Clarence Campbell after he took his seat in the Montreal Forum on St. Patrick's Day, 1955. Here, two Forum ushers restrain an attacking fan as Campbell presses his hand to his hat. Seconds later a tear-gas bomb exploded, and the riot reached its apex.

Canada

The Forum in ruins. The Richard riot lasted into the night as hundreds of marauding fans stormed down Ste. Catherine Street West, setting fires and smashing windows. The Forum itself was besieged as fans tossed everything from rubbers to railway lamps to register their protest. The Detroit-Montreal game was forfeited to the visitors, and I finally made a radio and television appeal to calm the population after what was one of sports' most notorious riots.

They call this the "Rocket's red glare." I swoop in on Boston Bruin goalie Sugar Jim Henry to put the puck on my backhand and then lift it over his left leg and into the net.

David

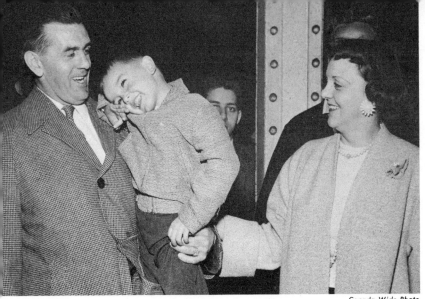

Home sweet home. My wife, Lucille, and son Normand greet me at Montreal's Central Railway Station after Les Canadiens won the Stanley Cup in 1958. Lucille has been a great inspiration to me since my early playing days in Montreal.

Wild about Harry. A superb goaltender, Harry Lumley always provided a challenge for me. Here I've outskated Toronto defenseman Fernie Flaman to fire a forehand shot past Lumley's stick and into the Toronto net during a game in 1953.

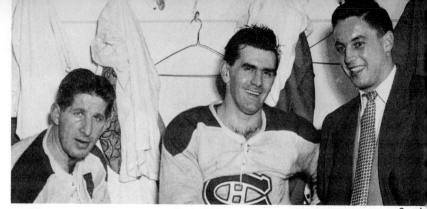

Three generations. Elmer Lach and Jean Béliveau share the limelight with me in November, 1952, after I scored my record-breaking 325th goal. Elmer was a member of the Canadiens before I joined the team and was my line mate for several years. Béliveau, at the time, played for the Quebec Aces. He later became my teammate and was named captain of the Canadiens after I retired.

One of my favorites. I have just circled the Ranger net from right to left and slipped the puck into the left-hand corner behind Ranger goalie Gump Worsley. It was my six hundredth goal, scored on November 26, 1958. If I seem far from the scene of the score it is because Lou Fontinato (left) had just knocked me to the ice, and I was getting back on my feet when the picture was taken.

Canada

Ups and downs. I didn't *always* score goals, as this picture amply indicates. As Jean Béliveau moves in on the left, I take a headfirst dive, no doubt the courtesy of a Boston Bruin stick—the meanie!

Les Trois Richards. Here I am surrounded by my brothers Henri (left) and Claude during a preseason workout. I always thought that Claude would have been good enough to make the N.H.L. but that he was not given enough of a chance by the Canadiens' management.

The Holy Grail. This is what we aim for every year—the Stanley Cup. The rather strained-looking man on the right is Bernie "Boom-Boom" Geoffrion. Watching proudly in the background are my old teammate Emile "Butch" Bouchard and my new teammate Jean Béliveau.

It was the sixteenth game of the N.H.L. season and, frankly, I had been doing a lot better than I thought I would. I already had five goals and six assists and was learning something new in every game. On this particular night we were playing the Bruins at the Forum. I had been out on the ice for close to three minutes. I was really tired when the puck skimmed over to my side in our own zone. I couldn't get off the ice, so I lunged for the puck, got it on my stick, and headed for Boston territory. The next thing I knew, big Johnny Crawford, the Bruins' defenseman who always wore a helmet, was looming directly in front of me. He smashed me with a terrific but fair body check and then fell on top of me on the ice. As I fell, my leg twisted under my body and my ankle turned in the process.

Once again I heard that deathly crack and I felt immediately that my ankle must be broken. As they carried me off the ice, I said to myself, "Maurice, when will these injuries ever end?"

The awful pattern was virtually the same as it had been the year before, and the year before that! I was out of action for the entire season and missed the Stanley Cup play-offs, too.

This time the depression I suffered was infinitely worse than it had been before. Now that I was with the Canadiens the newspapermen were concentrating on me much more than when I had played senior hockey. Pretty soon I began reading in the papers, "Richard too brittle for pro hockey" and things like that. It was terribly discouraging, and here I was, in my first year of marriage, with a very bleak future ahead. At the time I honestly never thought I'd be able to play hockey again. I thought, "Maurice, I don't know how you're going to do it next year." But, fortunately, neither Dick Irvin nor Tommy Gorman had given up on me and I was invited back to training camp for the 1943–1944 season.

By this time Les Canadiens looked like one of the best teams in the N.H.L. and I seriously wondered whether or not I had the ability or the strength to make the club. But I had a good training camp and was feeling fine when it happened again! We had only played a few games of the new season when somebody, I forget who, rapped me into the sideboards. It was my shoulder that snapped and I limped off the ice convinced that I was jinxed for life.

But luck was on my side this time. The injury turned out to be relatively minor and I returned to the lineup after missing only a couple of games. That was a small break. The big break came when Irvin decided to put me in Charlie Sand's place on a line with Blake and Elmer Lach. I didn't know Elmer that well, although he had been at training camp the year before. But being on a line with Toe was probably the greatest thrill I had experienced up until then.

Elmer was the center and Toe was the left wing. It was somewhat unusual for me to play on the right side because I had a left-handed shot. Originally I had been a left wing but when I played for the Senior Canadiens the coach, Dave Campbell, switched me to the right side and I remained there.

Some writers have remarked over the years that it was difficult for me, a left-handed shot, to play on the right side, but actually it was a blessing. When I was younger I used to turn with my right skate over my left and I did it much, much more than with the left skate over my right. When you bring your right skate over your left, you are making a left turn, which is what the right wing has to do when he is cutting in toward the goal. So as a youngster, even though I had been a left-hand shot, my skating was geared for the right wing.

When I started playing pro hockey with the Senior Canadiens, they put me on the left wing and I had difficulty turning in toward the right because of my early skating habits. Even as a left wing I tended to drift to the right side of the ice because that was my easy side. So When Campbell finally asked me to play on the right side I was delighted. I figured it would be a lot easier and it would also give me a chance to practice my backhand shot.

Another advantage I had on the right was the fact that by keeping the puck on my left side, I was able to have it that much closer to the net than a player who had it on his right or far side. For me, the angle on the net was a lot bigger than for the traditional right wings with the right-handed shots.

Playing was a lot of fun in those days, when I wasn't injured, but it was also difficult. I had to keep working at the wartime job and the team kept practicing at night, seven, eight, nine o'clock; sometimes we never knew when. And I was worried about the possibility of still another injury. Soon my anxiety disappeared and I managed to go six or seven years before any additional serious injury occurred.

Meanwhile our club had really started to jell. We were also fortunate because so many of the best players in the league had gone to war—Milt Schmidt, Bobby Bauer, and Woody Dumart of the Bruins and Chuck Rayner of the Rangers, among others. But there were still some good ones around. Chicago had the Bentley brothers, Doug and Max, and Bill Mosienko, and the Bruins still had their great center, Bill Cowley.

We were also lucky in obtaining Phil Watson who had been the star center for the Rangers for a number of years. We managed to acquire him just for the 1943–1944 season because of some wartime technicality. Watson really gave us the power down the center along with Lach.

Elmer was a good guy, but strange in some ways. He suffered a lot of injuries during his career, some of which were caused by deliberate efforts to injure him on the part of our opponents. Having played with Elmer for so long I can appreciate how he might antagonize another player. On the ice Lach was the kind of guy who used to get the other players mad with some trick or other. He would tease them by hooking or holding, but he never wanted to fight. All he wanted to do was get the others angry. He was also a very hard worker who would always go into the corners to get the puck. For me he was a good playmaker. He also talked a lot while he was on the ice.

Blake and I were just the opposite. Toe would hardly

say anything. Even if you made a mistake he'd never say a word about it to you. In that sense he was somewhat like me. I never wanted to be mad at anybody. One characteristic the three of us had in common was a love of work. Even though Toe was ten years older than I, he never stopped skating hard and, in that way, he was a tremendous inspiration to the line, especially to me.

Pretty soon I began really clicking. The goals came easier and my skating had never been better. It was in that second year, the first really good one for me, that I was given the nickname that stuck with me throughout my career, "the Rocket."

There have been many versions of the story of how I got the nickname so, now, once and for all, I'll set the record straight. Actually, I got the nickname from three players—all at once. It happened in practice. Toe, Elmer, and myself would infuriate the other guys with the way we'd score goals. Most of the time we'd scrimmage against the line of Watson, Murph Chamberlain, and Ray Getliffe. We used to go around them so fast they were amazed at our speed. At that time I was really flying and, one day, when I got up a full head of steam, one of them said, "Watch out, here comes the Rocket." The three of them picked up the expression and, whenever I'd get the puck, they'd yell, "Here comes the Rocket!"

There were a few newspapermen at the practice session that day and they heard Watson, Chamberlain, and Getliffe yelling at me, and calling me the Rocket. The next day the nickname appeared in the papers and it has stuck ever since.

It was up to me to make good on the reputation I was developing. One of the goals that helped support me was scored against the Chicago Black Hawks. Over the years people have asked me whether it was true that I actually scored a goal while carrying an opponent on my back and the answer is "yes."

The player was Earl Seibert, a big defenseman with the Black Hawks. It happened during one of my breakaways. Seibert tried to head me off from the side. As he cut across the ice he realized that he couldn't possibly get in front of me so he did the next best thing. He threw his arms right on top of my shoulders, trying to stop me. I kept skating and he kept following. Suddenly, I felt his skates lifting off the ice and flying up in the air and back down on the ice again. When I was about ten feet from the net he tried to throw all his weight on me. I think he weighed about 210 pounds. I felt as if I might cave right in. The goaltender moved straight out for me, and somehow I managed to jab the puck between his legs while Siebert kept riding on my back!

Siebert wasn't nearly as bad as some of the other pests. The Rangers had two of them, Tony Leswick and Eddie Kullman. They weren't very good hockey players but they would bug you in a dozen ways. One night Leswick was trying to push me around. I said, "Tony, I don't think you could fight a little mouse, you're so small." Well, he got mad as hell. Next time he came to town, he managed to get *my* goat and I went after *him*. The referee gave me a ten-minute misconduct and told me to stay away from Leswick. I said, "The hell with that, I'm gonna go after him. I want him to take a misconduct, too." I didn't stop until he finally swung at me and took his misconduct.

Apart from winning a lot of hockey games we had a lot of fun on that team. Usually Watson was in the middle of it. He organized a softball team and made sure that we all stuck together as a team during the off-season. We used to play on Saturdays and Sundays during the summer and had quite a good club. Our goalie, Bill Durnan, was the best softball pitcher in all of Canada. I played center field and third base.

Watson's idea for having the softball team developed a tremendous camaraderie on the team, one that has remained with it over the years. In the hockey season we'd have a party at one guy's place on one weekend and at another's place the next. You knew that after nearly every game at the Forum you didn't have to go out to celebrate on the town. There was always a party at a player's house. The wives and the players were together all the time, even on the road.

Another aspect of the team that surprised outsiders was the fact that there was never any trouble between the French-speaking players and the English-speaking players. In all the eighteen years I spent with the team there was never an argument between a Frenchman and an Englishman.

We ran away with the N.H.L. championship in 1943–1944 and people began saying that we played something known as "Firewagon hockey" because we seemed to be dashing all over the place all the time. This was all Irvin's doing. He always told the boys to skate, to work, to come back up ice when the other team takes the puck, to try to keep your position, and to play a two-way game.

Other teams seemed to concentrate more on defensive hockey, but we put as much emphasis on going for goals as we did on coming back with our wings. Irvin believed we should stay out on the ice at least two and a half to three minutes or longer. That's where the coaches are different today. Now they're satisfied with a minute or a minute and a half and they call for a line change.

Irvin couldn't do anything wrong in 1943–1944. We reached the Stanley Cup finals against Chicago and took them in four straight. What I remember most about that series was the last period of the last game. We were losing, 4–2, and the Forum crowd, for some reason, really got on our backs. They thought we had wanted to play still *another* game, which, incidentally, wasn't the case. Although we were doing our best the fans started booing us and yelling "fake, fake" until it was coming out of our ears. That made me good and mad. I got the next two goals, forcing the game into overtime and we won it in sudden death.

I played forty-six out of the fifty regular season games that season and scored thirty-two goals and twenty-two assists. But I had a fantastic play-off, scoring twelve goals, which was a record at the time, and five assists in nine games. Maybe I should have anticipated an even better season in 1944–1945, but I guess it wasn't a part of me to be overly optimistic until I was sure I was over the old injury jinx.

Looking back, there weren't many who thought I would score many more goals in 1944–1945. Right off the bat I injured my knee, and although it wasn't a serious enough injury to put me out of the lineup, I had to be careful and tape it before every game. And during the game there were always two or three times when the knee bothered me enough to force me to the bench. Still, everything went fine and the goals kept coming and coming and I wound up with fifty goals in fifty games.

What made me angry about that season was the fact that I didn't get the assists that I believe I deserved which would have given me the scoring championship. In the forties there was a great inequity in the distribution of assists. Many of the official scorers were "homers." They'd give an assist to one of their hometown players even if he was merely on the ice when a goal was scored, although he might not have participated in the score itself. There was nothing much that we could do about it.

In 1943–1944 and 1944–1945 we had what I consider one of the greatest teams of all time. Bill Durnan, our goalie, was the best goaltender I ever played in front of, and our defense, led by Butch Bouchard, was very solid. Up front, we had three good lines and excellent reserves.

Of course, I had to pay the price of scoring fifty goals. That meant the other teams would start assigning their most difficult "checkers" to guard me, and the honeymoon, for me at least, would be over. There were two opponents who stand out in my mind as the finest and cleanest players I've ever skated against. One of them was Bob Davidson of the Toronto Maple Leafs and the other was Kenny Smith of the Boston Bruins. Both of them did their job well—hard but clean—and neither, to my mind, ever handed out a dirty check.

I wish I could say the same thing for some of the others, but it wouldn't be the truth. For me, the worst player by far whom I've ever skated against was Ted Lindsay, of the Detroit Red Wings. It wasn't so much that he was a dirty player, but as far as I am concerned, he had a dirty mouth. He swore

at everybody on the ice. However, he wasn't very prominent
in the early forties because he was still quite young and he
wasn't really a star with the Red Wings.

The first player who gave me a hard time was Bob Dill,
the Rangers' defenseman. We were playing in Madison Square
Garden and I was behind the New York net at the time. An
argument started between a couple of players and Dill came
over and started yelling at me. I don't remember exactly
what he said but it was about me being a "French so-and-so."
That set me off. I went at him and dropped him with a couple
of punches. He got up and tried to get at me again and I hit
him again. Then we were both sent to the penalty box. He
went in first and when I walked in he jumped at me again.
This time I floored him in the penalty box and that was the
end of it.

The funniest part of the whole incident was after the game
when I walked out of the employee's exit on West Forty-ninth
Street. Right across the street was the Hotel Belvedere and there
was Dill waiting for me. I couldn't speak too much English
at the time but I asked Dill if he wanted to have dinner with
me. He said, "This is the first time I've ever been punched that
hard but I don't think I'll have dinner with you!" Dill was, and
still is, a helluva guy. Every time I see him now he gives me
a big handshake and a big smile.

Dill was different from some of the other opponents who
bothered me. As a defenseman, he guarded me all the time.
A lot of people have been mistaken over the years in thinking I was always disturbed by my tough checkers. Actually,
I wanted somebody on the other team to make me work harder. When somebody was checking me closely I wanted to get
away from him and I tried all the more to get my goals. If I
didn't have anyone on my back, or anybody to check me, I
don't think I would have accomplished all that I did. There's
no doubt that some of the opponents would get me good
once in a while. Mostly, they'd put me into the boards or trip
me and I'd get mad and retaliate. Most of the times that I

retaliated I was the one who got the penalty—not the other guy, who deserved it.

Don't get the mistaken impression that I was simon-pure. Players in the N.H.L. live by the Jungle Code. You have to make do in the best way you know how. I, too, had my little tricks. One of my favorites was using my left hand to hold off an opponent who was checking me closely. Since I was a left-handed shot I carried most of the weight of my stick in my right or upper hand. When you carry your stick that way you have your left arm on the side of the defense. You always have a chance to hold the man off and keep him from reaching at the puck. If I had been playing left wing it would have been a lot more difficult.

The only problem I had in the 1945–1946 season was with my knee. I slipped down to twenty-seven goals because the knee slowed me, but our line remained intact. We finished first and won the Stanley Cup. Basically, Irvin would never change our style, except in rare situations. Once, when we were going to Detroit where we hadn't done very well, he suggested we try dumping the puck into the Red Wing end of the rink and then try to retrieve it. If we couldn't get to the puck first, we were to tear back to our own end. Well, we wound up with a total of five shots on goal for the *entire* game, got beaten all the same, and Irvin quickly ended that experiment. I didn't blame him, though. He was always trying to help his men, off ice and on, and basically he was a nice guy, despite what some of his critics thought.

3

I Reach
My Prime

*I*rvin was a big help to me and the records prove it. In the 1946–1947 season I scored forty-five goals and just missed winning the scoring championship by one point. Frankly, I thought I was capable of having another fifty-goal year but, as it turned out, I never reached that level again. At the rate I was scoring then, I figured any season in which I scored fewer than forty goals was a poor one for me. I also knew that the better I became, the more trouble I'd get from the opposition.

One of the biggest brawls I remember occurred late in the 1946–1947 season in New York. It started when Cal Gardner of the Rangers clipped Kenny Reardon, our defenseman, in the mouth with his stick. Reardon was bleeding like a stuck pig and he went off toward the Ranger bench and the Garden's hospital. Suddenly a fight broke out in the aisle near the Ranger bench and poured out onto the ice. Soon every player on both teams seemed to be involved. There was a lot of stick-swinging and I wound up going after three guys without my stick. I punched one who had swung his stick at me. I had every intention of clouting him with my own stick, but once I saw him flat on the ice I decided to leave him alone. So I took my stick and rapped the ice near him but made sure not to hit him. It's one of those things that happen in the heat of a game. You think of using your stick on someone, but when you're about to do it, you change your mind at the last split second.

We didn't have much trouble with Boston in the 1947

Stanley Cup semifinals and then we went up against our old rivals from Toronto. The Leafs had rebuilt their club that season with a lot of good, tough youngsters such as Jim Thomson and Gus Mortson on defense and Howie Meeker and Vic Lynn up front.

In the first game at the Forum we beat the Leafs badly and we figured to romp through the series until all hell broke loose in the second game and I got myself into a lot of trouble. It started with Lynn. He hit me a dirty check, and as far as I can remember, no penalty was going to be called, so I went after him. As I went for him he lifted his stick in the air, and when I saw that, I swung my stick and hit him in the head. I didn't mean to get him there but it was done and he started bleeding a little. I got a five-minute penalty and I was seething.

Later in the game I got tangled up with Bill Ezinicki, a guy who gave me a lot of trouble through the years. For the most part he was a clean, hard checker but this time he had his stick up, so I lifted mine and hit him just before he hit me. I was very upset about it. Afterward I must have had some bad food and I really got sick. Clarence Campbell, the league president, had seen the fight and suspended me for one game, although in my condition I wasn't sure whether I'd have been able to play in the next game anyway.

Some people wonder whether I nursed a grudge against Ezinicki. Not really. But I always had my eye out for him because he had a habit of hitting players when they weren't looking. The sneaky check was his specialty. You had to watch him for that because he rarely carried the puck himself when he knew somebody was going to hit *him*. He was a hard guy, though, and he'd never say anything even though you'd give him a rough time. He had the knack of ducking at just the right moments. A couple of times I connected, but over the years he nailed me more times than I ever nailed him.

It's interesting; Ezinicki and I used to go after each other, season after season, but when we'd meet off the ice, at a banquet or other event, he was always a gentleman, a real gentleman. We never had an argument off the ice. In my estimation, he was a very nice guy.

Several writers, especially those in Toronto, believed that my one-game play-off suspension in 1947 hurt the Canadiens psychologically. It's true that Toronto upset us in the series, four games to two, but my bad leg hurt our team more than anything else. I just couldn't play my regular game when I returned to action.

By now I had been making headlines in the papers. My contacts with English-speaking people were more and more frequent. As a result I made up my mind to learn English as soon as possible. I didn't have much trouble during the hockey season because I was constantly in contact with English speaking players and was always in English-speaking cities. The problem was the summer. I would return home where no English was spoken. By fall, when I returned to training camp I had forgotten a lot of what I had learned.

With the exception of Kenny Mosdell, a very good and very underrated forward on our team, all my friends on the club were French-speaking. I wouldn't go out with the English-speaking players except when we played ball, and even then, I only talked to the French guys—in French, of course.

Mind you, there was no animosity on the team and there was plenty of spirit, especially with men like Ken Reardon and Butch Bouchard around. Reardon wasn't a very good defenseman, from the textbook point of view, but he had tremendous spirit and energy and never stopped working. He'd yell at us to be sure we were "in" the game and he was a great guy to team up with Bouchard. Butch was a big bull. When he was on the ice you knew that the smaller players on our team would be protected. If any of our men got pushed around Bouchard was right there to help. Butch and I were the first to step in if any of our teammates were involved in a fight. But I was never really friendly with Butch. As a matter of fact I never got along with him.

Life was beautiful for us in the mid-forties. We were like

kings in the province of Quebec. We couldn't do anything wrong as far as the public was concerned, but there always was the pressure to keep on winning. In some ways the pressure was greater on my wife than on me.

She was never relaxed. She was always afraid I might get hurt. Whenever we played on the road, her only contact with me was listening to the games on the radio and that was hard on her, home alone with the kids. But I'll say this—she never complained and she never missed a home game in which I played even before we were married.

Sometimes I felt better about Lucille not coming on the road because the fans in some of the American cities were pretty rough on visiting players. For me, New York and Chicago were the worst cities. On the whole the people were good fans but there were so many crazy kids and crazy guys who would come up behind our bench before and after the games and taunt us. It wasn't that I didn't like playing in these rinks but rather that, every so often, you'd get a really bad time from the fans. I remember times in New York when the fans behind us got into fights with the players. But that wasn't the worst of my problems in New York.

By far the most controversial incident involved a referee by the name of Hugh McLean. The trouble had started the night before in Montreal. McLean was refereeing the game at the Forum. Toward the end of the third period somebody clipped me in front of the net. Instead of the clipper getting the penalty, McLean whistled *me* off. That got me good and mad so I chased McLean and demanded to know what the penalty was all about. He didn't want to hear anything from me and he kept skating away. Suddenly, he wheeled around and said he was giving me a ten-minute misconduct penalty along with the minor penalty. Here was a rookie referee, just starting out in the league, acting kind of fresh and trying to make a name for himself by making a fool out of the Rocket.

After saying what I had to say I had no choice but to get into the penalty box and shut up or else he would hit me with another penalty. I was still furious about the whole incident and I still nursed my anger after the game and on the train to New York for the next night's game.

In those days referees and linesmen weren't supposed to stay at the same hotels as the players, but every so often they would drop over and fraternize between games. Customarily the Canadiens would stay at the Hotel Picadilly in New York. On Sunday afternoon I was outside the building getting some fresh air. McLean and the two linesmen were standing in the lobby talking to some players.

At that time, our goaltender was Gerry McNeil, who had a real sense of humor and was a great practical joker. McNeil was in the lobby with McLean when he saw me outside. He figured this would be a good time for a practical joke. McNeil came out, all excited, and said, "Rocket, that goddamned McLean is inside the lobby and he's talkin' about you." I didn't realize that McNeil was joking. I was still steaming over the events of the previous night and the thought of McLean talking about me was very infuriating to say the least.

I stormed into the lobby. There was McLean, sure enough. Whether he was talking about me or not didn't matter at that moment. I walked up to him and grabbed him by the neck. "Okay," I demanded, "what did you say?"

McLean didn't say a word but Camil Desroches, the Canadiens' publicity man who was there, rushed over to me and said, "Aww, c'mon, Rocket, leave him alone!"

But I was still mad. I just stood there with my hands around McLean's neck. Soon, some people intervened and I let him go. Naturally, the story leaked to the newspapers and I got a five-hundred-dollar fine. Some of the papers said I had hit the referee, but I did not hit the man.

Every so often I'd wonder whether these incidents would get me into so much trouble that the Canadiens' management would decide to trade me to another team. But I was lucky. Frank Selke, Sr., had succeeded Tommy Gorman as manager of Les Canadiens, and although he had trouble with some of the players, Selke and I got along pretty well.

One team that would have liked to get hold of me was Toronto. Conn Smythe, the Leafs' manager, was quite friendly. A lot of people thought we hated each other because of the rivalry between Toronto and Montreal but the opposite was true. Even when I had my troubles in Maple Leaf Gardens, Smythe would come over and try to cool me off.

One time he gave a story to the papers saying he would offer the Canadiens $100,000 to get me on the Maple Leafs. Personally, I think it was a publicity stunt on Smythe's part, more tongue than anything else, but it was interesting for me to think about what it would be like to play in Toronto. I know many writers have said that the Rocket couldn't think of playing anywhere but in Montreal. They believed that I represented the French-speaking people of Quebec province and that I couldn't conceive of playing for the English-speaking Maple Leafs. However, if I had to leave Montreal because of a trade I think I would have played in any of the other five cities in the N.H.L. without hesitation. But it's better to play in your hometown because it makes you work harder. And if I had had a choice of the five I would have picked Toronto. It's true that the Toronto fans were on my back in my first couple of years in the league but then they started to cheer me. I've always felt that the Toronto fan is the best in the entire circuit. Whenever he sees good hockey being played, he'll give the team and players a good hand even if they are bitter rivals of his home team.

Montreal fans were something else. They demanded perfection from us. When they didn't get it they would be quick to get on our backs. In the 1949–1950 season they were particularly tough on our goalie, Bill Durnan. This bothered me because Durnan was one of the nicest guys in the world. He had a smile for everybody and never said a word against anyone. As a teammate, you couldn't ask for anything more. He himself took the blame whenever a goal was scored against him and didn't put the rap on his defensemen.

But in 1949–1950 we didn't have one of our great years, although it wasn't a bad season. In Bill's case, though, it was below par and, being sensitive, he felt very unhappy about the way the fans reacted. After one bad game, he walked into the room and actually was crying. The crowd had been booing him.

We had Gerry McNeil with us in case of trouble, but Durnan started the 1950 Stanley Cup semifinal against the Rangers. We were the favorites because we had finished second and the Rangers had finished fourth. But the Rangers hit a hot hand and their right wing, Pentti Lund, caught fire and just about killed us single-handedly. Lund was a good, clean hockey player with a hard shot. In that series I thought we had played well enough to win, but every time Lund took a shot at our goal, he scored.

With Durnan in the nets we lost the first three games of the series. The Montreal fans were unmerciful. Finally, Irvin threw McNeil in for the fourth game and we won, but New York bounced back and took the fifth game, and we were eliminated from the play-offs. Durnan couldn't take the punishment from the fans anymore, so he quit. On top of that he had had a lot of trouble with his knees and they were hurting him so it was all for the best that he got out of the game. But as far as I'm concerned, Durnan was the best goaltender I've ever seen, with Boston's Frankie Brimsek right behind.

What put Durnan head and shoulders above the others was his style. He could switch hands with ease and use either his left or his right glove to spear shots. Very few goaltenders have ever been ambidextrous like Durnan and none has ever mastered the art the way he did. He'd rarely commit himself on a play and had a great knack of waiting for the forward to make the first move, which was the reason he was so hard to beat on breakaways. Brimsek was almost the same, but Brimsek could use only one hand.

For me, the easiest goalie to play against was Harry Lumley, who started out with the Red Wings and later played for Chicago, Toronto, and Boston. Lumley was big and filled out a lot of the net, but somehow I was able to beat him with ease.

We managed to recover from the debacle of 1950, although I can't say that I kept out of trouble as much as I would have liked. Most of the time, it was just a case of the opposition sending some clown player out on the ice to pester me. The Leafs did that once with a third-rate forward named Bob Bailey, who did something to me that never happened to me before or since and I'll never forget him for that.

The incident started when he hit me with a dirty check. I started after him hoping to get even, and when I finally caught him we were in the middle of the ice. He managed to get on top of me, so naturally I tried to protect myself by hiding my head in my hands. He couldn't hit me but what he did was much worse. He took his fingers and shoved them in my eyes. Mind you, this wasn't a gentle act. Bailey was actually pushing my eyes inside my head! Can you imagine a guy resorting to something as low as that—putting his fingers in my eyes.

When I got up I was madder'n hell. But I couldn't see very well. George Hayes, the linesman, was trying to hold me off, and that got me even angrier, because all I wanted to do was get back at Bailey. Hayes didn't mean any harm to me but I was furious over anybody trying to hold me so I went after Hayes. I didn't hit him with my fist; just my gloves with a sort of "get away, man, you're bothering me" kind of push. I just didn't want to see anybody around me. But Hayes was big and strong and he managed to keep me away. I got fined good for that one and, even worse, I didn't catch up with Bailey. Before I knew it he was back in the minors again, where as far as I'm concerned, he belonged.

All these difficulties managed to get me into a lot of trouble with N.H.L. president Clarence Campbell. I was never particularly crazy about his attitude. He was always very standoffish. He reminded me of members of the English aristocracy of Canada who tend to look down on the French-

Canadians as second-class citizens. At the time, I had begun to write a weekly sports column for a French-language paper in Montreal with a sportswriter acting as my guide. I often criticized Campbell in the column, and he finally demanded that I stop writing the column as long as I was playing in the N.H.L. He forced me to deposit a thousand-dollar bond with the league which would be returned when I was finished playing.

My relationship with the sportswriters was a lot better than it was with Campbell and it was a lot better than people have been led to believe. As far as I can remember I never got into a real argument with any of the writers. In fact, the only time most writers thought I was kind of rough or didn't have a smile for them was in the dressing room after a game. That was because I would be so pent up emotionally from the game that it was difficult for me to think straight. As a result I didn't answer some of their questions. It was tough for me to talk to them after losing because it feels as if the world had ended and here are guys pumping questions at you while everything seems to be crumbling around you. I've always felt they should have waited ten to fifteen minutes before coming into the dressing room and then we could talk. But I'll say this—I never got mad at any newspaperman who wrote negative stories about me.

I did get angry at fans from time to time, particularly in out-of-town rinks. One night in Chicago one big, fat spectator needled the daylights out of me. I had told the ushers in Chicago Stadium that this fellow was overdoing it and that there might be trouble if they didn't contain him.

He kept coming at me and I kept telling him to go away. I didn't want to talk to him. Suddenly he took a swing at me. One usher grabbed him and took him away and that seemed to be the end of it. After the game I deliberately took a different exit than usual to avoid trouble. Somehow the guy found me and came at me again. This time I didn't give him a chance to do anything. I socked him right between the eyes. I hit him so hard I could see his eyes puffing, and he went down, in a heap.

I thought I would be sued over that incident, but two days later when I returned to the stadium his brother came over and identified himself, I thought I was going to have more trouble, but he told me I had done him a big favor by flattening the pest.

"I'm the happiest guy in the world," the brother said. "Now that fat bully doesn't shoot his mouth off anymore and doesn't bother anybody. You did us all a service!"

That's one of the crazy things about the hockey business. But hockey players themselves are strange. For example, they never bother to phone a newspaperman to thank him for a good story, but they are always quick to criticize if a bad one appears. In my day I can't remember any player ever thanking a reporter for a story.

Of course not all of the men on the team took the games as seriously as I did. We had quite a few jokers on the club. Doug Harvey, who became the best defenseman in hockey, was one, and Boom Boom Geoffrion, another.

Doug and the Boomer loved to mess your bed up when you were away from your sleeping compartment on the train. They'd manage to find out about a guy's allergies and then come up with whatever made him allergic and put it in his bed. Sometimes they'd hide our belongings on the train. We had plenty of fun and some strange incidents, too.

At one time, Queen Elizabeth and Prince Philip visited the Forum when we played the Rangers. Prince Philip is quite a guy; he knows his sports and loves them. Prior to the game we were asked by the league to try to make a good impression on the royalty. "No fights, no arguments," that was the word.

I made up my mind that I would stay out of trouble. There was a little argument going along the boards not far from where the Prince and Queen were sitting. Normally, I would have barged in and started pushing and shoving, but

I decided to play it cool. Suddenly Prince Philip walked over to where we were standing and said, "What's the matter, Rocket, don't you want to fight?"

As things turned out, Floyd Curry, a third-line forward on the team, upstaged me and scored a three-goal hat trick that night. I think I scored a goal or two but it was Curry's night. After the game Prince Philip walked into the dressing room and bawled me out. "How come you let that other guy beat you out?" he kidded. "I don't even know him. I wanted *you* to get the goals!"

Actually, Curry was a splendid hockey player and, like so many of the lesser lights on the club, was overshadowed by our stars. The Canadiens were an interesting bunch of characters who would surprise you in a lot of ways. Take Doug Harvey as an example.

A lot of people don't realize that Doug was one of the first hockey players to start the movement to organize a player's association. That took a lot of guts in my day. Nowadays the N.H.L. Players' Association is taken for granted, but in the early fifties any player who talked about a union faced reprisal from management. Doug was our leader in Montreal and Ted Lindsay started the movement in Detroit. Unfortunately, it never got off the ground and some of the leaders, including Lindsay, got themselves into a lot of trouble with management. I know that Jack Adams, the Detroit manager, was angry with Lindsay and wound up sending him to the then lowly Chicago Black Hawks as punishment.

Harvey asked me to join the association at that time. I didn't have anything against it but I decided not to. I was sure that if I did, especially someone like me, who was already in a lot of trouble with the N.H.L. I would have been in even more hot water, particularly with Frank Selke. He didn't want me to have any part of the union. Since he had always been nice and I didn't want to hurt him or get into an argument, I decided against joining.

As the years went by Doug changed. Toward the end of his career in Montreal he became too direct in his criticism of the various players and began getting the others angry at him so that his effectiveness in the dressing room was lost.

After I had been around the league for ten years I began to hear murmurings about "another Richard" joining the Canadiens. The next in line, as far as my hockey-playing brothers were concerned, was Jacques. He played junior and senior hockey and one year, he joined the Canadiens' training camp. But he only lasted about a week.

This disappointed me a great deal because Jacques reminded me, in style, of myself. He was tall and stocky and had a good shot. Personally, I think he could have made it to the N.H.L. if he had tried harder, but he didn't try. He also had a very negative attitude and didn't want to speak English. Wherever he played, if anybody spoke English to him, he wouldn't listen. He would leave and sit elsewhere. He wouldn't play with an English player on his line, and he wouldn't talk to anybody on his team who was English-speaking. The funny thing is that he wants to learn English now!

After Jacques, there was Henri. He was fifteen years younger than I and different in almost every respect. Unlike me, Henri was a natural, especially with his skating, which had come easy. I immediately knew that Henri would make the big team as soon as he tried out for it and he proved I was right.

The baby of the family was Claude. He got as far as the Montreal Junior Canadiens and also played a little senior hockey. To this day I believe that Claude had the makings of a big-leaguer but I think he was mishandled by Sammy Pollock, who didn't play him enough in junior hockey. Had he gotten more ice, he would have developed his skills and he would have been able to play on the same line with Henri and me. Claude had a good shot, he was a hard worker and a good skater, but he couldn't make it because nobody gave him a regular turn. I think if Claude had been coming up now, when the Canadiens are not getting the players they did then, he would have been put on a line with Henri and myself. But the kid never got the chance.

I think I can say without fear of being accused of immodesty that in the middle and late forties I was the biggest drawing card in big-league hockey. But by the beginning of the fifties it had become apparent to me and most other hockey people that there was a great new star on the N.H.L. horizon, young Gordie Howe of the Red Wings.

He was big and strong and skated with great ease. He could do what no other player in the league could do, shoot the puck from either the left or right side. I noticed Howe when he first joined the Red Wings in the late forties and he impressed me as a good, but not a great, hockey player. I never thought he would develop into the player he is today. But he kept coming along and from one year to the next he seemed to come on stronger. Looking back, I would say that Howe is the best all-around hockey player I've ever seen, and that includes Bobby Hull and Bobby Orr. Hull has the big shot and great strength and skating ability but Howe had all these and was a great stick-handler and playmaker as well; something Hull never was. Orr, on the other hand, has a lot of Howe's attributes but he has not been around long enough to merit a judgment on a scale with Howe and Hull.

Another thing about Gordie that I experienced firsthand was that he was a dirty hockey player, not tough, mind you, but *dirty*—and he would take absolutely nothing from anybody. If you gave him a bad check, you could be sure he'd get even with you, in spades! But he wouldn't start it. In that sense, Howe and I were the same. I would never hit anybody first if he hadn't done anything to me before.

That's not to say that Howe didn't give me trouble. He played on the great Production Line with Sid Abel and Ted Lindsay and anytime Lindsay was on the ice there was apt to be trouble—for me! One night I had to fight all three of them. First, Lindsay started it, as usual.

I got the best of Lindsay that time but the fight tired me out. Before I could turn around Abel jumped on me and clouted me a few times. As I staggered away Howe came along and got the best of me. But it was Lindsay who was the culprit. For sheer troublemaking, he was at the very top of my list. He was a bad man with everything—his mouth, his stick —and off the ice, believe it or not, it was the same thing. Even his wife would yell and swear at me if she spotted me outside the dressing room at Olympia Stadium in Detroit. I'd hear everything in the book from both of them.

A lot of players seemed to want to get a reputation just by taking a shot at the Rocket. The Rangers had a mediocre defenseman named Ivan "The Terrible" Irwin. He was terrible, all right, as a hockey player! But he loved to hit and he gave me quite a few solid body checks and, once, he and I nearly had a stick fight. Toronto also had a tough, chunky defenseman, Bill Juzda, who was a railroad engineer in the off-season. One night I was busy fighting with one of the Leafs. After the fight was broken up there was still a lot of arguing going on near the penalty box.

There was one big circle with everybody jawing away when Juzda came along, yapping a mile a minute. Then he turned to me and said something unpleasant. It struck a sensitive nerve. I reared back and—*foom!*—I hit him a good one and he went down flat on his back. I never remember the Forum crowd being more pleased than they were over that punch. Poor Juzda was out cold. But he deserved it. He was one of those typical N.H.L. bullies who thought he could push everybody around without retaliation.

There were a few others like him. The Bruins had Leo Labine. He was built like Lindsay and played the same kind of game but he wasn't as talented a player. Every once in a while I run into Lindsay but I don't speak to him much. He knows that I *still* don't like him! Labine isn't quite as bad. In fact, I'm beginning to think he's a nice old guy but he talks too much.

I'll never forget some of those Boston incidents involving Labine and a few of the other Bruins. They say the greatest goal I ever scored came against the Bruins in the seventh game of the 1952 Stanley Cup semifinal, and Labine, indirectly, was the cause of it all. Early in the game I tried to go between two Bruin defensemen. They got a piece of me and just as I was falling to the ice Labine came along and hit me on the head with his knee. He cut me wide open, knocking me out. Later, I was told that I was taken to the Forum clinic but I don't remember that. I was unconscious at the time. They stitched me up and let me come back to the bench and I sat there, not knowing where I was or what team I was playing against. I do know that the doctors had wanted to send me to the hospital but I said "nothing doing," I wanted to finish the game. After all, it was the seventh game of the series!

I was really dizzy when I stepped on the ice. I didn't know which way to skate. Slowly, very slowly, I began to regain some of my senses. Then came the big play, although at the time I wasn't too sure what I was doing. It was just sort of a reflex action. All I know is that the puck came to me, I skated past a few Boston forwards, then alongside the boards and, finally, there was defenseman Bill Quackenbush. I went around him and got the shot off that beat goalie Jim Henry. I really didn't know how it happened at the time. The only reason I remember it now is because I saw movies of the play later on. When I did it the whole play was more or less of a blur. In retrospect I can honestly say that I've scored goals that were as good as that one, but somehow that particular one stands out because it was the winning goal in the seventh game of the play-offs and I had come back to the game after that injury.

4

The
Riot

I've had my trouble with the Bruins down through the years. The biggest fuss of all and the one that damaged my career more than anything else happened at Boston Garden in March, 1955. That year I was leading the league in scoring and I was desperately trying to win the scoring crown because it had eluded me for more than ten years.

We had come off a tough Saturday night game at the Forum and were in pretty lousy spirits before the Sunday night game at Boston Garden. Nevertheless, we did have a first-place edge over the Red Wings and I was holding the scoring lead, so things weren't really that bad, considering that we were entering the final week of the schedule. On this particular night the Bruins were really up for us. They laid on the lumber at every opportunity, and by the time the game had reached the end of the first period we were a very bruised bunch of men.

One of the Boston defensemen was tall Hal Laycoe, one of the few men in hockey to play the game wearing a regular pair of glasses. Laycoe had originally broken into the league with the Rangers and then was a teammate of mine for a couple of seasons before moving on to the Bruins. He wasn't a particularly rough or dirty player but he wasn't the cleanest player in the world either. All I know is that on the play in question he had hit me a bad check and I was trying to get even with him. It happened in the middle of the ice. I hit him and he fell. As he fell he hit me in the eye with his stick, opening up a bleeding wound over my eye. Mind you, he wasn't even cut.

When I discovered I was bleeding I got good and mad and started skating after Laycoe. As I was running for him Cliff Thompson, a linesman who had once played defense for the Bruins, jumped on my back and tried to stop me. It was the first time in all my years in the N.H.L. that a referee or linesman had done that. It was a stupid thing to do. I started to shake him off.

I managed to push him off twice and while I was doing it Laycoe took a good swing at me. Thompson kept returning and when he jumped me for the third time we were backing up near the boards. After getting him off my back again I turned around and took a good swing at him. I felt he deserved it because I had already warned him twice to stop jumping on me. "Stop me from the front, if you want," I told him, "but not from behind." But he wouldn't listen. That's why I hit him. Of course, I was thrown out of the game.

The incident caused a much bigger uproar than I thought it would, especially since I didn't think I had started it. There was Laycoe who cut me and there was that "homer" linesman, Thompson, who continued to provoke me by jumping me from the rear. But Campbell ordered a hearing in his office two days later and I showed up with Irvin and Kenny Reardon. Laycoe was there as well as Lynn Patrick, the Bruin coach.

It would be foolish for me to go on record that I wasn't at fault. There's no doubt that I hit Laycoe and had also hit Thompson. The point is that there was a great deal of provocation in both instances. I think my penalty would have been lighter if Lynn Patrick had told the absolute truth to Campbell at the hearing. To this day I can't forgive him. Patrick said that I had started the fracas and had hit Laycoe first. Everything Patrick said to Campbell was completely different from the way I remembered it or the way the referee, Frank Udvari recalled. Overall, Laycoe wasn't a bad guy but his testimony left much to be desired.

When I left Campbell's office I thought to myself that I should have expected to be punished. I probably deserved to be suspended for the final three games of the season and

possibly ten or fifteen games in the following season but not
for the play-offs. I could see no justification for Campbell
punishing my teammates or me by docking me from the
Stanley Cup round. I still say that if justice was truly done I
wouldn't have been kept out of any of the Stanley Cup games.

Our next game was scheduled for Thursday night, St.
Patrick's Day, at the Forum against the Red Wings. It was the
biggest game of the season until then because we were still
holding a slim first-place lead over Detroit. I went to the
Forum that morning to check my skates and equipment.
That's when I got the news—suspended for the remaining
three regular season games *and* the entire play-offs!

I've never been so shocked in my life. I felt numb from
head to toe. All I wanted to do was to get out of the Forum
and go home. By the time I arrived home the news had spread
all over the city. As soon as I walked into the house I knew
there would be big trouble.

One after another, people phoned me. "Rocket," they
would say, "we're going to get even with Campbell. There's
going to be a lot of trouble at the Forum tonight."

Some of the callers were strangers but I knew others. One
in particular sounded like he was really going to do something violent. "Listen," I warned him, "don't do anything
stupid. You're going too far already!"

From the gist of the conversations I sensed that these guys
weren't about to be calmed. I wasn't exactly sure what I
should do—stay home and brood about the suspension, or go
to the game and root for my teammates. In the end I made up
my mind I'd be doing the boys, and myself, the most good
if I went to the Forum.

When I got to the rink I could see all the elements of a
disturbance. People were marching around the building with
placards denouncing Campbell. They were shouting and their
mood was very ugly. When I got to my seat near the ice the
game had already started and the Canadiens couldn't seem to
get untracked.

Then Campbell made his grand entrance. I looked up and

I could see some fans beginning to menace him. On one hand I felt pleased because I hated him for what he had done to me, and on the other hand I didn't want to see harm come to him. He was doing his job. The crowd began pelting Campbell with fruits and vegetables. I saw a tear-gas bomb go off. The first thing I thought about was the safety of my wife who was in the stands.

I could see her from my seat and I waved to her to meet me. We had previously worked out a plan in case of emergency: We would meet in the Forum clinic. When I beckoned to her to leave her seat, she knew exactly what to do. As soon as the bomb exploded, I knew the game couldn't continue because the gas was spreading and tears were coming to people's eyes.

I took off for the clinic, and when I arrived, Lucille was already there. To my amazement, who else was there but Campbell! Just the sight of him infuriated me. I felt like punching him right in the face but Police Director Leggett was also there and he must have known what was on my mind. "Rocket," he warned, "don't even *talk* to him. Everybody is on your side. Just stay until the place clears out."

I never did get to Campbell. They led him out the back exit before I left the clinic. My wife and I stayed until the whole place emptied before we left. The uproar was increasing outside on Ste. Catherine Street West. We could hear yelling and screaming and store windows cracking as rocks sailed through them. They hadn't started on their rampage down Ste. Catherine Street as yet, but from the mood of the crowd I could tell the worst was yet to come.

Needless to say, the looting and destruction were appalling to me. In all honesty, I felt sympathetic to those who carried banners endorsing me and denouncing Campbell. I think the whole thing could have been averted if Campbell had done what the police had advised him to do—stay home. But he had insisted on coming to the Forum that night. To my mind that was as irresponsible an act as any that occurred.

What Campbell did was no more sensible than waving a red flag in front of an angry bull.

I've always had mixed emotions about Campbell. In my earlier years I believed that he was anti-French-Canadian and that many of his decisions against me and other players reflected that point of view. Later, I began to doubt that viewpoint. But I never really liked him as a person. He always struck me as snobbish. When you talked to him, he would look somewhere else, not straight at you. In all fairness, however, I have to admit that after the first few seasons be began to issue nothing but positive statements about me and very rarely criticized any of the players in the league.

When Lucille and I returned home that night we heard the news about the hoodlums rampaging up and down Ste. Catherine Street West. Then I received a call from Frank Selke asking if I would go on radio and television the next day, urging the people of Montreal to be calm. I said I would and I did because I sincerely believed that the damage that had been done was senseless and a blemish on the city. At the same time I couldn't conceal my distaste for Campbell and his ill-handling of the whole situation, from my suspension to his foolish decision to show up at the Forum for the game. I told the people that I had deserved my penalty, although I didn't believe it should have been as severe as it was, but I also told close friends exactly how I felt about the whole business.

The game, naturally, had been forfeited to Detroit. Over the weekend the Red Wings overtook Les Canadiens and clinched first place. As if that wasn't bad enough, my teammate Boomer Geoffrion beat me out for the scoring championship that I had wanted so dearly. I don't think it's possible to describe how brokenhearted I was over losing the championship. I certainly can't blame the Boomer. He was trying to win games for the team. He was also playing to win the scoring championship, but there were a few assists that he received over the season that were cheap. When I think of them and the fact that it was my last chance at the title, I can't help but feel resentful.

After the riot it was felt that my presence at the Forum for the rest of the season would do more harm than good. I immediately received invitations from all over Canada to make speeches, attend banquets, and referee hockey games. I accepted some of the offers and did some refereeing. I didn't see any of the play-off games that spring.

was funny, always pulling off a joke in the dressing room. Lots of times he'd talk nonsense and just talked for the sake of hearing himself talk. On the whole, he was well liked by the players.

I felt a much closer kinship to the Boomer than to Béliveau because Geoffrion and I were more alike personality-wise. Boomer was explosive like me. Sometimes if the coach would reprimand him or if he was in a long scoring slump, the Boomer would get moody and sulk. But, eventually, he'd get out of it and would bull around like the Boomer of old. After I had retired and Doug Harvey had left the team a new captain was needed. The club had to choose between Béliveau and Geoffrion. The players voted and Béliveau won, but personally I think the management pressured the players to pick Béliveau. I think it was a great mistake. For one thing, Geoffrion had seniority on the team; and that was something that should have been respected. For another, I think being by-passed that way was the worst thing that could have happened to the sensitive Boomer. After he was rejected by his teammates, the Boomer was never the same guy for Les Canadiens. It changed him completely. Had he been named captain I think the Canadiens would have been just as good as they were with Béliveau, if not better, and the players would have had more fun with him than with Béliveau.

Boomer was like me in other ways. Every so often the Boomer would lose his temper on the ice. I remember one time in New York when he flattened Ron Murphy of the Rangers with his stick. Here was another instance where the referee was more at fault than anybody. The Boomer had dropped his stick and was scuffling along the boards when Murphy, *who hadn't dropped his stick,* kept clubbing Boomer in the face. If the referee had been doing his job properly, he would have penalized Murphy and that would have been the end of it. But, no. What did he do? He overlooked Murphy giving Boomer the business. Well, there's just so much one man can take without blowing his stack and the Boomer did it. He couldn't take it anymore and he went after Murphy. It was the old story of the referee missing the guy who started the trouble and penalizing the poor guy who is forced to retaliate.

I don't want to give the impression that I was a crusader against referees. That wasn't the case. There were a few like Bill Chadwick and Hugh McLean I could have done without, but there were also some I thought were good referees. For my money, King Clancy and Red Storey were about the best. What made them the best is that they would at least let you talk to them. They didn't act superior or ignore you when you had something to say. I always felt that that was important because it gave a player a chance to let off some steam and that never hurt anyone. Chadwick was a good referee but I never liked him because he always struck me as being too fresh, especially when he handled French-Canadians. I always thought he held a grudge against us.

Frank Udvari was another referee who gave me a lot of trouble, especially during his early years as an official. In my opinion. he was much too flamboyant. He was a show-off and had a sharp tongue that was not appropriate for an official. Lots of times I went after him just to warn him not to be so high-handed with our players and not to be so fresh. He gave me quite a few misconducts for that alone. But after a few years' experience he developed into a better official, and before he retired, he was one of the best in the league.

One of the biggest shocks—and biggest losses—of my career occurred the day that Dick Irvin stepped down as coach of Les Canadiens to take a similar job with the Black Hawks. Irvin had been my coach since the first day I put on the Montreal uniform. I don't think I am out of order in saying that he was like a second father to me. I know there have been those, including Selke, who have charged that Irvin, in his last year or so, had a detrimental effect on me; that he incited me to cause all kinds of commotion and was doing me more harm than good.

But that was a lot of bunk. I think what happened would have happened if anybody else was behind the bench. Irvin's problem was with the hierarchy at the Forum. He was having more and more difficulties with the owners, and finally they felt that he had to go. He accepted the Chicago offer. Unfortunately, Dick was already a sick man and only a few of us realized it. Dick had told Elmer Lach and myself that he didn't have too many years to live but he loved hockey so much he wouldn't quit as long as he was well enough to walk to the rink.

Once we learned that Irvin was no longer with us we began speculating about his successor. A lot of names were tossed around in the newspapers. One, Billy Reay, a teammate on the Canadiens, was a pretty good hockey player. Another, Roger Leger, was also a teammate who played defense. We felt that the next coach would have to be at least partly French-Canadian. That ruled out Reay. Leger was a good man who knew his hockey, but he had his off moments and I think that militated against him.

That left only one man, Toe Blake. As far as I was concerned, no other man was qualified for the job but Toe, for lots of reasons.

Most of the team had played with Toe. They knew the kind of competitor he was, a fellow who hated to lose, who knew his hockey, and was liked by everyone who ever met him. The French players knew he was half French Canadian so that solved one problem. There was also the important fact that Toe had had coaching experience with Valleyfield in the Quebec League, so he wasn't coming into the job cold. And, of course, I had idolized Toe as a kid and had played with him on the Punch Line for many years. As far as I was concerned, there couldn't have been a more perfect choice.

It didn't take long to realize that we would work very well under Blake, perhaps even better than under Irvin. Toe had one quality that marked him from Dick. It was Irvin's policy to roast a player publicly for his mistakes. Blake would never give anybody hell in front of the other players. When he had something to say he would take them out to a private room, or his compartment on the train, or into his office and discuss it.

Make no mistake, Blake was a tough man. You never heard a good word from him on the bench. If you made a good play he wouldn't walk over and pat you on the back. But that really didn't matter. In the dressing room you knew he was behind you, and as long as I played for him Toe was well liked by the players.

As for coaching technique, Blake and Irvin were practically alike. Toe emphasized skating and more skating, "head-manning" the puck, and shooting whenever possible. Of course, we had an advantage then, with shooters like myself, the Boomer, Béliveau, and Dickie Moore. We had one of the greatest scoring teams of all time and, maybe, the greatest all-round hockey team of all time. Along with all those stars we also had my brother, Henri, coming up. Which was something of a surprise at the time.

Henri showed up at training camp in the fall of 1955 and everybody figured he'd be around for a few days and then the Canadiens would ship him down to one of their minor-league teams. But every time you looked around he had the puck and he stuck with the team right through training camp. Naturally, I was very proud of the kid. I realized he was small, but I also knew how tough he was. He also had ability—he could skate, stick-handle, and shoot. He had always played against older and bigger guys and handled himself well.

At first, I was tempted to take him in hand and give him a lesson in the facts of life in the N.H.L. Then I decided maybe we'd both be better off if I just left him alone. As it turned out Henri never came to me for advice and I never tried to give it to him. Whatever he accomplished—which was plenty—he accomplished on his own. Come to think of it, what kind of advice could I have given him? He was a better stick-handler than I was, and a better skater. As an all-round hockey player he was better than I. The only difference was that he couldn't score goals the way I could but he made up for that by becoming a terrific playmaker which, in its way, was just as important.

The only time I ever interfered on Henri's behalf was in his rookie year. Everybody in the league was out to test him because his name was Richard and he was a little guy. So, once in a while, when a big fellow like Lou Fontinato would run at him, I'd go up and hit the guy. That ended after the first year when I discovered that Henri didn't need any protection. In fact, I found out that the rougher the game, the better Henri would play.

Henri wasn't the only Richard to feel the pressure. My two oldest sons, Maurice, Jr., and Normand, went through hell themselves because of the name Richard. Maurice, Jr., my oldest boy, really had a tough time of it. He played organized hockey in Montreal and wasn't a bad little hockey player, but the kids made life miserable for him. Wherever he played they bothered him, not only the players but the public, too. They knew that he was my boy and they thought he should be the best player on the ice. Unfortunately, he was not. It was so tough for him that he finally quit playing hockey and concentrated on his college studies.

My second oldest boy, Normand, was also a good hockey player. He got as high as Junior A and then he decided that he would throw in the towel. It was the same story, the pressure was just too much with everybody expecting him to be a super hockey player. I have a younger son, André, who's also playing and he doesn't seem to be bothered as much by the Richard name. The reason is that the kids he plays with today are too young to remember me, so they don't give him the big reminder about his father.

But back to my brother, Henri. With him on my line I seemed to mellow quite a bit. I had made my resolution to "cool it" and I was making it stick. Blake was also a soothing influence. When he took over as coach he said, "If I ever say anything that hurts you, don't come back and say anything to the press. Wait, and come and see me and we'll talk about it." Toe was always afraid that I was going to talk in front of the other guys and to the newspapermen and hurt the team morale, but that never happened. In some ways, it was difficult for me to retain my composure when there were needlers like Fernie Flaman of the Bruins in the league. But I minded my business the last five years and managed to stay out of trouble.

My resolution to stay out of trouble was part of the reason for that. Also, I was older and heavier and slower. Even if I had wanted to retaliate I couldn't get the guys as easily as I had before. In my last five seasons, playing with Henri and Dickie Moore, I weighed over 200 pounds. I was only 160 when I started playing pro hockey.

With my weight that high I just wasn't the same Rocket. I tried dieting a couple of times and lost about ten pounds each time, but it made me feel weak. What I should have done, as I look back, is gone on a diet during the summer, lost about fifteen pounds, and then started eating when the season started. That way I'd have felt a lot stronger and I probably would have been able to add a few years to my career. But I was always trying diets in the winter and it did me more harm than good.

With my weight up I was more of an easy mark for opposing defensemen. In the mid-fifties I got into a couple of tangles with Lou Fontinato of the Rangers. One night he hit me a good one, right under the eye, that nearly brought down the house at Madison Square Garden. The old Rocket wouldn't have stood there and absorbed all the catcalls and the needling. I was mad as hell and I wanted to get back at Fontinato but the other men on the team cautioned me and pretty soon I cooled off. I actually didn't have all that big of a feud with Fontinato. At least not the kind of feud the newspapers made it out to be. I never thought he was a good hockey player but he was a hard worker and he could hit you a good body check which was not all that dirty. The guy whom Fontinato *really* feuded with was Bert Olmstead, who played left wing for us on the line with Béliveau and Geoffrion. One night Fontinato cross-checked Olmstead across the head with his stick after taking a flying leap. He hit Bert so hard that his stick cracked right across Olmstead's head and Bert fell to the ice as if he were dead. Fortunately, the check wasn't as bad as it looked, but I'll say this—I'm glad I wasn't on the receiving end.

Bert wasn't the most likeable guy in the world even to his own teammates. I didn't mind having him on the team because he was a hard worker and a good player but I never wanted him on the same line with me. I played two games with him on the line and then asked that he be taken off. He had a foul mouth, and when we played together, he would get mad when we made a bad pass or a bad play. Then he'd come to the bench and give us more hell. After two games I couldn't take it anymore—not from him or anyone else!

Otherwise, he was good for the team because he pepped up a lot of the players and he was marvelous at getting the puck out of the corners. As far as I'm concerned, Olmstead never played a bad game. But he was strange. He'd never say a word in the dressing room and after the games he wouldn't mix with anybody. He'd never go to parties and was always alone.

Not that I wasn't somewhat of a loner myself. I was very friendly with Ken Mosdell. Although he was one of the English-speaking players on the team, Kenny was always the guy I stayed with. His wife and my wife got along well together, which helped. Kenny was one of the most under-rated players on the Canadiens. He was good defensively, a good skater and playmaker and a very hard worker, as well as a very nice guy. I liked him and I also liked Bill Durnan. They were very much alike.

Durnan had long since retired and had been replaced by Gerry McNeil and then Jacques Plante. McNeil didn't last too long. As a goalie he was just fair, never a natural. He had to work for his job but not Plante. Jacques was one of the best goaltenders I've ever seen, probably ranking behind Durnan and Brimsek. He's the kind of athlete who is unbeatable when he *wants* to play the game, even in practice. Lots of times we'd want Jacques to play a good practice game so we'd make a two-dollar bet with him and then he'd be at his best.

I liked Jacques better as a player than as a personality. He popped off to the press and never seemed to want to take the blame for anything, especially when he was beaten and looked bad. As a result some of the players developed a dislike for him. Eventually, the Canadiens traded him. If he'd been smart, he would have been a lot more careful with what he said, especially to his own teammates. He would have been better liked and would have lasted in Montreal a lot longer than he did. The record shows that he didn't get along with Dick Irvin and he didn't get along with Toe Blake; in New York, he didn't get along with Red Sullivan.

To my mind there *had* to be something wrong if a guy couldn't get along with Blake. I know that Blake didn't like Plante's ways. If I had been the coach of the Canadiens, I would have felt the same way. I don't think I would have kept Plante one year!

However, you have to give Jacques credit where credit is due. He was the first goaltender to wear a mask. I can remember the night he first put it on. We were playing the Rangers at Madison Square Garden and Andy Bathgate, who had a terrific shot, hit Jacques in the face with one of his drives. Plante was a bloody mess as he went into the dressing room for repairs. By this time he had already been experimenting with the mask, although Blake wasn't crazy about it. He had one of them in the dressing room. When Plante came into that room, dripping with blood, he said, "If I don't wear the mask I'm not going out there anymore!" So Blake said, "Go ahead, wear the mask."

Jacques put on the mask and went out on the ice. He hasn't taken it off in a game since. That mask must have lengthened his career about ten years. Now just about every kid coming up from the juniors wears one, and pretty soon we'll be seeing the day when not one of the twenty-eight goalies in the N.H.L. goes out on the ice without one.

Jacques was lucky, too, because he had a fine defense in

front of him especially Doug Harvey. Doug was one of the greatest defensemen of all time, mostly because he had a terrifically cool attitude when the action got hot and heavy. Absolutely nothing bothered him, on or off the ice. He might be late for a workout or for the train, but he never rushed. His attitude was "everything's fine, everything's good." Which was just the opposite of Blake's approach. Toe couldn't stand Harvey's attitude and soon Harvey as well as Plante were traded to New York. Frankly, I don't think I'd have put up with Harvey either if I was his coach.

Each year my kid brother kept getting better and better which partly explains why we were able to take one Stanley Cup after another. Conn Smythe of the Leafs once said the key to a team's success is "strength down the center" and we sure had it. There was Henri, Béliveau, and young Ralph Backstrom but Henri and Béliveau were one-two, depending on how you like your centers. It's hard to compare the two because their styles differed so much. My brother is a better puck-carrier and a better skater and he can take more of the rough stuff than Béliveau, even though he's much smaller. Béliveau, of course, has been a better scorer, but I always felt that Henri was sort of skating in Béliveau's shadow and he really shouldn't have been. Henri was on the puck all the time and if he didn't have the puck, you knew he was always around. His one mistake always was not shooting enough.

Henri was such a speedy skater I had to work hard to keep up with him and Dickie Moore, but with each passing year it became harder and harder for me. The injuries started to occur more frequently. The worst, by far, was an injury to my Achilles tendon. That happened in a game against Toronto. Like so many hockey injuries, it was the result of a freak accident.

There was a pile-up in front of the Toronto net. I fell to the ice and the Leaf defenseman, Marc Reaume, fell on top of me. First, he tried to get up while I was still on the ice.

His skate was immediately behind my leather tendon guard that was connected to the back of my boot. The toe of his skate blade went behind my tendon guard and cut down the back of my foot, between the tendon guard and my stocking. His skate was very sharp and it sliced through the stocking *and* my tendon! For a while I thought it was the end of my career. I was out for three months with my foot in a cast. When I came back I wasn't too sure of myself and, I thought, if it was too difficult to play I'd hang up my skates for good. But I got two goals in my first game and two more in the second game and eleven goals in the play-offs. That gave me confidence again, and I kept playing, although my tendon was stiff and kept hurting me. The next season it was still stiff but not enough to keep me from playing.

The fact is I didn't really give any serious consideration to retiring until my last season in the league. That's when my weight started to bother me and I knew I was slowing down. Every so often Selke would come over and sort of encourage me to quit. "If you want to play next year, Rocket, that's okay," he'd say. "You can play. But if you don't want to play, we'll give you the same salary you're getting now and you'll be our public-relations man. You'll go on the road and visit different organizations." I listened to him, and I was getting the message, but I said, "I'll think about it during the summer and when I go back to training camp I'll decide what I'm going to do."

When I arrived at the 1960 training camp I surprised myself. I played very well and I was scoring goals, but also I was feeling it. I was obviously forcing myself and I seemed to be trying too hard. Back on the bench I'd get dizzy spells. And I started to fear getting hurt.

I don't think I had lost my scoring touch, though—not that I ever had any "secret" to scoring. That was one aspect of the game that I always blocked out of my mind. I never planned a play in advance. Whenever there was a break, a chance in front of the net, I'd try to pick a spot or try to beat the goalkeeper. Everything I did was spontaneous and every play I made seemed to be different from the one before.

Right in the middle of training camp I made up my mind that I had had it. The dizziness, the pushing, and the fact that it was so hard to lose weight convinced me that I'd be better off retiring. There were other considerations. My kids were growing up and they were watching every game. I didn't like the idea that they would see their father playing less than his best.

My wife went along with the decision. She and I had talked it over during the summer. She had said the decision had to be mine alone. I had no trouble telling Lucille about it but it was awfully difficult telling the kids, especially my son Normand. I felt bad about telling them. In fact, I didn't tell them about it until the day that I made the official announcement to the press, the radio, and the team officials.

When I told Selke, he didn't mind a bit. He told Senator Molson who was president of the team and they agreed that I would work for the team in the public-relations department. "We'll give you lots of work," Selke said at the time and he wasn't kidding! They really got their money's worth out of me. I traveled all over the place, from Vancouver to Halifax, right across the continent, four, five, six times a week for five months. It was then that I realized that this wasn't for me. I should have played another year or two. It would have been a lot easier.

I finally told Selke that I wasn't crazy about the new job. I saw him a couple of times about it. He asked me to keep at it a little longer. If anyone else had asked, I'd have said "no." But because it was Selke I kept going a little longer and then, finally, I wouldn't go anymore. Selke was still in power then, although the Molson family had bought the team. The real big change came a few years later when David Molson became president and Sammy Pollock was named general manager to replace Selke. That was the start of the new regime.

The appointment of David Molson and Sam Pollock in 1965 was made with a lot of fuss and fanfare. While they were at it they also announced that I was given the job of "assistant to the president," which, you will have to admit, is an impressive title. At first, I was very pleased with the appointment because they told the newspapermen that I would be working as a consultant to Pollock and Molson and would be active in the affairs of the team. All this was printed in the press and I assumed it would be the case. I approached the job with a great deal of enthusiasm.

It didn't take very long for me to realize that the whole thing wasn't quite as represented. To begin with, my salary was smaller than it had been under Selke. That was the first clue that something was wrong. But I was willing to make a few concessions here and there as long as I was a member of the Canadiens' team. Then they gave me a tiny office and I set myself up waiting for some work.

Right off the bat the new administration began holding meetings, to discuss player personnel and other aspects of the team. Since I was assistant to the president I assumed that I would participate in these meetings. Somehow, I was never asked to any of the meetings. I eventually discovered that there was really nothing for me to do. Apparently, the new administration didn't want me to do anything! I was just a showpiece sitting around the Forum like a potted plant! They didn't even show me the courtesy of asking my advice about some of the players whom I knew so much about. The only thing I did was go to an occasional banquet and make a few speeches —at half the salary I had made before. It was obvious to me that the new big man on the campus was Pollock and I didn't fit into his plans. I couldn't really have worked for him anyway because I didn't like his style of operating. Not that I have anything against him personally. He's a hard worker, he knows the game and the players, and, if I was the boss, I'd hire him anytime.

6

Blake

Retires

When Pollock and David Molson moved in, the whole atmosphere of the organization changed. It became more high-pressure than it had been under Selke. Hockey wasn't as much fun as it had been and I'm sure Toe Blake felt the same way. I think he would have quit a lot sooner than he did but Pollock kept urging him to stay. Toe didn't like the change in the organization any more than I did, although he wasn't the kind who would come out and say so. He wasn't wild about Pollock either and he finally left the team even though his club had finished on top and won the Stanley Cup.

There was always pressure playing in Montreal without this new group making it worse. Hockey in Montreal is different than in most cities. It's a religion in Montreal. When I was playing and went a couple of games without scoring, I wouldn't want to leave the house. If I went to the supermarket somebody was sure to say, "Hey, Rocket, what's the matter with you?" They'd give you hell wherever you went. As a result, a guy who plays hockey in Montreal has to work that much harder than in any other city in the league. You can imagine how much pressure there was on Blake. Toe had been brought up in the system under Tommy Gorman who was easygoing, and then under Selke who was a reasonable man. Pollock was something else again and Toe finally got out.

Now a big decision had to be made. Filling Blake's shoes would be just about the toughest job for a general manager. Toe was probably the best coach hockey has ever known, and his record with the Canadiens proves it. There's no doubt that Pollock was on the spot to come up with an able successor, possibly as much pressure as Selke faced when Dick Irvin left Montreal to go to Chicago.

Blake had been a natural in the job; there was no doubt about that. Now, Pollock knew that Blake had to retire sooner or later and Sammy is no dummy. He must have been thinking for some time about a replacement. His decision to pick Claude Ruel reveals something about Pollock's thinking.

Sam has always been an organization man. He had worked his way up through the Canadiens' system, coaching minor-league teams and then managing and scouting. There's no quarreling with that background. So it's not surprising that he'd choose a man who had been an organization man just as he was. Ruel had been a good defenseman with the Junior Canadiens before he lost an eye in a game. Then he turned to coaching and did pretty well. Finally, he had become the club's chief scout, which meant that he was in a good position to know nearly all the players in the Canadiens' organization.

Plain and simple, Ruel was Pollock's prodigy. Ruel had worked for Pollock ever since he had been a junior and Pollock wanted a man who knew what he wanted with no back talk. Sammy always wants to be top man in the organization, and Ruel, for all intents and purposes, would do what he asked. As a person, Claude is a good kid. For the organization he was ideal because he wasn't going to demand a big salary.

Right from the start Ruel had his troubles, although the Canadiens were able to conceal them in his rookie season. The club still had a lot of momentum from the previous year under Blake, and Béliveau had a year of good hockey left in him. As it turned out the club was lucky to squeeze into first place and beat the Bruins in the East Division finals. But the handwriting was on the wall. The centers were getting old and their replacements simply weren't good enough. After all, a club can go along with Henri and Béliveau for just so long. On top of that Backstrom was slowing down.

It didn't take a genius to realize that Ruel was not commanding the same kind of respect from the players that Irvin and Blake had inspired. Claude has a tendency to get overly excited. This plus his inexperience soon made him the butt of jokes from some of the veterans. Pretty soon it became clear that a lot of guys on the team didn't want to work for him. By the middle of the 1969–1970 season the evidence was there. First Dick Duff, a very fine left wing, began to have problems with him and then Gump Worsley. These men were two of the stars of the 1969 play-offs. Whenever veterans of their caliber have difficulties with the coach you know there's dissension on the team. I don't ever remember this happening under Irvin or Blake.

Pollock stuck by his man, Ruel. So Duff was traded to Los Angeles and Worsley was eventually dealt to Minnesota. Meanwhile, the team that had won the Prince of Wales Trophy and the Stanley Cup was suddenly fighting for a play-off berth! Some writers, like John Robertson of the Montreal *Star*, blamed Ruel directly. Others said that injuries were a factor and that some of the old stars like Béliveau were over the hill. Actually, it was a combination of all three.

By early March the pressure really tightened around Pollock. He could have fired Ruel then and there but he decided to give him a "vote of confidence." He signed him to a new contract and warned the players they would have to produce, or else. On paper this was not a bad hockey team; not by a long shot. But it was not a great one either; not in the sense of the teams I played on.

Consider some of the players. Jacques Laperrière has been an All-Star defenseman and he was a good junior. But I never liked him very much as a defenseman. Although he does play a good game once in a while, it's not enough to suit me. Terry Harper, another defenseman, is a good guy to have on the team. At first the Montreal fans, mostly the French-Canadians, took a dislike to Harper. He's a crude skater and he can look bad at times. But he kept working and now he's about the best defenseman on the team. He's learned to carry the puck and make a pass; the only thing he's missing is a good shot. Now, all of a sudden, everybody likes him in Montreal.

By contrast, J. C. Tremblay, a big hero on defense a few years ago, is booed regularly by the fans. Tremblay can be an excellent defenseman when he wants to work, but he has a tendency to get lazy and he doesn't play the man enough. He tries to be fancy and, very often, that can backfire on him.

After Harper, I'd say Serge Savard is the team's best defenseman. He was playing well during the 1969–1970 season until he broke his leg, crashing against the goalpost in March, 1970. What I like about him is his versatility. Savard can not only play defense but can be used as a utility forward and he can kill penalties.

Up front the Canadiens have too many little men. A typical example is Yvan Cournoyer. He's got a good shot and he's strong for his size and he can be pushed around a lot. Yvan has a good wrist shot and a quick slapshot, but he has a habit of shooting too often from the center zone and not enough from in close.

The forward I like best on the club is John Ferguson. He's a throwback to the old-time hockey players. He's absolutely fearless and he's strong. He likes to fight and doesn't waste time helping other guys on the team when they're in trouble. There aren't too many Fergusons left in the N.H.L. and the league is all the worse for that.

Ferguson has played quite a bit with Ralph Backstrom, a center who never really fulfilled his potential. He always manages to get into the enemy zone where he makes a bad pass and winds up in the corners.

The two most essential men in the Canadiens' drive for the championship in 1969–1970 were defenseman Serge Savard and right wing Bob Rousseau. Although they differ in physical stature the two French-Canadian skaters have much in common on the ice. At any given time they can play both an offensive and a defensive game. They are both expert at killing penalties.

Rousseau fell into disfavor and wound up in Minnesota after the 1969–1970 season. His small stature was one of Bobby's drawbacks. In contrast, Savard uses his huge body to great advantage and, despite his size, is a fast skater. Serge won the Conn Smythe Trophy as the most valuable player in the 1969 Stanley Cup play-offs and he fully deserved the award. In my opinion he ranks right behind Bobby Orr as the best young defenseman in hockey. Savard is extremely solid at the blue line and is excellent at blocking the enemy.

Savard's injury late in the 1969–1970 season and the inconsistent play of Rousseau throughout the campaign were two of the key reasons that the Canadiens failed to gain the play-off berth. It is ironic that Savard broke his leg while he was in the act of making a typically spectacular attempt to prevent a goal.

Another Canadien worth mentioning is Claude Provost, a former teammate of mine and one of the unsung heroes of the N.H.L. Provost was never a star in the true sense of the word, but because of his great desire, his perseverance and his love of work, he became one of the most valuable of the Habitants and the best defensive forward in hockey.

While Provost was in the twilight of his career another player was just hitching his wagon to a star; that was huge Peter Mahovlich, the big kid brother of Frank Mahovlich. When Peter came to the Canadiens' training camp in the fall of 1969, I predicted that he would make a name for himself with the Montreal team.

It is history that Peter did not immediately score a big hit with the Canadiens. He was assigned to the Montreal Voyageurs of the American League but, from time to time, the Canadiens would call him up to the N.H.L. Peter found his groove late in the season when he was ordered to replace the injured Jacques Lemaire. Mahovlich worked on a line with my brother Henri and Mickey Redmond and showed that by adding a little more muscle to his game he could make it in the N.H.L.

One of the most perplexing characters on the Canadiens

and the center of great controversy was the coach, Claude Ruel. Nobody could dispute Ruel's success in the 1968–1969 season, but the 1969–1970 campaign would prove to be Claude's moment of truth. Naturally, nobody could expect Ruel to better his rookie season but he was expected to do at least as well. To miss a play-off berth was out of the question. Ruel had a big plus going for him in his second year. The Canadiens loaded Les Voyageurs with some of the best young players in their farm system. Thus, if any of the players on the big team got hurt, Ruel simply had to yell downstairs, so to speak, and he would immediately have one of the Voyageurs' stars. In October, 1969, it certainly looked as if the Canadiens were capable of repeating their previous triumphs.

Apparently Montreal had escaped many of the problems that had hurt the other clubs. All the players had signed their contracts early and it seemed that Ruel would have a harmonious team, but this was not to be, as was discovered later in the season. Meanwhile, other clubs were having their woes. Bobby Hull refused to report to the Black Hawks over a contract dispute and Tim Horton said he was "retiring" from the Maple Leafs. Horton later "unretired" and won himself a fat contract. Personally, I thought Horton was putting on an act, and judging by his play later in the season, he did very little to help the Leafs. In my opinion he hardly earned his money.

The Hull–Black Hawk dispute was interesting because Bobby had earlier been blasted by his teammate, Pit Martin, for getting special privileges from management. Martin made a wholesale indictment of his team and said there were too many individuals and not enough team men on the club. Hull finally came to terms with management, and Martin somehow managed to keep his job. The Hawks made a dramatic change in style and high-scoring Bobby was suddenly reduced to a defensive checking forward. He didn't especially like his new role but he adapted to it and soon the Black Hawks became a contender.

Training camp explosions weren't confined to contract negotiations. In Ottawa the Bruins and Blues played an exhibition game, and in the middle of it Ted Green of Boston and Wayne Maki of St. Louis became embroiled in a vicious stick-swinging duel. Green fell to the ice, the victim of a fractured skull, and for a time it appeared that he might lose his life.

Once again, I believe that Clarence Campbell failed in his duty as president of the N.H.L. He suspended and fined each of the players and issued his usual reprimand about such behavior; the same old Campbell song I have heard going back to 1946. Actually, the punishment was light in relation to the nature of the offense. In this situation, a player was involved in a close brush with death.

Campbell's sentence was so light as to have virtually no curbing effect on future stick-swinging incidents and merely served to underline his weakness as president. To the other players in the N.H.L., Campbell's failure to take more severe action was nothing more than an invitation to resume the kind of behavior that led to the Maki-Green affair.

7

The Fall
of the Canadiens

*T*he signs that the Canadiens were about to crumble were very faint. Captain Jean Béliveau spent a very busy summer during 1969 working for his new public-relations company and turned up at training camp virtually exhausted. This was to be a terrific blow to the Canadiens because Béliveau never regained the form that had made him so important to the team in previous years.

Then more problems developed. Ruel decided to start Rogatien Vachon in the goal, while keeping Gump Worsley in reserve. This was a big mistake. Although Vachon had played superbly against Boston and St. Louis in the 1969 Stanley Cup triumph, he seemed to have lost his edge in the fall and he was blowing both hot and cold. A season earlier I had thought it would be wise to bench Worsley and use Vachon. This time, however, it was a mistake. Ruel should have been using Worsley on a more regular basis while keeping Vachon in reserve. Ruel's failure to do so ultimately led to a team crisis and would directly result in the Canadiens missing a play-off berth.

If anything, Ruel should have at least alternated them consistently rather than play Vachon the majority of the time. It is well known in hockey circles that an inactive goaltender turns stale very easily, which is what happened to Worsley. It would have been much more sensible had the coach alternated them on Saturday and Sunday nights right from the start of the season. My theory is that it's much more practical to use two goaltenders in the high-speed seventy-eight-game schedule N.H.L. hockey of today. But they must be alternated equally so that they both remain in top shape. This is exactly what Harry Sinden did at Boston in the 1969–1970 season and he just missed finishing in first place but won the Stanley Cup.

With Vachon getting the majority of the work, Worsley became rusty and was soon asked to report to the Voyageurs of the American League.

Worsley has always been a proud man and he rightfully refused the demotion. It was a foolish move on the Canadiens' part to order Gump to the Voyageurs because he could have worked himself into shape with the big team. Once Gump refused, management was backed against the wall. The bosses at the Forum wouldn't relent and the two positions hardened until it became apparent that Worsley could never again play for the Canadiens.

If the management believed that Worsley was over the hill, I, for one, didn't, and I said so at the time in my weekly column in the French-language paper *Dimanche-Matin*. My feeling was that Worsley, always a great competitor, still had a couple of years of good hockey in him just as Jacques Plante and Glenn Hall were proving they had at St. Louis. But Sam Pollock refused to talk with Worsley and eventually dealt him to Minnesota where he proved he was still sharp and in good condition. He led the North Stars to a play-off berth. By the same token, Worsley's departure was directly linked to the Canadiens' failure to make the play-offs because Vachon played mediocre hockey too often and Worsley's replacement, Phil Myre, just wasn't experienced enough to adequately substitute for the Gump. Pollock and Ruel were to pay dearly for their handling of Worsley.

I should put more emphasis on Pollock's role in the strategy than Ruel's. The fact of the matter is that Pollock called the shots for the Canadiens. It is the Pollock formula that has both made and broken the Canadiens. Ruel, like Blake before him, had to follow Sammy's orders, or else!

The Worsley affair was just one of several that disturbed the Canadiens as the 1969–1970 season moved along. There was also the dilemma concerning Dick Duff, the veteran left wing who had played so well in the 1969 Stanley Cup play-offs.

Duff missed several games because of some minor surgery, but when he returned to the Canadiens he remained out of shape and began to miss practices. Frankly, I was astonished at the patience the management had with Duff before he was finally traded to Los Angeles. In this case I believe the Canadiens did the right thing because Duff's departure meant there was more room for a younger player who would do the job as well as if not better than Duff and with considerably more enthusiasm.

Meanwhile, the injury jinx began hitting the Canadiens with unbelievable frequency. My brother Henri, who had emerged as the leader of the 1969–1970 Canadiens, was injured on December 27, 1969, which, in itself, was a remarkable coincidence. It was on that same date during my season with the Montreal Senior Canadiens that I fractured my ankle. Henri had been skating better than he had in years and was off to a sensational start.

Apart from Henri, there was Béliveau, who had been sidelined, and John Ferguson, the valuable left wing who was enduring a series of injuries that would plague him throughout the year. For that reason alone I began to wonder whether the Canadiens could summon enough power to finish first. I concluded that they would be fortunate to finish third behind the Bruins and Rangers. Mind you, it was in December when I thought that.

There were other symptoms of a Montreal malaise. One of the most surprising, from my point of view, was the negative reaction of the Forum spectators. I say surprising because when I was a player, there was no question that the Montreal fans were nearly 100 percent behind the Canadiens. In 1970 the whole sentiment of the audience was shifting. In all my career I can never recall the crowd lacking so much enthusiasm as it did then.

This lack of enthusiasm seemed to be contagious. Not

only were the fans on the quiet side but this feeling apparently affected the players as well. The old-time *joie de vivre* was gone and replaced by a more cynical attitude. No doubt part of this was due to the fact that the Canadiens have been so successful for so long that the customers have become accustomed to perfection, first place, and the Stanley Cup. They almost seemed to have become bored by triumph and, it is possible, now that the Canadiens are once again among the hoi polloi, the crowd will regain its verve.

There were times, though, in the 1969–1970 season, when the visiting team received as much or even more applause than the Canadiens. This inevitably has a destructive effect on the players and they performed more capably on the road than they did at home.

The man who paced the Canadiens' attack through the early part of January was Jacques Lemaire, a third-year man who had run up a fine total of twenty-five goals before the end of January. This was a case of a player doing well, yet capable of doing even better if he could shake himself of a bad habit. Lemaire possesses one of the hardest shots in the league; perhaps second only to Bobby Hull. Yet Jacques fell into the foolish habit of shooting the puck from far distances from the goal. He became a slave to his slapshot and instead of moving in close he began to shoot more and more from great distances. I mentioned this publicly in mid-January but I don't think Lemaire got my message. He scored only seven more goals during the second half of the season and finished with thirty-two when he might have even reached fifty.

Lemaire's case symbolized the Canadiens' plight in February, 1970. Man for man the Montreal sextet had the best team in the league but the Canadiens were not playing up to their capabilities; which was the fault of the players themselves, the coach, and the manager, not to mention the continuous string of injuries.

While the Canadiens fought to remain in play-off contention the tension of the homestretch become apparent among some of the players. There were reports of a rift between the English- and French-speaking players, rumors that the players were quietly mocking Ruel and that they had lost the will to win. I heard that the organization was having severe inner troubles. There was wrangling among Pollock, Ruel, and Molson and arguments between players and management.

Every so often an ugly incident would surface. A sportswriter named Guy Emond traveled with the team in February, 1970. Emond is an excellent raconteur with a wonderful sense of humor and is a good friend of many of the French-Canadian players on the team. They like him for his amiability and his funny stories. On one occasion Emond was sitting with some of the players in the rear of the airplane en route to Montreal from Chicago.

Les Canadiens had beaten the Black Hawks, 3–2, and there was a certain air of joviality on the plane, which was helped by Emond's stories. Guy was sitting with Serge Savard and a few other French-Canadian players when Ted Harris, the big English-speaking defenseman, walked to the back of the plane and saw Emond. "You have no business here," said Harris. "Leave!"

Emond didn't know whether Harris was kidding or not, but he had no intentions of giving up his seat, particularly after Savard had backed him up. "He's our friend," said Savard in defense of Emond.

It appeared that the incident would be closed at this point but Harris returned again and demanded that Emond leave. The Montreal defenseman then swung at the writer, missing his head and hitting him in the chest. At this point Emond got out of his seat and said he would find another. "Not because of you," he told Harris, "but in deference to the other players on the team."

The incident occurred early in February. When Emond returned to Montreal he told his editor, Jean-Paul Jarry, of *Dimanche-Matin*, about the episode. Jarry suggested that Emond wait a day or two so that the Canadiens' management would have enough time to formulate an apology. There was good precedent for this because a year earlier Ted Blackman, the Montreal *Gazette* sportswriter, had been struck by Maury Wills of the Expos. Almost immediately, the Expos, as well as major-league baseball leaders, came up with an apology to the newspaperman.

A week went by and still there was no reply from the Forum. "The Canadiens' executives didn't even apologize for Harris's stupid gesture," wrote Jarry in his weekly column. "There was no excuse for that. It is because of this bush-league attitude that I feel obliged to make this public." By the fall of 1970, however, Harris had become a member of the Minnesota North Stars.

Such unfortunate incidents contributed to the dissension in the Canadiens' camp. By late February it had become apparent that despite the terrible fall of the Rangers, the Canadiens could well tumble out of a play-off berth. To some viewers this was an impossible thought, but I recalled how the 1947–1948 team, on which I played, failed to make the play-offs and were beaten out by a scrappy New York team.

It had also become obvious that some of the genuine stars of the team were not giving 100 percent of their ability, for one reason or another. The captain Béliveau had his injuries but they had healed. He still was not the old Béliveau. One theory had it that Le Gros Bill never wanted to make a comeback in the 1969–1970 season. As I did, he wanted to retire on top after the Canadiens clinched the Stanley Cup in May, 1969. But Béliveau has long worked for the Molson Brewery, which owns Les Canadiens. When the Molsons suggested Béliveau make a comeback for 1969–1970, I believe he had no choice. But he couldn't give his best as a result of the pressure.

Others were also skating below par. Bobby Rousseau, whom I had mentioned as one of the most important members of the Canadiens, left a lot to be desired, as did J. C. Tremblay, formerly a great defenseman. On the other hand, Henri Richard, John Ferguson, Terry Harper, and Rogatien

Vachon gave all they had. As the schedule moved toward the first week of March, it was obvious that the Canadiens would require an all-out effort to regain any of the past glory.

This all-out effort seemed possible from time to time but then it would fizzle out into another "lost weekend." In early March a concerted effort began among some sportswriters, especially John Robertson of the Montreal *Star*, to fix the blame on Ruel's shoulders and Ruel alone. I believe this was grossly unfair. After all, Ruel was the same coach he had been the season before when he won the Prince of Wales Trophy and the Stanley Cup. As I've said it wasn't Ruel as much as the long sequence of injuries, the loss of Worsley to Minnesota, as well as the fact that some of the key veterans just weren't earning their money! A pair of losses to the Red Wings and Boston led one writer to suggest the theme of Montreal hockey in 1970 should be "The Rise and Fall of the Canadiens."

In addition an anti-Forum sentiment appeared to be surfacing in some areas. The quality of hockey had deteriorated especially in the games against West Division teams; yet the ticket prices were at an all-time high. Certain moves, or lack of moves, by Pollock angered the French-Canadian press. Jarry, for example, took Pollock to task for his failure to bring up Pierre Bouchard, a promising young defenseman with Les Voyageurs.

When Savard was injured and obviously finished for the season, Pollock executed another of his questionable decisions. He elevated Jean Gauthier, a veteran defenseman, who had failed in his earlier attempts with the Canadiens, Bruins, and Flyers. Mind you, I have considerable admiration for Gauthier's ability but I've always believed he didn't take his role seriously enough and, therefore, was less than at his best for the N.H.L. It seemed to me that Pollock should have elevated Pierre Bouchard, who was only twenty-two years old, compared with Gauthier's thirty-two years. Pierre is the son of my former teammate, Butch Bouchard, and a fine prospect if there ever was one. To my mind, Bouchard was the best young defenseman on Les Voyageurs. The failure to elevate him to Les Canadiens was an insult to French-Canadian hockey fans.

Fortunately for Ruel, J. C. Tremblay regained a measure of his old-time form and was a pillar of strength in the absence of Savard. But Gauthier was hardly ever used in the home-stretch as the Canadiens tried to stave off the Rangers' challenge.

Montreal could have solved all its problems on Saturday night, March 25, when the Rangers invaded the Forum for the first of a home-and-home series. Les Canadiens took a 1–0 lead late in the game on a goal by Peter Mahovlich, who had developed into a very valuable player. But the Rangers tied the score in the closing minutes and therein lies the cause of the Canadiens' demise. Too many times they were unable to hold on to leads in the late minutes of a game. In my day we would sustain the offense at all times. But the latter-day Canadiens tended to go into a defensive shell, which is the worst technique to use to protect a lead. A day later the Rangers whipped the Canadiens in New York and it was obvious that now the New Yorkers had revived themselves and Montreal would have to win by itself if it was to gain a play-off berth. The onus was on Béliveau. He had regained some of his championship form; but he would have to be at his best in the final three games of the season if Montreal was to survive.

Béliveau did become the Béliveau of old in the midweek game against Boston when he scored twice and led Les Canadiens to a one-sided victory. But New York had hung in there by defeating Toronto. So, now, on the final weekend, Montreal faced Chicago in a home-and-home series starting in the Forum. A win for Les Canadiens on Saturday night at home would put them in the play-offs. Even a tie would do it because the Rangers were losing to the Red Wings at Detroit that night.

But the Canadiens failed. Chicago, playing one of its best games in years, completely outclassed Montreal and romped to a 4–1 win. Béliveau was just another man on the ice and scored nothing. Fortunately, John Ferguson broke the shut-out late in the game and the Canadiens remained alive, thanks to the Ranger loss in Detroit.

It still looked good for Montreal. Even if the Canadiens lost to Chicago on Sunday and the Rangers defeated Detroit in New York they would be tied for fourth and Montreal would take the play-off berth on the basis of most goals scored; that is, if they could preserve their five-goal lead over the Rangers.

New York's game with Detroit was played on Sunday afternoon and it was a disgrace to hockey. Instead of icing his best team, Red Wing manager-coach Sid Abel started a third-string line and used his top line of Frank Mahovlich–Gordie Howe–Alex Delvecchio only sporadically throughout the game. Instead of using his ace goalie, Roy Edwards, he used Roger Crozier. Of course, it wasn't a "dump" but it was obvious that Abel was not sending out his best players; what mattered was that the Red Wings didn't appear to be trying their best. Hockey has rarely suffered such a black eye and the Detroit club should never be permitted to forget it. As a result, the Rangers breezed to a 9–5 win and, suddenly, had taken the goal lead away from the Canadiens.

I want to make it abundantly clear at this point that I take nothing away from the Rangers who played their hearts out and did get the goals. What matters more, as far as hockey's integrity is concerned, is Detroit's failure to send out its best possible team on Sunday, April 5, 1970.

As Dick Young, the New York *Daily News* columnist, pointed out: "You have a moral responsibility to your league, to your sport, to your conscience, to put out 100 percent as long as something is at stake, as there was to the Rangers and to Montreal.

"If Crozier is as good as Edwards, why was Edwards in the nets the night before when the game meant so much to De-troit? If I'm the Rangers, I'd much rather be shooting at Crozier than at one of the two men who shut me out in three years,

Roy Edwards. There are two days of rest between the final game and the play-offs, and why couldn't a victory party have waited till then? Why was Roy Edwards in the locker room during the game, sleeping off his sickness?"

When such incidents take place, hockey has to suffer just as it must suffer when you have a situation where two opponents, Mike Walton and Bobby Orr, are working as partners in a business enterprise as they have for the past few years. It is hard for me to believe that Orr and Walton, who are close friends as business partners, are going to play as hard against each other as two players who are not linked up by business. Certainly, in my day it would have been unheard-of for me, say, to go into business with Gordie Howe. It's downright unhealthy for hockey to have a situation like Walton and Orr working together in the off-season. Which is not to suggest that I'm critical of Orr as a player. In my opinion he is in a class by himself. He has revolutionized the defensive style of play and could eventually develop into hockey's all-time greatest star.

However, the Canadiens still had an opportunity to stay ahead of the Rangers when they skated out on Chicago Stadium ice the night of April 5, 1970. A win, a tie, or at least the ability to score five goals, even in defeat, would have saved them. They tried, to be sure, but they simply did not have it and they left the ice thoroughly disgraced by a 10–2 defeat.

History has demonstrated that all dynasties eventually come to an end. It happened in Green Bay with Vince Lombardi and it happened in New York to the Yankees. Eventually, it had to happen to Les Canadiens and now the question remains whether or not Sam Pollock and the Molsons can rebuild the team and the organization. Pollock started the rebuilding by dropping Ted Harris and Bobby Rousseau. But more had to be done.

It won't be easy. Many of the stars of yesteryear, such as Béliveau, Provost, Backstrom, and Richard, are getting older. Pollock will have to find a new leader to replace Béliveau, and I, for one, believe that that man should be Savard! In addition new blood is needed to rejuvenate the team and there must be a new feeling of rapport between players, coach, manager, and the upper-front office; otherwise the problems that beset the team in 1969–1970 will happen all over again and Les Canadiens will find themselves in trouble once more.

As a philosopher once said, "Pain and progress are inseparable." This is true in the case of Les Canadiens. The Montreal club has finally known the suffering of a fifth-place finish after twenty-two years of leadership. They may never again enjoy the domination they once experienced, but with proper direction they could once again rise from the ashes of defeat back to the top of the N.H.L. I, for one, hope this happens.

8

Hockey Was
a Better Game in My Day

When I played for the Montreal Canadiens in the 1940's and
1950's, the Stanley Cup play-offs always climaxed the National
Hockey League season. Every player seemed to reach his peak
then, and these games were usually the most exciting of the
season.

That's not true anymore.

In 1968 and 1969 the Cup games between the Eastern
Division Canadiens and the Western Division St. Louis Blues
were something of a joke. The teams played eight times and
St. Louis didn't win a game. In the 1968 series the Blues made
it close, but in 1969 the games were so bad and so one-sided
that one critic said the series was "like Sominex on the rocks."
In 1970 St. Louis lost four straight games to Boston in the finals.

The problem, of course, was that the best team in the
expansion West was just not ready yet to engage the best
team in the established East in a showdown series. The truly
great Stanley Cup games in the spring of 1969 were between
the Canadiens and Boston Bruins in the Eastern Division finals.
For most hockey fans this was when the season really ended;
the Montreal–St. Louis series was mere formality.

There is something drastically wrong when hockey's
showcase series is suddenly meaningless. But there is more
to hockey's ills than just a mismatch in the Stanley Cup
finals. The game of hockey—from the first face-off in October
to the last one in April—is simply not the game it was in my
day. Shooting was more accurate then. Passing cleverer. Stick-
handling was an art practiced not by just a few but by many.
And, most important, there was much more individuality. In

short, the game is hurting today, and if you want to find the causes, you have to start with the biggest one—expansion.

I'm afraid I have to agree with Toronto *Daily Star* columnist Jim Proudfoot when he says, "The N.H.L. never has been motivated by what its customers might or might not like. It has been guided, instead, by its estimate of what the public will hold still for. . . . The only trouble is that the hockey is no longer exciting very often."

One example of what Proudfoot is talking about is found in the schedule since expansion. In 1968–1969 the Canadiens played only forty of their seventy-six games against Eastern teams. That meant that Montreal's great rivals, such as the Bruins and the Maple Leafs, came to the Forum just four times each, instead of seven times as they used to. That's a big difference, especially when the replacement is an inferior team. St. Louis has yet to beat an East team in the play-offs. The league bosses thought they would help the expansion teams at the gate by having the established clubs play them more often, but this is a mistake. A well-matched contest lures the customer, and one poorly matched keeps them away.

Overall, in 216 interdivisional games in 1968–1969, the West won just 51 and lost 129. It was no different in 1969–1970. Some people will boast that 51 wins is plenty for new teams, but really, it's not so much the *fact* of winning as it is the *act* of winning. When a Western team won, it was often done with an unappetizing, defense-minded style. Some people call it "kitty-bar-the-door" hockey, but the tactic by any other name would still be as boring. The idea is to keep each of the opposing players closely checked, hoping that sooner or later they themselves will get a break and score. If they do get a goal, they can return to the defensive, trying to protect the lead until the end of the game. But it's also a device that greatly limits the moments of enjoyable hockey. When the defending team is constantly holding back, the game is slowed down considerably, and at that point hockey can no longer pride itself on being called "the fastest game on earth." Even the players find themselves bored. Ed Giacomin, the

Ranger's goalie, once said he couldn't keep awake because there was so little action in the game.

Another reason the players tend to hold back is the expanded schedule which doesn't even include exhibition games. By adding more teams the owners felt obliged to lengthen the schedule, and when that happened players began watching themselves more carefully, trying to last out the longer year. It makes for a situation where the players just don't put out all they can.

Still another evil of expansion has been the downgrading of scoring values. There was a time when it was an honor to score twenty goals in a season. It was like hitting .300 in baseball. But now twenty goals don't mean beans at contract time. Nearly a month before the season had ended in 1968–1969, a bunch of unknowns had scored twenty goals— players like Garry Unger, Bill Flett, André Lacroix, Ed Joyal, Gary Sabourin, and Gary Jarrett. I don't want to take anything away from these players, but I just can't include them among the All-Stars. Too many of their goals are against weak expansion defenses, and when two expansion teams get together they play a more wide open game than when one of them is up against an established team.

You know what else has changed? *The game isn't as tough as it used to be.* You can count on the fingers of less than two hands the really tough fighters in the game: Ted Harris, Ted Green, John Ferguson, Gordie Howe, Gilles Marotte, and Orland Kurtenbach are the best ones. And there really isn't what I would consider a fine body-checker among them.

When I was playing, nearly every team was loaded with policemen. The Toronto Maple Leafs of 1947–1948, for example, had a whole roster of hitters: Bill Ezinicki, Gus Mortson, Bill Barilko, Garth Boesch, Vic Lynn, Howie Meeker, Harry Watson, and Jim Thomson, to name just a few. It was like that all over. Detroit had Black Jack Stewart and Ted Lindsay; even their goalie, Harry Lumley, liked to fight. Montreal had hitters like Ken Reardon, Butch Bouchard, Glen Harmon, and on and on.

You really had to watch out for the heavy body-checkers back then. Ezinicki was typical. He'd circle center ice and roam around until he thought you were off guard, and then he'd go into orbit and try to hit you from the blind side. He got me a few times, and not always legally either. I also remember a fellow on the Rangers named Bill Moe. He could catch you with his hip and send you somersaulting onto the ice. That kind of body checking is a lost art today and the game is all the worse for it.

Another aspect of hockey you see less and less is the magic of stick-handling. There are still a couple of good magicians left such as Gordie Howe, of Detroit, and Stan Mikita, of the Black Hawks, but not many others. It seems as if the youngsters coming up have not been taught properly. They just skate and slap the puck wildly. There's nobody around like Max Bentley, who could do fantastic things with the puck, and Edgar Laprade and Buddy O'Connor and many, many more. Their stick-handling gave a certain individuality to the game that you don't see much of anymore. Today, players are always trying to pass the puck ahead, instead of taking the time to stick-handle.

This also makes for a sloppier game. More and more of the goals come as a result of a puck bouncing in off somebody's leg or a mad scramble around the net, and that's directly linked to the disappearance of the great forward lines. In 1948, for instance, we had the Punch Line (Richard, Elmer Lach, Toe Blake) in Montreal. Detroit had the Production Line (Howe, Lindsay, and Sid Abel). Toronto had the Kid Line (Howie Meeker, Vic Lynn, Ted Kennedy), and the Rangers had the Atomic Line (Cal Gardner, Church Russell, and Rene Trudell).

Fifteen and twenty years ago every team had at least one good line, and some of them had three. Today, with fewer good players, every club changes the players around con-

stantly, like parts in a machine. That hurts the quality of the
game because the players don't get a chance to work ex-
clusively with two other men and develop the pretty plays
that come only through anticipating your linemates' moves.

In the 1968–1969 season the Red Wings had one of the
best lines in the league in Gordie Howe, Frank Mahovlich,
and Alex Delvecchio. Yet as soon as the season ended, coach
Bill Gadsby said he'd have to break up the line because his
second and third units were so weak he needed to add more
balance to the attack. That's typical of what's happening
today.

The decline in stick-handling and creative line-passing
has been accompanied by a decline in the art of shooting. I
remember during the 1969 All-Star Game, when Red Berenson
scored a goal against Ed Giacomin. Many people were
amazed that Berenson did it on a back hand shot, they see
so few of them. It was almost as if the backhander had just
been invented by Berenson, right before their eyes. But when
I was playing, nearly every player had a good backhander; in
fact, I scored most of my goals that way.

The difference in the two eras, of course, is that most
players use a curved stick nowadays, which means: (1) It's
practically impossible to stick-handle the puck as well as
with a flat stick and (2) it's just as impossible to get off a
backhander from the "wrong" side of the curved blade. Since
most kids now use the curved stick as soon as they begin
playing hockey, few are learning to backhand.

Young players are also slapping the puck too much—the
way Bobby Hull does—and not learning how to release a
solid wrist shot, which is far easier to control. Ten years ago
nobody would have thought of shooting the puck from the
center red line and expect to score a goal. We would have
attempted to go in on the goalkeeper. But now that there are
players who aren't competent enough to stick-handle around
a defense, they'll get rid of the puck with an erratic slapshot. So the combined effect of the curved stick and slapshot

lowers the quality of the game, despite an exception like Hull who puts both to spectacular use.

Despite all these grumblings from this particular gray-beard, the hockey picture is not all bleak. For one thing, the modern player is more independent and conscious of his value than I ever was. Some players are getting $50,000 to $100,000 contracts, and there is a union to protect the average player. On the other hand, the player of today has been spoiled by the new riches. Some expansion players, for example, realize that the reserves behind them aren't very talented, so they are not apt to work as hard as we used to. We knew that if we didn't produce there was plenty of good material in the minors.

And the attitude of opposing players has changed. Rivals are going into business with each other, as I mentioned, like Bobby Orr of Boston and Mike Walton of Toronto, who are running a summer camp. I feel all this fraternizing takes something off the competitive edge, and I know that when I played, fraternizing with the enemy was out.

By now you may find this hard to believe, but I really do love the game of hockey. Not only that, but I think the owners can straighten things out and make the game better than ever. All it will take is a little time. The big hope for the West lies with the young kids coming up. After two or three years they'll be showing considerable improvement and some of them could turn into superstars the way others already have in the East. When that happens, the West will be competing favorably with the older division.

In the meantime, the league governors should make sure there's better distribution of talent to future expansion teams than there has been in the past. Instead of permitting a team to protect eighteen or fourteen players in the draft, cut the figure to ten and let the new teams have a chance. Now that Vancouver and Buffalo have the latest new franchises in the N.H.L., I, for one, would like to see them make it because it would be good for hockey. I'm sure there are enough hockey players in Canada to meet the demand. All they need is the proper training and the ability to play in an atmosphere of even competition.

A couple of rules changes might help, too. Something should be done to put more of the class back in the game—the stick-handling and the wrist shot and the pattern plays that are so beautiful. Maybe it would be a good idea to eliminate the center red line and allow passing all the way up to the opponent's blue line. And maybe we should eliminate the slapshot until the puck is carried over the enemy blue line. And perhaps the curved stick should be eliminated altogether.

It would also be a good idea if the schedule makers saw to it that some of the teams weren't forced to play three games in three days after making long plane trips. When the owners permit such tight scheduling, they are begging for an inferior product that will be rejected sooner or later by the fans.

We shouldn't argue with progress, which is what expansion amounts to, but, at the same time, we shouldn't permit it to ruin the game as it has the last few years. I hope the N.H.L. takes swift measures to improve the situation so that we won't ever have to see again the headline that ran in the Toronto *Daily Star*. It read: "Stanley Cup Is Tarnished."

That's no way to run a hockey league.

PART III

RECORDS
OF THE CANADIENS

Canadiens' Team Standing by Season

Season	GP	Won	Lost	Tied	GF	GA	Points	Standing
1917–1918	22	13	9	0	115	72	26	1st
1918–1919	18	10	8	0	88	78	20	2nd
1919–1920	24	13	11	0	129	113	26	2nd
1920–1921	24	13	11	0	112	99	26	3rd
1921–1922	24	12	11	1	88	105	25	3rd
1922–1923	24	13	9	2	73	61	28	2nd
1923–1924	24	13	11	0	59	48	26	2nd
1924–1925	30	17	11	2	93	56	36	3rd
1925–1926	36	11	24	1	79	108	23	7th
1926–1927	44	28	14	2	99	67	58	2nd
1927–1928	44	26	11	7	116	48	59	1st
1928–1929	44	22	7	15	71	43	59	1st
1929–1930	44	21	14	9	142	114	51	2nd
1930–1931	44	26	10	8	129	89	60	1st
1931–1932	48	25	16	7	128	111	57	1st
1932–1933	48	18	25	5	92	115	41	3rd
1933–1934	48	22	20	6	99	101	50	2nd
1934–1935	48	19	23	6	110	145	44	3rd
1935–1936	48	11	26	11	82	123	33	4th
1936–1937	48	24	18	6	115	111	54	1st
1937–1938	48	18	17	13	123	128	49	3rd
1938–1939	48	15	24	9	115	146	39	6th
1939–1940	48	10	33	5	90	167	25	7th
1940–1941	48	16	26	6	121	147	38	6th
1941–1942	48	18	27	3	134	173	39	6th
1942–1943	50	19	19	12	181	191	50	4th
1943–1944	50	38	5	7	234	109	83	1st
1944–1945	50	38	8	4	228	121	80	1st

Season	GP	Won	Lost	Tied	GF	GA	Points	Standing
1945–1946	50	28	17	5	172	134	61	1st
1946–1947	60	34	16	10	189	138	78	1st
1947–1948	60	20	29	11	147	169	51	5th
1948–1949	60	28	23	9	152	126	65	3rd
1949–1950	70	29	22	19	172	150	77	2nd
1950–1951	70	25	30	15	173	184	65	3rd
1951–1952	70	34	26	10	195	164	78	2nd
1952–1953	70	28	23	19	155	148	75	2nd
1953–1954	70	35	24	11	195	141	81	2nd
1954–1955	70	41	18	11	228	157	93	2nd
1955–1956	70	45	15	10	222	131	100	1st
1956–1957	70	35	23	12	210	155	82	2nd
1957–1958	70	43	17	10	250	158	96	1st
1958–1959	70	39	18	13	258	158	91	1st
1959–1960	70	40	18	12	255	178	92	1st
1960–1961	70	41	19	10	254	188	92	1st
1961–1962	70	42	14	14	259	166	98	1st
1962–1963	70	28	19	23	225	183	79	3rd
1963–1964	70	36	21	13	209	167	85	1st
1964–1965	70	36	23	11	211	185	83	2nd
1965–1966	70	41	21	8	239	173	90	1st
1966–1967	70	32	25	13	202	188	77	2nd
1967–1968	74	42	22	10	236	167	94	1st
1968–1969	76	46	19	11	271	202	103	1st
1969–1970	76	38	22	16	244	201	92	5th

(Eastern
Division)

Canadiens' Scoring and Penalty Leaders
Since 1917–1918

Season	Player	Goals	Player	Ass.	Player	G	A	TP	Player	TPM
1917–1918	J. Malone	44x	League did not record assists or penalties this season.							
1918–1919	N. Lalonde	23x	N. Lalonde	9x	N. Lalonde	23	9	32x	J. Hall	85x
1919–1920	N. Lalonde	36	D. Pitre	7	N. Lalonde	36	6	42	B. Corbeau	59
			L. Berlinguette	7						
1920–1921	N. Lalonde	33	L. Berlinguette	9x	N. Lalonde	33	8	41	B. Corbeau	86x
1921–1922	O. Cleghorn	21	L. Berlinguette	7	O. Cleghorn	21	3	24	S. Cleghorn	63x
			S. Cleghorn	7	S. Cleghorn	17	7	24		
1922–1923	B. Boucher	23	A. Joliat	9	B. Boucher	23	4	27	B. Boucher	52x
1923–1924	B. Boucher	16	B. Boucher	6	B. Boucher	16	6	22	S. Cleghorn	39
1924–1925	A. Joliat	29	B. Boucher	13	A. Joliat	29	11	40	B. Boucher	92x
1925–1926	H. Morenz	23	A. Joliat	9	H. Morenz	23	3	26	B. Boucher	112
					A. Joliat	17	9	26		
*										
1926–1927	H. Morenz	25x	H. Morenz	7	H. Morenz	25	7	32x	A. Joliat	79
1927–1928	H. Morenz	33x	H. Morenz	18x	H. Morenz	33	18	51x	A. Joliat	105
1928–1929	H. Morenz	17	H. Morenz	10	H. Morenz	17	10	27	A. Leduc	79

Season	Player	Goals	Player	Ass.	Player	G	A	TP	Player	TPM
1929–1930	H. Morenz	40x	A. Joliat	12	H. Morenz	40	10	50	S. Mantha	108
1930–1931	H. Morenz	28	H. Morenz	23	H. Morenz	28	23	51x	M. Burke	91x
1931–1932	H. Morenz	24	H. Morenz	25	H. Morenz	24	25	49	S. Mantha	62
1932–1933	A. Joliat	18	J. Gagnon	23	A. Joliat	18	21	39	J. Gagnon	64
1933–1934	A. Joliat	22	A. Joliat	15	A. Joliat	22	15	37	G. Carson	51
			J. Gagnon	15						
1934–1935	L. Goldsworthy	20	P. Lépine	19	P. Lépine	12	19	31	R. Jenkins	63
			W. Larochelle	19						
1935–1936	L. Goldsworthy	15	P. Haynes	19	L. Goldsworthy	15	11	26	J. Gagnon	42
	A. Joliat	15								
1936–1937	J. Gagnon	20	B. Siebert	20	J. Gagnon	20	16	36	J. Gagnon	38
**									B. Siebert	38
1937–1938	G. Mantha	23	P. Haynes	22	G. Mantha	23	19	42	B. Siebert	56
1938–1939	H. Blake	24	P. Haynes	33	H. Blake	24	23	47x	S. Evans	58
1939–1940	H. Blake	17	C. Sands	20	H. Blake	17	19	36	P. Drouin	51
1940–1941	J. Quilty	18	H. Blake	20	J. Quilty	18	16	34	E. Chamberlain	75
1941–1942	J. Benoît	20	H. Blake	28	H. Blake	17	28	45	K. Reardon	93
1942–1943	J. Benoît	30	H. O'Connor	43	H. Blake	23	36	59	L. Lamoureux	53
1943–1944	M. Richard	32	E. Lach	48	E. Lach	24	48	72	M. McMahon	98x
1944–1945	M. Richard	50x	E. Lach	54x	E. Lach	26	54	80x	L. Lamoureux	58
1945–1946	H. Blake	29	E. Lach	34x	H. Blake	29	21	50	E. Bouchard	52
1946–1947	M. Richard	45x	H. Blake	29	M. Richard	45	26	71	E. Chamberlain	97
1947–1948	E. Lach	30	E. Lach	31	E. Lach	30	31	61x	K. Reardon	129
1948–1949	W. Reay	22	W. Reay	22	W. Reay	22	23	45	E. Chamberlain	111

Season										
1950–1951	M. Richard	42	E. Lach / M. Richard / D. Harvey	24	M. Richard	42	24	66	T. Johnson	
1951–1952	B. Geoffrion	30	E. Lach	50x	E. Lach	15	50	65	D. Harvey	82
1952–1953	M. Richard	28	M. Richard	33	M. Richard	28	33	61	M. Richard	112x
1953–1954	M. Richard	37x	B. Olmstead	37	M. Richard	37	30	67	M. Richard	112
1954–1955	B. Geoffrion / M. Richard	38x / 38x	B. Olmstead	48x	B. Geoffrion	38	37	75x	M. Richard	125
1955–1956	J. Béliveau	47x	B. Olmstead	56x	J. Béliveau	47	41	88x	J. Béliveau	143
1956–1957	J. Béliveau / M. Richard	33 / 33	J. Béliveau	51	J. Béliveau	33	51	84	J. Béliveau	105
1957–1958	D. Moore	36x	H. Richard	52x	D. Moore	36	48	84x	D. Harvey	107
1958–1959	J. Béliveau	45x	D. Moore	55x	D. Moore	41	55	96x	J.-G. Talbot	77
1959–1960	J. Béliveau	34	H. Richard	43	J. Béliveau	34	40	74	H. Richard	66
1960–1961	B. Geoffrion	50x	J.-G. Talbot	58x	B. Geoffrion	50	45	95x	J.-G. Talbot	143
1961–1962	C. Provost	33	H. Richard	42	R. Backstrom	27	38	65	L. Fontinato	167
1962–1963	G. Tremblay	25	J. Béliveau	50x	H. Richard	23	50	73	L. Fontinato	141
1963–1964	J. Béliveau	28	C. Provost	50	J. Béliveau	28	50	78	J. Ferguson	125
1964–1965	C. Provost	27	R. Rousseau	37	C. Provost	27	37	64	J. Ferguson	156
1965–1966	R. Rousseau	30	R. Rousseau	48	R. Rousseau	30	48	78	J. Ferguson	153
1966–1967	R. Rousseau	19	R. Rousseau	44	R. Rousseau	19	44	63	J. Ferguson	177
1967–1968	J. Béliveau	31	J. Béliveau	46	J. Béliveau	31	37	68	J. Ferguson	117
1968–1969	Y. Cournoyer	43	Y. Cournoyer	49	Y. Cournoyer	43	44	87	J. Ferguson	185
1969–1970	J. Lemaire	32	H. Richard	36	Y. Cournoyer	27	36	63	J. Ferguson	139

* to **: League was divided into two sections, Canadian and American. Only the Canadian section of which Canadiens were a member has been taken into consideration as regards records for goals, assists, etc.

Canadiens' National Hockey League Team Records

Most games won in a single season..46
Set by Montreal Canadiens in a seventy-six game schedule, 1968–1969, winning forty-six, losing nineteen, and tying eleven.

Most goals scored by one team in one game...........................16
Canadiens scored sixteen goals March 3, 1920, at Quebec in defeating Quebec Bulldogs, 16–3.

Most total goals scored in one game...21
Canadiens 14, Toronto 7, at Montreal, January 10, 1920.

Most penalties in one game..36
Seventeen minors, four majors, and fifteen misconducts were given for a total of thirty-six on December 9, 1953, at Toronto in a game between Canadiens and Toronto.

Most penalty minutes in one game...204
Canadiens had eight misconducts, two majors, and eight minors for 106 minutes; Toronto had seven misconducts, two majors, and nine minors for 98 minutes for total of 204 minutes in game of December 9, 1953, at Toronto.

Most penalties in one period...26
Fifteen misconducts, four majors, and seven minors were given by Frank Udvari in third period of game in Toronto, December 9, 1953, between Toronto and Canadiens.

Most penalty minutes in one period...184
184 minutes in penalties, comprised of fifteen misconducts, four majors, and seven minors were handed out by Frank Udvari in Toronto, December 9, 1953.

Most shutouts by a team in one season...................................22

Scored by Canadiens in a forty-four game schedule in 1928–1929.

Longest undefeated record at home..28
Set by Canadiens. Began March 13, 1943, with a 6–6 draw with Chicago and ended November 2, 1944, when they lost, 4–1, to Toronto. They played the entire 1943–1944 season without a loss at home, winning twenty-two and tying three. In the twenty-eight games Canadiens won twenty-four and tied four.

Most tie games in one season..23
Canadiens (1962–1963).

Fewest losses, one season..5
Ottawa Senators, 1919–1920 (twenty-four game schedule); Boston Bruins, 1929–1930 (four-forty-game schedule); Montreal Canadiens, 1943–1944 (fifty-game schedule).

Fewest goals against, one season (seventy-game schedule) 131 Toronto Maple Leafs (1953–1954), Montreal Canadiens (1955–1956).

PLAY-OFFS

Most times Stanley Cup winners...16
Since its presentation by Lord Stanley of Preston in 1893, the Stanley Cup has been won sixteen times by the Montreal Canadiens, seven times more than the Toronto Maple Leafs and eight more than Detroit Red Wings.
The Canadiens first won the Cup in 1915–1916 and since have won it in 1923–1924, 1929–1930, 1930–1931, 1943–1944, 1945–1946, 1952–1953, 1955–1956, 1956–1957, 1957–1958, 1958–1959, 1959–1960, 1964–1965, 1965–1966, 1967–1968, 1968–1969.

Most conscecutive years Stanley Cup finalists........................10
Canadiens played in ten Stanley Cup Finals, from 1950–1951 to 1959–1960.

Most years in play-off...40
Canadiens.

Most consecutive Stanley Cup championships.......................5
Canadiens (1956–1960).

Most consecutive play-off appearances 21
Canadiens (1949–1969).

Most final series appearances 20
Canadiens.

Most goals, one team, four-game series...............................26
Canadiens in 1946 semifinal.

Most goals, both teams, four-game series.............................33
Canadiens, Chicago, in 1946 semifinal. Canadiens won best-
of-seven series, 4–0, outscoring Chicago, 26–7.

Most goals, one team, five-game series................................24
Canadiens in 1956 semifinal. Canadiens defeated New York
Rangers, 4–1, in best-of-seven series, outscoring Rangers, 24–9.

Most goals both teams, five-game series..............................35
Boston, Canadiens, in 1943 semifinal. Boston won best-of-seven
series, 4–1, outscoring Canadiens, 18–17.

Fewest goals, one team, four-game series...............................2
Boston Bruins in 1935 semifinal, outscored by Toronto 7–2;
Canadiens in 1952 final, outscored by Red Wings, 11–2.

Most goals, one team, one game..11
Canadiens at Montreal, March 30, 1944. Canadiens 11, Toronto
0.

Most goals, both teams, one game..13
Detroit, Toronto, at Detroit, April 7, 1936. Detroit 9, Leafs 4.
Canadiens, Toronto, at Montreal, March 29, 1945. Canadiens
10, Toronto 3.

Most goals, one team, one period...7
Canadiens, March 30, 1944, at Montreal in third period against
Toronto.

Most goals, both teams, one period..7
Toronto, Boston, at Toronto, March 26, 1936, in second period.
Toronto won game, 8–3, scored six of the second-period goals.
New York Americans, Detroit, at New York, March 22, 1940, in
third period. Americans scored four of the goals winning game,
5–4; Canadiens, Toronto, at Montreal, March 30, 1944, in third
period. Canadiens scored all seven goals winning game, 11–0.

Most overtime games, final series..5
Toronto, Canadiens, in 1951. Leafs beat Canadiens, 4–1, in
best-of-seven series.

Most consecutive play-off game victories....................................11
Canadiens. Streak began April 16, 1959, at Toronto with 3–2
win in fourth game of final series won by Canadiens, 4–1, and
ended March 23, 1961, when Chicago defeated Canadiens,
4–3, in second game of semifinal series. Included in the streak
were eight straight victories in 1960.
Streak began April 28, 1968, at Montreal with 4–3 win in fifth
game of semifinal series against Chicago won by Canadiens,
4–1, and ended April 17, 1969, when Boston defeated Canadiens, 5–0, in third game of semifinal series.

Fastest two goals, both teams..10 seconds
Toronto, Detroit, at Detroit, April 5, 1936. Wally Kilrea scored
at 12:05 of first period for Detroit and Buzz Boll of Toronto
scored at 12:15. Detroit won game, 3–1. Toronto, Canadiens, at
Toronto, April 12, 1947. Vic Lynn of Toronto scored at 12:23 of
second period and Leo Gravelle of Montreal at 12:33. Toronto
won game, 4–2.

Fastest three goals, one team..56 seconds
Canadiens at Detroit, April 6, 1954, against Red Wings. Dickie
Moore scored at 15:03 of first period, Maurice Richard at 15:28
and again at 15:59. Canadiens won game, 3–1.

Fastest three goals, both teams....................................38 seconds
Canadiens, Toronto, April 13, 1965, at Toronto. Red Kelly of
Toronto scored at 3:11 of first period, John Ferguson of Cana-

diens at 3:32, and Ron Ellis of Toronto at 3:49. Canadiens won game, 4–3, in overtime.

Fastest four goals, one team.......................2 minutes, 35 seconds
Canadiens at Montreal, March 30, 1944, against Toronto. Toe Blake scored at 7:58 of third period and again at 8:37, Maurice Richard at 9:17 and Ray Getlifie at 10:33. Canadiens won game, 11–0.

Fastest four goals, both teams....................1 minute, 39 seconds
Canadiens and Toronto, April 13, 1965, at Toronto. Dave Keon scored for Toronto at 2:10 of first period, Red Kelly of Toronto at 3:11, John Ferguson of Canadiens at 3:32, and Ron Ellis of Toronto at 3:49. Canadiens won game, 4–3, in overtime.

Fastest five goals.......................................3 minutes, 36 seconds
Five goals were scored in third period in 3 minutes and 36 seconds as Canadiens defeated Toronto, 11–0, at Montreal, March 30, 1944.

Highest shutout game...11–0
Canadiens defeated Toronto, 11–0, in Montreal, in fifth game of semifinal round, March 30, 1944.

Most games home team winless....................................9
Nine play-off games involving Montreal-Detroit and Toronto-Boston were played before the home team finally won, in play-offs of 1950–1951. Five in Montreal-Detroit series and four in Toronto-Boston series were played before Canadiens and Toronto won in their home rinks the night of Saturday, April 7, 1951.

Consecutive game record for wins...............................8
Shared by Detroit Red Wings and Canadiens. Wings won Stanley Cup in eight straight games in 1951–1952, defeating Toronto and Canadiens. Canadiens won Stanley Cup in eight straight games in 1959–1960, defeating Chicago and Toronto.

Canadiens' National Hockey League Individual Records

Most points in one game..8
Set by Maurice Richard at Montreal on December 28, 1944, when he scored five goals and three assists as Canadiens defeated Detroit, 9–1. Record was tied by Bert Olmstead of Canadiens with four goals and four assists on January 9, 1954, as Canadiens defeated Chicago at Montreal, 12–1.

Most goals in one season by a right wing..............................50
Set by Maurice Richard of Canadiens in a fifty-game schedule in 1944–1945. Tied by Bernie Geoffrion of Canadiens in a seventy-game schedule in 1960–1961.

Most shutouts by a goalkeeper in one season...........................22
Set by George Hainsworth of Canadiens who scored twenty-two shutouts in a forty-four-game schedule in 1928–1929.

Least goals scored against a goalkeeper.................................43
Set by George Hainsworth of Canadiens who allowed forty-three goals in forty-four games in 1928–1929.

Most goals, one season including play-offs..............................59
Jean Béliveau, Canadiens, 1955–1956, forty-seven goals in seventy regular season games; twelve goals in ten play-off games.

Most assists, one period..4
Buddy O'Connor, Canadiens, November 8, 1942, at Montreal, third period. Montreal 10, New York Rangers 4. Doug Bentley, Chicago Black Hawks, January 28, 1943, at Chicago, third period. Chicago 10, New York 1. Joe Carveth, Detroit Red Wings, January 28, 1944, at Detroit, third period. Detroit 15, New York 0. Phil Watson, Canadiens, March 18, 1944, at Mont-

real, third period. Montreal 11, New York 2. Bill Mosienko, Chicago Black Hawks, March 4, 1945, at Chicago, third period. Chicago 6, Montreal 4. J.-C. Tremblay, Canadiens, December 29, 1962, at Montreal, second period. Montreal 5, Detroit 1. Phil Goyette, New York Rangers, October 20, 1963, at New York, first period. New York 5, Boston 1.

Longest modern shutout sequence........309 minutes, 21 seconds
Set by Bill Durnan of Canadiens who racked up four consecutive shutouts in 1948–1949. Durnan started streak at Chicago on February 24 and ended it at Chicago on March 9, 1949.

Most winning goals including play-offs........................101 goals
Set by Maurice Richard in eighteen seasons with Canadiens. He has scored eighteen winning goals in play-offs, six of those in overtime, along with eighty-three regular season winners for a total of 101 winning goals.

Most three-goal hat tricks in career..26
Set by Maurice Richard in eighteen seasons with Canadiens.

Most three-goal hat tricks including play-offs............................33
Set by Maurice Richard in eighteen seasons with Canadiens. He has seven play-off hat tricks and twenty-six in regular season play for a total of thirty-three.

Most times winner of Vézina Trophy with same team............6
Set by Bill Durnan of Canadiens who won the trophy six times in seven years with Canadiens, from 1943–1944 to 1949–1950, missing out in 1947–1948. Tied by Jacques Plante with six Vézinas in eight years with Canadiens.

Most consecutive years Vézina Trophy winner........................5
Set by Jacques Plante who has won Vézina Trophy five straight seasons, from 1955–1956 to 1959–1960.

Most leading scorers since 1917–1918............................13 times
Canadiens' players have won the league scoring crown thirteen times since the formation of the N.H.L.

PLAY-OFFS

Most consecutive years in play-off series................................16
Set by Jean Béliveau (1954–1969).

Most goals in play-off series...12
Set by Maurice Richard with twelve goals in nine games in
1943–1944 play-offs against Toronto and Chicago. Record
equaled by Jean Béliveau of Canadiens with twelve goals in
ten games in 1955–1956 play-offs against New York and
Detroit.

Most goals in play-off competition...82
Set by Maurice Richard in fifteen play-off series.

Most goals scored in single play-off game.....................................5
Set by Maurice Richard who scored five goals as Canadiens
defeated Toronto, 5–1, in second game of semifinals in Montreal, March 23, 1944.

Most winning goals in play-offs.....................................18
Set by Maurice Richard in fifteen play-off series. Six of these
goals were scored in sudden-death overtime.

Most three-goal hat tricks in play-offs...7
Set by Maurice Richard in fifteen play-off series.

Most assists in single play-off game...5
Toe Blake of Canadiens had five assists on March 23, 1944, as
Canadiens defeated Toronto, 5–1, in Montreal. Shared by
Maurice Richard, who had five assists on March 27, 1956, in
Montreal as Canadiens defeated New York, 7–0, and by Bert
Olmstead of Canadiens who had five assists as Canadiens de-
feated New York, 8–3, on March 30, 1957. Record is shared
by Don McKenney of Boston who scored five assists on April
5, 1958, in Boston as Bruins defeated New York, 8–2.

Most points in a single play-off game...6
Set by Dickie Moore of Canadiens with two goals and four
assists as Canadiens defeated Boston, 8–1, in semifinal round

at Montreal, March 25, 1954. Tied by Phil Esposito of Boston with four goals and two assists as Boston defeated Toronto, 10–0, in quarter-final round at Boston, April 2, 1969.

Most goals in final series...7
Jean Béliveau, Canadiens, in 1956 during five games against Detroit.

Most assists in final series...8
Bert Olmstead, Canadiens, in 1956, during five games against Detroit.

Most points, one period..4
Maurice Richard, Canadiens, March 29, 1945, at Montreal, against Toronto. Third period, three goals, one assist. Final score: Canadiens 10, Toronto 3. Dickie Moore, Canadiens, March 25, 1954, at Montreal against Boston. First period, two goals, two assists. Final score: Canadiens 8, Boston 1.

Most goals, one period...3
Harvey Jackson, Toronto Maple Leafs, April 5, 1932, at New York against Rangers, third period. Final score: Toronto 6, Rangers 4. Maurice Richard, Canadiens, March 23, 1944, at Montreal against Toronto, second period. Final score: Canadiens 5, Toronto 1. March 29, 1945, at Montreal against Toronto, third period. Final score: Canadiens 10, Toronto 3. April 6, 1957, at Montreal against Boston, second period. Final score: Canadiens 5, Boston 1. Ted Lindsay, Detroit Red Wings, April 5, 1955, at Detroit against Canadiens, second period. Final score: Detroit 7, Canadiens 1.

Most assists, one period...3
Mick Metz, Toronto Maple Leafs, March 25, 1941, at Toronto against Boston, second period. Final score: Toronto 7, Boston 2. Toe Blake, Canadiens, March 23, 1944, at Montreal against Toronto, second period. Final score: Canadiens 5, Toronto 1. April 13, 1944, at Montreal against Chicago, third period. Final score: Canadiens 5, Chicago 4. Elmer Lach, Canadiens, March 30, 1944, at Montreal against Toronto, third period. Final score:

Canadiens 11, Toronto 0. Bobby Bauer, Boston Bruins, March 24, 1946, at Boston against Detroit, third period. Final score: Boston 5, Detroit 2. Jean Béliveau, Canadiens, March 25, 1954, at Montreal against Boston, first period. Final score: Canadiens 8, Boston 1. Maurice Richard, Canadiens, March 27, 1956, at Montreal against Rangers, second period. Final score: Canadiens 7, Rangers 0. Doug Harvey, Canadiens, April 6, 1957, at Montreal against Boston, second period. Final score: Canadiens 5, Boston 1. April 2, 1959, at Montreal against Chicago, first period. Final score: Canadiens 4, Chicago 2. Don McKenney, Boston Bruins, April 5, 1958, at Boston against Rangers, third period. Final score: Boston 8, Rangers 2. Dickie Moore, Canadiens, April 2, 1959, at Montreal against Chicago, first period. Final score: Canadiens 4, Chicago 2. Henri Richard, Canadiens, April 7, 1960, at Montreal against Toronto, first period. Final score: Canadiens 4, Toronto 2.

Most consecutive games with goals..8
Maurice Richard, Canadiens. Twice. First streak started March 27, 1945, at Toronto, and ended April 2, 1946, at Montreal. He scored one goal in each of seven games and four in another. Second streak started April 5, 1951, at Detroit, and ended March 27, 1952, at Montreal. He scored one goal in each of seven games and two in another.

Most overtime goals...6
Maurice Richard, Canadiens (one in 1946, three in 1951, one in 1957, one in 1958).

Members of the First and Second All-Star Teams

1930–1931	1st team	Howie Morenz, Aurel Joliat
	2nd team	Sylvio Mantha
1931–1932	1st team	Howie Morenz
	2nd team	Sylvio Mantha, Aurel Joliat
1932–1933	2nd team	Howie Morenz
1933–1934	2nd team	Aurel Joliat
1934–1935	2nd team	Aurel Joliat
1935–1936	2nd team	Wilf Cude
1936–1937	1st team	Babe Siebert
	2nd team	Wilf Cude
1937–1938	1st team	Babe Siebert
	2nd team	Toe Blake
1938–1939	1st team	Toe Blake
1939–1940	1st team	Toe Blake
1940–1943	none	
1943–1944	1st team	Bill Durnan
	2nd team	Emile Bouchard, Elmer Lach, Maurice Richard
1944–1945	1st team	Bill Durnan, Elmer Lach, Maurice Richard, Toe Blake, Emile Bouchard
	2nd team	Glen Harmon
1945–1946	1st team	Bill Durnan, Emile Bouchard, Maurice Richard
	2nd team	Kenny Reardon, Elmer Lach, Toe Blake
1946–1947	1st team	Bill Durnan, Kenny Reardon, Emile Bouchard, Maurice Richard
1947–1948	1st team	Elmer Lach, Maurice Richard
	2nd team	Kenny Reardon

1948–1949	1st team	Bill Durnan, Maurice Richard
	2nd team	Glen Harmon, Kenny Reardon
1949–1950	1st team	Bill Durnan, Kenny Reardon, Maurice Richard
1950–1951	2nd team	Maurice Richard
1951–1952	1st team	Doug Harvey, Elmer Lach
	2nd team	Maurice Richard
1952–1953	1st team	Doug Harvey
	2nd team	Gerry McNeil, Bert Olmstead, Maurice Richard
1953–1954	1st team	Doug Harvey, Ken Mosdell
	2nd team	Maurice Richard
1954–1955	1st team	Doug Harvey, Jean Béliveau, Maurice Richard
	2nd team	Ken Mosdell, Bernard Geoffrion
1955–1956	1st team	Jacques Plante, Doug Harvey, Maurice Richard, Jean Béliveau
	2nd team	Tom Johnson, Bert Olmstead
1956–1957	1st team	Doug Harvey, Jean Béliveau
	2nd team	Jacques Plante, Maurice Richard
1957–1958	1st team	Doug Harvey, Henri Richard, Dickie Moore
	2nd team	Jacques Plante, Jean Béliveau
1958–1959	1st team	Jacques Plante, Tom Johnson, Dickie Moore, Jean Béliveau
	2nd team	Doug Harvey, Jean Béliveau
1959–1960	1st team	Doug Harvey, Henri Richard
	2nd team	Jacques Plante, Bernard Geoffrion
1960–1961	1st team	Doug Harvey, Jean Béliveau, Bernard Geoffrion
	2nd team	Henri Richard, Dickie Moore
1961–1962	1st team	Jacques Plante, Jean-Guy Talbot
1962–1963	2nd team	Henri Richard
1963–1964	2nd team	Charlie Hodge, Jean Béliveau, Jacques Laperrière
1964–1965	1st team	Claude Provost, Jacques Laperrière
	2nd team	Charlie Hodge

1965–1966	1st team	Jacques Laperriere
	2nd team	Jean Béliveau, Robert Rousseau, Lorne Worsley
1967–1968	1st team	Lorne Worsley
	2nd team	J. C. Tremblay
1968–1969	2nd team	Jean Béliveau, Ted Harris, Yvan Cournoyer

Special Award
Winners

The Hart Trophy

1926–1927 Herb Gardiner
1927–1928 ⎫
1930–1931 ⎬ Howie Morenz
1931–1932 ⎭
1933–1934 Aurel Joliat
1936–1937 Babe Siebert
1938–1939 Toe Blake
1944–1945 Elmer Lach
1946–1947 Maurice Richard
1955–1956 Jean Béliveau
1960–1961 Bernard Geoffrion
1961–1962 Jacques Plante
1963–1964 Jean Béliveau

Art Ross Trophy

1947–1948 Elmer Lach
1954–1955 Bernard Geoffrion
1955–1956 Jean Béliveau
1957–1958 ⎫
1958–1959 ⎬ Dickie Moore
1960–1961 Bernard Geoffrion

Leading scorer prior to Ross Trophy

1917–1918 Joe Malone
1918–1919 ⎫
1920–1921 ⎬ Newsy Lalonde
1927–1928 ⎫
1930–1931 ⎬ Howie Morenz
1938–1939 Toe Blake
1944–1945 Elmer Lach

Lady Byng Trophy

1945–1946   Toe Blake

Calder Trophy

1940–1941   John Quilty
1951–1952   Bernard Geoffrion
1958–1959   Ralph Backstrom
1961–1962   Bob Rousseau
1963–1964   Jacques Laperrière

Conn Smythe Trophy

1964–1965   Jean Béliveau
1968–1969   Serge Savard

Vézina Trophy

1926–1927 ⎫
1927–1928 ⎬ George
1928–1929 ⎭ Hainsworth
1943–1944 ⎫
1944–1945 ⎪
1945–1946 ⎪
1946–1947 ⎬ Bill Durnan
1948–1949 ⎪
1949–1950 ⎭
1955–1956 ⎫
1956–1957 ⎪
1957–1958 ⎪
1958–1959 ⎬ Jacques Plante
1959–1960 ⎪
1961–1962 ⎭
1963–1964   Charlie Hodge
1965–1966   Lorne Worsley,
            Charlie Hodge
1967–1968   L. Worsley,
            R. Vachon

Norris Trophy

1954–1955 ⎫
1955–1956 ⎪
1956–1957 ⎬ Doug Harvey
1957–1958 ⎭
1958–1959   Tom Johnson
1959–1960   Doug Harvey
1960–1961   Doug Harvey
1965–1966   Jacques Laperrière

Members Hockey Hall of Fame

Georges Vézina

Howie Morenz

Aurel Joliat

Joe Malone

Newsy Lalonde

Herb Gardiner

Sylvio Mantha

Maurice Richard

George Hainsworth

Joe Hall

Sprague Cleghorn

Tommy Gorman

Frank Patrick

Dick Irvin

George McNamara

Hon. Donat Raymond

William Northey

Frank J. Selke

Jack Laviolette

Didier Pitre

J. Ambrose O'Brien

Leo Dandurand

Babe Siebert

Bill Durnan
Toe Blake
Kenny Reardon
Butch Bouchard
Elmer Lach
Tom Johnson